Practical

Papers and discussions by:

G. E. M. ANSCOMBE
RODERICK CHISHOLM
ROY EDGLEY
G. R. GRICE
R. M. HARE
JAAKKO HINTIKKA
J. L. MACKIE
ANTHONY MANSER
D. E. MILLIGAN
ANSELM WINFRIED MÜLLER
J. RAZ
M. J. SCOTT-TAGGART
AMARTYA SEN
W. H. WALSH
J. W. N. WATKINS

Edited by
STEPHAN KÖRNER

New Haven   Yale University Press   1974

Library of Congress catalog card number: 74-77066

International standard book number: 0-300-01759-6

Printed in Great Britain

Preface

The papers, comments and replies contained in this volume constitute the Proceedings of the First Bristol Conference on Critical Philosophy, held under the auspices of the Society for the Furtherance of Critical Philosophy—the sponsors of *Ratio*—and the University of Bristol. The task of editing the volume was made easy by the contributors and by my colleagues Mr. David Hirschmann and Mr. Michael Welbourne who also helped me in all other matters connected with the organization of the conference. The main purpose of this preface is to express my thanks to the persons and institutions mentioned in it.

STEPHAN KÖRNER

Contents

I / Practical Reason and the Logic of Requirement[1]

Roderick Chisholm

1. To deal with the problems of practical reason we must understand certain general principles about what I will call 'the logic of requirement'. Some of these principles, I believe, have not yet been clearly articulated. I will attempt to formulate a number of them here and to discuss their philosophical significance.

The following passage from Leonard Nelson's *Kritik der praktischen Vernunft* should be sufficient to convey what I mean by 'the problems of practical reason':

What rules guide us when we pass a judgment on what is duty? The first answer that presents itself is: In general we are guided in such decisions by certain rules of morality. In general, when we are confronted with an ethical decision, we have a rule at hand that indicates to us what is to be looked upon as duty. Such rules are, for example, the rule of courtesy in social intercourse, of honesty in the communication of our thoughts, of readiness to help those in need, of loyalty toward our friends, of tolerance for the weaknesses of others. But on closer scrutiny we find that such moral rules are not, strictly speaking, universally valid. It happens to us often enough that these rules fail us. We find ourselves in situations not provided for in this set of rules, or in situations in which a given rule is applicable

[1] With the permission of the editor of the *American Philosophical Quarterly*, I have incorporated certain passages from my article 'The Ethics of Requirement', which appeared in that journal, Vol. I (1964), pp. 147–53.

but in which we feel ourselves justified in violating the rule. This second situation occurs whenever there is a conflict between one rule and another. For example, we are sometimes confronted with an inner conflict when we wish to observe the rule of courtesy as well as that of honesty. The decision as to which of these rules is to be given preference cannot lie in either of the two rules in question. In the case of such conflict one moral rule must be waived in favor of another; here we require a principle of selection enabling us to know which rule we are to waive and which we are to uphold. In other words, we require a strictly universal criterion to determine the validity of each of the two rules in question; and this criterion alone can properly be called the moral law.[2]

But let us make the subject of the final sentence plural: 'such criteria alone can properly be called laws of morality.'

2. We will consider the logic of the following types of argument:

(A)   (1) p occurs
        (2) p requires that S perform A
∴ (3) S has a duty to perform A

(B)   (1) q occurs
        (2) q requires that S perform an act incompatible
            with his performing A
∴ (3) S has a duty not to perform A

(C)   (1) r, as well as q, occurs
        (2) r and p does not require that S perform A
∴ (3) The requirement, imposed by p, that S perform A has
        been overridden

The second premiss in an argument of the form of (A) would formulate what Nelson calls a 'rule of morality'; the second premiss in an argument of the form of (B) could be said, in a certain sense, to formulate an extension of such a rule; and the

[2] The first edition of Nelson's book appeared in 1917; a second, unchanged edition is published by Felix Meiner Verlag (Hamburg, 1972). An English edition, entitled *Critique of Practical Reason*, translated by Norbert Guterman, is published by the Leonard Nelson Foundation (Scarsdale, N.Y., 1970). The above passage is from p. 116 of the English edition; it appears on pages 126–7 of the German edition.

second premiss in an argument of the form of (C) might be said
to formulate a 'rule of moral permission'. The conclusions of
arguments of the form of (A) and of (B) could be said to formulate '*prima facie* duties'. And the conclusion of an argument of
the form of (C) could be said to describe a situation in which
such a duty could be said, in Nelson's term, to be waived.

I would assert the following: (1) A significant part of our
practical reasoning—our exhorting, justifying, and excusing,
to ourselves and to others—can be cast in these three forms.
(2) Each of the arguments is a valid logical argument. Moreover
(3) the three arguments may be said to be consistent with each
other in the sense that one may consistently affirm the premisses
and conclusions of all three arguments, where A, p, q, r, and S
are replaced, completely and consistently, by actual terms. And,
finally, (4) once we have made the explications that are necessary in order to see the second and third of these points, we will
have grasped certain concepts which will help us in dealing with
a number of fundamental puzzles about what we ought to do.

3. We must understand, then, the concept I have tried to
single out with the term 'requirement'.

Examples of requirement, as here understood, are: making
a promise requires keeping the promise; wronging a person
requires compensating the person; virtue (if Kant is right)
requires being rewarded; performing a sinful act requires
punishment and repentance. Other examples of requirement
have been studied by the Gestalt psychologists: 'It is a basic
fact of perceptual experience that some things belong or fit
together, and that others do not. A curve may demand a certain
completion and seem to reject all others; this completion
appears as appropriate to the nature of the curve.'[3] As the
quotation suggests, the terms 'fitting' and 'unfitting' might also

---

[3] Maurice Mandelbaum, *The Phenomenology of Moral Experience*
(Glencoe, 1955), pp. 95–6. Compare Wolfgang Köhler, *The Place of
Value in a World of Facts* (New York, 1938), especially ch. 3 ('An
Analysis of Requiredness'). Köhler refers to M. Wertheimer, 'Some
Problems in the Theory of Ethics', *Social Research*, vol. 2 (1935), pp.
353 ff.

be used to express the phenomena of requirement. Thus '*p* is fitting to *q*', in one of the senses in which philosophers have used this expression, could be taken to mean the same as '*p* requires *q*'; in another one of the senses in which philosophers have used it, it might be taken to mean the same as '*p* does not require not-*q*'.

We will take as our primitive locution the schema '*pRq*'—'*p* when it obtains requires *q*'—where the letters *p* and *q* may be replaced by terms designating states of affairs. The schema '*pRq*' may be read in English either as '*p* would require *q*', or as '*p* when it obtains requires *q*', or as '*p* is such that if it were to obtain it would require *q*'. ('States of affairs' will be understood in what I take to be the usual way. For example: states of affairs stand in logical relations to other states of affairs; some of these logical relations constitute the subject-matter of the logic of propositions; for every state of affairs *p*, there is another state of affairs which is the negation of *p* and which obtains, takes place, or occurs when and only when *p* does not obtain, take place, or occur. I will use 'obtains', 'takes place' and 'occurs' interchangeably.)

To facilitate exposition let us begin with a definition:

D1   *p* requires *q* = Df *p* obtains and *pRq*

In other words, *p* does require *q*, or *p* in fact requires *q*, when *p* is such that (i) it obtains and (ii) if it were to obtain it would require *q*. Thus the defined '*p* requires *q*', unlike the undefined '*pRq*', implies that *p* obtains. (This contrast between the defined '*p* requires *q*' and the undefined '*pRq*' points to a certain ambiguity in the ordinary use of 'requires'. Sometimes philosophers who talk about the ethics of requirement use the locution '*p* requires *q*' in the sense here defined, and sometimes they use it in the sense of our undefined '*pRq*', i.e. '*p* when it obtains requires *q*'. The expression '*p* confirms *q*', which resembles '*pRq*' in a number of significant respects, has an analogous ambiguity. Sometimes '*p* confirms *q*' is used to refer to a relation that holds necessarily between propositions, or states of affairs, without implying anything as to the epistemic status of p; but sometimes 'p confirms q' is used to imply, not only that a certain relation holds between p and q, but also that p is known to be true, or that it is evident that p is true.)

I will now attempt to set forth certain general principles that hold of requirement as here understood. I will presuppose a principle of substitutivity according to which logically equivalent expressions may replace each other in any R-formula. The list of principles is by no means exhaustive. Additional principles will suggest themselves when we consider some of the concepts that may be defined in terms of requirement. It will be simplest, I believe, to formulate the principles as axiom schemata:

The first principle reflects our commitment to states of affairs:

A1 $pRq \supset (\exists x)(\exists y)(xRy)$

Consider, for example, 'Jones promising to meet his friend, when it occurs, requires Jones meeting his friend'. This implies that there *is* something—namely, Jones promising to meet his friend, which is such that when it occurs it requires Jones meeting his friend; and it implies that there *is* something—namely, Jones meeting his friend, which is such that Jones promising to meet his friend, when it occurs, requires it. But when we say of the first of these two things that when it occurs it requires the second, our statement does not imply that either one occurs. More generally, 'pRq' does not imply either that p obtains or that q obtains. And 's obtains and pRq' does not imply either '$(p\&s)Rq$' or '$pR(q\&s)$'.

Our second general principle tells us that the relation of requirement is like the relations of logic: if it holds between any two states of affairs, then it holds necessarily between those states of affairs.

A2 $pRq \supset N(pRq)$

Our third principle is reflected in the principle that 'ought' implies 'can'. If one state of affairs is such that when it occurs it requires a certain other, then the two states of affairs are logically compatible with each other

A3 $pRq \supset \sim N[(p\&q)$ does not obtain$]$

Our fourth principle tell us, on the other hand, that two states of affairs that are logically compatible with each other may yet have requirements that are *not* logically compatible with each other:

A4 $(\exists x)(\exists y)(\exists z)\{\sim N[(x\&y)$ does not obtain$]\ \&\ xRz\ \&\ yR\sim z\}$

There is, therefore, the possibility of a *conflict* of actual requirements. That is to say, there may occur one state of affairs which requires a certain thing q and another state of affairs which requires not-q. If I promise one man to go and promise another man not to go, then there is something requiring me to go and something requiring me not to go. A man may be subject to conflicting requirements through no fault of his own. For example, he may find himself in the position of being the only one who is able to rescue either, but not both, of two equally worthy men in distress.

We may compare 'confirms' once again: one true proposition may confirm q, and another true proposition may confirm not-q. Indeed, one proposition that is known to be true may confirm q, and another proposition that is known to be true may confirm not-q.

We add two obvious principles pertaining to disjunctive and conjunctive states of affairs:

A5 $(pRs\ \&\ qRs) \supset (p\,v\,q)Rs$
A6 $(pRq\ \&\ pRs) \supset pR(q\ \&\ s)$

If two states of affairs are each such that they would require a given state of affairs, then their disjunction would also require that state of affairs (A5). Every state of affairs is such that it would require the conjunction of all those states of affairs it would require (A6).[4] It should be noted that we cannot affirm the converse of (A5), viz.,

[4] These two principles were suggested to me by Ernest Sosa.

$(p \vee q)Rs \supset (pRs \& qRs)$

For suppose, what (A4) allows, that (i) p would require s but (ii) the conjunction of p and r would not require s. Then the principle of substitutivity for logically equivalent expressions would allow us to infer, from (i), that $[(p \& r) \vee (p \& \sim r)]$ would require s. And then the converse, above, of (A5) would allow us to infer that $(p \& r)$ would require s, which contradicts (ii).

But the following, closely related formula would seem to be axiomatic:

A7 $(p \vee q)Rs \supset (pRs \vee qRs)$

One might put this principle, somewhat loosely, by saying that if a given state of affairs requires a certain other state of affairs, then, of the possible ways of extending or making 'more determinate' the first state of affairs, one at least will also require the second state of affairs.

4. Among the consequences that can readily be drawn from our axioms are the following:

T1 $pRq \supset \sim N(p \text{ does not obtain})$
T2 $pRq \supset \sim N(q \text{ does not obtain})$
T3 $pRq \supset \sim(pR \sim q)$
T4 $(pRq \& sR \sim q) \supset \{\sim[(p\&s)Rq] \vee \sim[(p\&s)R \sim q]\}$
T5 $pRq \supset [(p\&s)Rq \vee (p \& \sim s)Rq]$

A self-contradictory state of affairs would not require anything (T1) and would not be required by anything (T2). No state of affairs would impose incompatible requirements (T3). Thus if, in accordance with the possibility countenanced by (A3), two states of affairs that are compatible with each other happen to impose requirements that are incompatible with each other, then at least one of those requirements is not imposed by the conjunction of those two states of affairs (T4). Much of the sting of (A5), then, is removed by (T3) and (T4). Principle (T4), then, allows for the possibility that, although p is such that if it were to obtain it would require q, there occurs a wider state of affairs that entails p and that does not require q. But principle T5, which is a consequence of (A5), tells us that this is *only* a possibility. For, according to (T5), it is also possible that, if p requires q, then, for every wider state of affairs that obtains and entails p, that wider state of affairs also requires q.

We can say, then, that there may be requirements that conflict with each other (A4). But if there occurs something p which requires q, then this same thing p does not also require not-q (T3). Similarly, if there is a true proposition p which confirms another proposition q, then p does not also confirm not-q. If p and s have incompatible requirements, the larger situation, consisting of both p and s, will not have these incompatible requirements (T4). The analogy with confirmation is obvious, once again.

5. Our theorem T4, above, may be given this alternative formulation: if two states of affairs are such that they would impose incompatible requirements, then one or the other of those incompatible requirements would be *overridden* by the conjunction of the two states of affairs. The concept of a requirement being overridden is central to the logic of requirement and we will now consider it briefly.

Let us first define the case where one state of affairs is such that it *would* override the requirement that would be imposed by another:

D2   The requirement for q, that would be imposed by p, would be overridden by s = Df (i) pRq, (ii) $\sim[(p\&s)Rq]$, and (iii) $p\&s$ is logically compatible with q.

If s is such that it would override the requirement for q that would be imposed by p, then: p is such that it would require q, but the conjunction of p and s is *not* such that it would require q, and the conjunction of p and s does not entail the negation of q.[5]

---

[5] The third condition in the definiens of D2 is needed because of the consequences that would otherwise follow, given our general principles, from the assumption that a requirement for q had not been fulfilled. Without the third condition we would have to say that if p required q, and not-q obtained, then the conjunction of p and not-q would override the requirement q imposed by p.

We may now say that a state of affairs *does* in fact override a certain requirement if the state of affairs obtains and is such that it would override that requirement:

D3   The requirement for q that is imposed by p is overridden by s = Df (i) the requirement for q that would be imposed by p would be overridden by s and (ii) $p\&s$ obtains.

W. D. Ross has given us a clear example: 'If I have promised to meet a friend at a particular time for some trivial purpose, I should certainly think myself justified in breaking my engagement if by doing so I could prevent a serious accident or bring relief to the victims of one.'[6] His promise (p) to meet the friend requires his meeting the friend (q), but the accident or the dangerous situation (s) creates a new situation (p and s) which does not require that he meet the friend.

In Ross's example, of course, the new situation not only overrides a requirement but creates a new one—the requirement to prevent the accident or to relieve distress—and the new requirement is incompatible with the requirement that is overridden; the requirement for q is replaced by a requirement for not-q. But a requirement for something q may be overridden without being replaced by a requirement for not-q. If I am required to go to Boston in order to meet a friend, and then learn that he is dead, the requirement may be overridden without my being required not to go to Boston.

6. An overriding may itself be overridden. If, as I go to assist the man in distress, I learn that an even greater disaster will result should I fail to keep my appointment with the friend, then this new and more inclusive situation may require me once again to keep the appointment with the friend. Thus there may occur a set of events (there may be a set of true propositions) p, q, r, s, and t, such that:

> p requires q
> p and r requires not-q

[6] W. D. Ross, *The Right and the Good* (Oxford, 1930), p. 18.
BPR

> *p* and *r* and *s* requires *q*
> *p* and *r* and *s* and *t* requires not-*q*

Once again, therefore, we find that requirement is like the logical concept of confirmation. For there may be true propositions, *p*, *r*, *s*, and *t*, such that:

> *p* confirms *q*
> *p* and *r* confirms not-*q*
> *p* and *r* and *s* confirms *q*
> *p* and *r* and *s* and *t* confirms not-*q*

The following propositions provide an example: 'Most of the people in this room are Democrats, and John is in this room' (*p*); 'John is a Democrat' (*q*); 'Most of the people on the left side of the room are not Democrats, and John is on the left side of the room' (*r*); '45 of the 50 people who arrived on time are Democrats, and John arrived on time' (*s*); '99 of the 100 people who voted for the measure are not Democrats, and John voted for the measure' (*t*). We do not say, in such cases, that one confirmation has been 'overridden' or 'defeated' in virtue of another, but we could.

Let us consider still another feature of this example of confirmation. Should we say that, in the situation described, the proposition *q* is probable, or should we say that it is improbable? One of the clearest answers to this question is suggested by Bernard Bolzano. We may say that a relational, or relative, probability of a proposition for a given person is the probability which the proposition has in relation to any part of what the person knows to be true. Thus, for a man who knows the propositions, *p*, *r*, *s*, and *t*, to be true, the proposition *q* has various relational probabilities—depending upon which of these propositions it is that *q* is being related to. But the absolute probability of a proposition, for any given person, is the probability which the proposition has in relation to the totality of those propositions which the person knows to be true.[7] Abso-

---

[7] Bernard Bolzano, *Wissenschaftslehre*, vol. 3 (Leipzig, 1930), pp. 267–8. Bolzano also made a distinction between a real or objective probability and a supposed or subjective probability which we might

lute probability is thus 'toti-resultant'. Normally, when we speak of 'the probability' of a proposition, we are referring to its absolute probability. And it is absolute probability that should constitute the guide of life.

7. From the fact that a state of affairs q is required by a certain state of affairs p such that p obtains, we may not infer that q is a state of affairs that *ought* to obtain. For the requirement imposed by p may be overridden by some other state of affairs s. But from the fact that a requirement for q has thus been overridden, we may not infer that q is a state of affairs that 'need not' obtain—i.e. a state of affairs such that it is not true that that state of affairs ought to obtain. For there may be some *other* state of affairs that requires q—indeed, some wider state of affairs that includes (entails) both p and s. We will say that a state of affairs ought to obtain provided there is a requirement for it that has not been overridden:

D4   It ought to be that q obtains $=$ Df. There is an x such that x requires q and it is false that the requirement for q imposed by x is overridden.

The relation between what is merely required and what ought to be is thus analogous to the relation between what was called relative and absolute probability above. Thus one might also consider defining the 'ought to be' by reference to what is required by the totality of relevant considerations. But D4 is simpler and, I believe, accomplishes the same purpose.

8. Another pair of concepts that are useful in formulating certain ethical issues are singled out by the following definitions:

D5 p would indefeasibly require q $=$ Df (i) pRq and (ii) there is

put as follows: a real or objective probability of a proposition, for a given person, is the probability which that proposition bears to something that the person knows; the supposed or subjective probability is the probability the proposition bears to something the person thinks (possibly mistakenly) that he knows. (Unfortunately, Bolzano's own definitions are marred by the fact that he attempts to get along with an epistemic term which is weaker than 'knows'.) The more important parts of Bolzano's book have been translated by Rolf George as *Theory of Science*, The University of California Press: Berkeley and Los Angeles, 1972). Compare pp. 359–65 of the English edition.

> no *x* such that the requirement for *q* that would be imposed by *p* would be overridden by *x*.

D6   *p* indefeasibly requires *q* = Df (i) *p* requires *q* and (ii) *p* would indefeasibly require *q*.

If we know that *p* indefeasibly requires *q*, then we can know that, no matter what wider states of affairs may happen to obtain, *q* is such that it ought to obtain.

There is a temptation to say that most ethical disputes are concerned, not merely with what requires what, but with what *indefeasibly* requires what. But any dispute about what indefeasibly requires what will turn upon some question about what requires what. (If you think, and I do not, that promise-making indefeasibly requires promise-keeping, then presumably there will be some state of affairs *p* which is such that I think, but you do not, that *p* would override the requirement imposed by promise-making. Our dispute would then turn on the question whether the conjunction of *p* and promise-making requires promise-keeping.)

The concept singled out in D6 is also relevant, of course, to the problems of theodicy.[8]

9. We are now in a position to introduce three definitions enabling us to see the validity of the three types of practical inference with which we began. The three types of inference were exhibited by:

(A)   (1) *p* occurs
       (2) *p* requires that *S* perform *A*
∴ (3) *S* has a duty to perform *A*

(B)   (1) *q* occurs
       (2) *q* requires that *S* perform an act logically
           incompatible with his performing *A*
∴ (3) *S* has a duty not to perform *A*

(C)   (1) *r*, as well as *p*, occurs

---

[8] I have discussed this point in 'The Defeat of Good and Evil', in *Proceedings and Addresses of the American Philosophical Association*, vol. XLII (1968–9), pp. 21–38. This paper is reprinted in J. E. Smith, ed., *Contemporary American Philosophy: Second Series* (George Allen & Unwin: London, 1970), pp. 152–69.

(2) *r* and *p* does not require that *S* perform *A*

∴ (3) The requirement, imposed by *p*, that *S* perform *A* has been overridden.

To remove a certain ambiguity, to be noted below, let us re-express the conclusion of argument (A) by saying '*S* has a *prima facie* duty to perform *A*' and that of argument (B) by saying '*S* has a *prima facie* duty not to perform *A*'. We now add definitions of these two concepts:

D7 *S* has a *prima facie* duty to perform *A* = Df. There is an *x* such that *x* requires *S*'s performing *A*.

D8 *S* has a *prima facie* duty not to perform *A* = Df. There is an *x* and a *y* such that (a) *x* requires *S*'s performing *y* and (b) *S*'s performing *y* is logically incompatible with *S*'s performing *A*.

Definitions D7 and D8 enable us to see that arguments (A) and (B) are valid. Our earlier definition D3—the definition of the concept of *overriding*—enables us to see that argument (C) is valid. The three definitions together, taken with what we have said about the logic of requirement, are sufficient to justify the following remark that was made at the outset; namely, that the three arguments (A), (B), and (C), may be said to be consistent with each other in the sense that one may consistently affirm the premises and conclusions of all three arguments, where *A, p, q, r*, and *S* are replaced, completely and consistently, by actual terms.

We may now define 'the ought to do' by reference to 'the ought to be':

D9 *S* ought to perform *A* = Df. It ought to be that *S*'s performing *A* obtains.

Having defined 'the ought to be' in terms of requirement, and having characterized requirement in terms of relations holding necessarily among propositions or states of affairs, we may say, with Samuel Clarke, that our duties are a function of the eternal relations of fitness that hold among things.[9]

10. Thus, if I am not mistaken, we have a clear-cut distinction between what it is that a person ought to do and what it is

[9] Samuel Clarke, *Discourse upon Natural Religion* (London, 1706).

that something may require him to do. We have defined the nonrelative term 'ought' by reference to the relative term 'requires'. I suggest that the way in which we have drawn this distinction may throw light upon a number of questions of moral philosophy. I shall mention six such questions.

(i) We can now better understand the distinction W. D. Ross wished to make, in saying that certain acts are '*prima facie* duties' and others are 'duties proper'—that certain acts are '*prima facie* obligatory' and others 'absolutely obligatory.' We may say that a man has a *prima facie* duty to perform a certain act *a*, if there is a requirement that he perform *a*, and that he has a duty proper to perform *a* if he ought to perform *a*.

There are circumstances under which it makes good sense to say: 'You ought to do it even though you are under obligation not to do it.' In this use, the expression 'You ought to do it' is more authoritative, more stringent than 'You are under obligation to do it.' We could say to the man of Ross's example, 'You ought to miss the appointment, in order to prevent the accident, even though you are under obligation to your friend not to miss the appointment.' The man's *prima facie* duty is the duty to keep the appointment, and had it not been overridden by the danger of the accident, it would have been his duty proper. The distinction between *prima facie* and absolute duty is thus the analogue of Bolzano's distinction between relational and absolute probability. Ross's 'duty proper', like Bolzano's 'absolute probability', is 'toti-resultant'.[10]

---

[10] Professor Strawson has argued that Ross's distinction is untenable on the ground that it comes to little more than the following: *x* is *prima facie* obligatory provided *x* has a property such that everything having that property tends to be obligatory; and *x* is absolutely obligatory provided *x* has no property such that, having that property entails being absolutely wrong. The first definition obviously leaves something to be desired, and the second leaves us with the concept of wrong, which involves all of the difficulties of obligatory; 'besides having this theoretical defect, the suggested model is, of course, practically absurd'. P. F. Strawson, 'Ethical Intuitionism', *Philosophy*, vol. 24 (1949). It must be conceded that without a concept such as that of overriding which I have attempted to define, Ross's distinction would involve serious theoretical difficulties.

(ii) This type of distinction enables us to solve at least one of the theoretical problems which the fact of moral conflict involves. A man may be able to formulate two practical arguments having premises that are true, but conclusions that contradict each other: '*a*'s occurring obligates me to do *b*; *a* has occurred; therefore I ought to do *b*. But *c*'s occurring obligates me not to do *b*; *c* has occurred; therefore I ought not to do *b*'. Shall we say—what seems implausible—that there really are no such conflicts? Or shall we say—what seems intolerable—that a person may have conflicting absolute obligations?[11] We may avoid both extremes by saying that the two arguments are formally invalid: The premises refer to *prima facie* obligations, or requirements; and the conclusions refer to absolute obligations, or what it is that one ought to do.

A valid practical argument, with premises referring to requirement, and with a conclusion referring to what one ought to do, would have this form: '*a*'s occurring requires me to do *b*; *a* has occurred; and nothing has occurred to override this requirement; therefore I ought to do *b*'.

Thus we may say that there are moral conflicts and also, if we choose, that whenever there is such a conflict, there is a reasonable and proper way out. As our theorem T3 makes explicit, we may assume that if there occurs something *p* which requires *q*, then this same thing *p* does not also require not-*q*. And we may also assume that, wherever there are conflicting requirements, then at least one of the requirements is overridden. The difficult problem is that of deciding which.

(iii) Let us now consider one of the problems involved in supposing that people are capable of acquiring knowledge in ethics. Our ethical judgements, if some of them constitute knowledge, resemble those judgements which are traditionally called '*a priori*' in the following way: An 'intuitive induction'

[11] A clear formulation of the theoretical problem may be found in John Ladd's 'Remarks on the Conflict of Obligation', *Journal of Philosophy*, vol. 55 (1958), pp. 811–19. Ladd attempts to get between the horns, but I believe he is committed to the first of the two courses noted.

or an 'experiment in the imagination' seems to be all that is needed to establish a universal generalization. To know, for example, that malice is reprehensible wherever and under whatever conditions it occurs (if one can know such a thing), it would seem to be necessary only to know what malice is, or to contemplate a single instance of it. Thus we have said, in A2, that the relation of requirement holds *necessarily*. Yet our ethical judgements, unlike those which are traditionally called *a priori*, are notoriously corrigible. Not only do we fail to agree with each other; we come to realize that many of our own ethical judgements, even those made under conditions which seem ideal for such deliberation, have been mistaken. The problem, then, is this: How can an *a priori* judgement be so obviously corrigible?

I suggest that we are now in a position to solve the problem in the following way. A judgement to the effect that something *p* requires something *q* may be *a priori* and incorrigible; so, too, for the judgement that *p* and *r* taken together do not require *q*—i.e., the judgement that the addition of *r* to *p* overrides *p*'s requirement for *q*. The judgement that there is in fact a requirement for *q* and that this requirement has not been overridden— hence the judgement that *p* ought to obtain (or that *p* ought to be true)—is not *a priori*, but requires a survey of all of the relevant *a posteriori* evidence that is available.

(iv) These distinctions may also throw light upon the nature of moral disagreement and of *akrasia*. If, as often happens, two people agree upon all the facts and accept the same principles of morality and yet find themselves in disagreement about a particular moral issue, then at least one of the people has failed to consider the moral relevance of some particular fact. In consequence he has failed to see that some requirement has been overridden, or that some overriding has been overridden. And the incontinent man may be said, in the following sense, to 'do what he knows he ought not to do'. His act is one such that his information and moral principles imply that it ought not to be performed; but he restricts his view to only a part of the relevant situation, making use only of enough of his information to be able to draw the conclusion that the act is not one which ought not to be performed.[12]

(v) What is the status of 'Small Moralls'—the requirements of etiquette and esthetics ? We may say that these requirements are 'small', for not much is needed to override them. But they are requirements, and therefore when they are not overridden—when the only question is whether or not to follow the requirements of 'good taste'—then they are absolute obligations. Our principle (A5) and its consequence (T5), tell us that, if p requires q, then it is possible that, for every wider state of affairs that obtains and entails p, that wider state of affairs requires q. Every requirement, however small it may be, is such that, under certain possible circumstances, it would be an absolute obligation.

(vi) Finally, let us consider what is sometimes called 'subjective' obligation. What shall we say of the man who has an obligation to perform a certain act a, but who believes that he has an obligation to do something which is incompatible with his performing a? We can hardly say that it is obligatory for him to do what is not obligatory. But it would be equally wrong to say that his beliefs about what is obligatory have no moral relevance. What we must conclude, I think, is this: The fact that a man believes that a certain act is obligatory is morally relevant precisely because it is a fact which requires him to perform that act; but the requirement is one that may easily be overridden. An erring conscience may not bind, but it does require.

Comment:

BY G. E. M. ANSCOMBE

It is characteristic of Professor Chisholm to carry one always by a succession of small harmless looking moves which then

[12] Compare William James, *Talks to Teachers on Psychology, and to Students on Some of Life's Ideals* (New York, 1906), pp. 186 ff.; W. D. Ross, *Foundations of Ethics* (Oxford, 1939), p. 84; Jean-Paul Sartre, *L'Être et le Néant* (Paris, 1943), Pt. i, ch. 2 ('La mauvaise foi').

suddenly enable him to pull out some large kicking rabbits like a conjurer operating with a hat. This time he has produced the large kicking rabbits, but the initial movements do not seem as unsuspicious as usual.

Note first, that he uses the proposition variables generally, i.e. not as standing in for the Propositions we are accustomed to in the writings of Russell, Church, Reichenbach, etc. This is not an accident—viz. the 'eternal relations of fitness that hold among things'.

Second, a connected point, he uses 'There is an x such that . . .', with x ranging over states of affairs, not meaning that any state of affairs such that . . . actually counts or obtains. 'For every state of affairs p there is another which is the negation of p and which obtains when and only when p does not occur.' But in the light of the first point that won't be true. P might obtain in one place and p in another (It's raining). This needs some clarification. It may be possible to give a good account. Just as we assume in the course of an argument that names have constant reference, so we assume that sentences and clauses do not change their truth-values. We can make this assumption without introducing an abstract entity, a Proposition, which *cannot* change its truth-value.

So I am not out of sympathy with this way of proceeding—but it does need investigation. Where I am out of sympathy is over the whole assimilation of practical reasoning to a trivial move of speculative reasoning. What on this view is special about practical reasoning except its subject matter?

Professor Chisholm tells us that: p requires that S perform A ∴ S has a duty to perform A, is a valid argument (I leave out the first premiss 'p occurs' since by his explanation of 'requires' it is redundant).

The validity is later vindicated by appropriate definition of 'S has a *prima facie* duty to perform A'. It is defined as 'there is an x such that x requires S's performing A'. So the argument is: p requires that S perform A ∴ there is a state of affairs that require S's performing A. Which is just like: the colour red occurs in the spectrum ∴ some colour occurs in the spectrum.

I have always objected to accounts of practical reasoning which reduce it to theoretical, i.e. to the argument from the truth of premises to the truth of a conclusion implied by them. This is an example, mediated by a definition.

My own view is that the conclusion of a practical syllogism is an action or decision—that a man draws this conclusion shows that he wants to have or avoid something mentioned in the premisses, and the premisses show what the point of the decision or action was. For example: 'Nicotine is a deadly poison, what's in this bottle is nicotine, so I'd drink it.' But this isn't the place to develop my views.

Pursuing Professor Chisholm's approach: *logical* incompatibility between an overriding requirement and an overridden one is surely not necessary to enable the latter to be overridden. It is surely enough if it is physically impossible that both requirements should be met.

I jump over his interesting comparisons between requirement and confirmation, as I have no contribution to make here.

His puzzle about judgements being *a priori* and incorrigible is surely a muddle. I don't use the term *a priori* myself. It once meant 'from cause to effect' and nowadays teachers have to persuade undergraduates to adopt a different and far fishier meaning for it. But I take it to imply: without recourse to experiment or to observation, or particular facts which may be this way or that; necessarily true, or the like. If so, we can get our (would be) *a priori* judgements wrong and correct them just as when we make mistakes in our sums. So there just wasn't the problem that Professor Chisholm conjured up.

However, I find his solution of it interesting; it is that when people disagree about a particular moral issue then at least one of them has failed to consider the moral relevance of some particular fact. He also thinks the same holds for *akrasia*.

There is an ambiguity here. A particular moral issue might be whether gambling or adultery are wicked kinds of action, or it might be like: 'What should we do, kill these prisoners?'

or 'pay this amount out to these people?'; that is it might be a specific problem of a general nature; or it might be concerned with here and now.

On the 'specific' interpretation his 'There is an x . . .' may have deleterious consequences. If x ranges over all conceivable states of affairs, science-fiction fantasy might be in if it were coherent, like one I once had in which the human race was always born female and changed sex to male at the age of 30. Clearly this would affect the morals of marriage! So if one were discussing the merits of adultery, someone who thought it indefeasibly excluded would be saying that no *conceivable* situation would override the requirement not to commit it. Morality is more tied to the actual than that. Possibly there are things like malice—evil will—and lying whose concepts are so general and abstract that one could get some indefeasibility even under these conditions. But the issues which often burn are not to be deprived of their fire by giving Chisholm's meaning to indefeasibility.

In both cases—moral disagreement and *akrasia*—and in both interpretations—the 'specific' one and the one that concerns here and now—a man makes a judgement which is wrong, and that is how Chisholm regards the problems.

On *akrasia*, it seems to me he is plainly wrong. Certainly ignorance of particular facts in a situation is sometimes operative in *akrasia*, but what makes it that as opposed to counter-voluntariness (what Aristotle called *akousion*) is that the ignorance is voluntary, e.g., careless; or even chosen, as when someone has the attitude: 'I don't want to know about that because I might have to think or act differently if I did.' But *also* a man may let his principles lose their grip on him through fear or rage or desire, so that his enunciation of them is like a drunk recitation of the verses of Empedocles.

About theoretical disagreement in morals the case is different, and here I think Professor Chisholm may be right—and yet, I suspect, not quite in the way the earlier part of his paper suggested. Take the case of gambling, which some people think so wrong that they think it a bad action to even bet a trifling amount which the bettor can well spare. It's not that 'can well spare' that they overlook or fail to see the relevance of. If you ask such a man, he tells you, say, that it's a sort of dishonesty, trying to get something for nothing, trying to get what hasn't been earned. What facts, then, is he overlooking? Not, I suggest, the facts of the particular situation, but that we all get lots for nothing, that property is luck (good or bad), that no one earns all the good things he has, that misfortune isn't necessarily earned either. He is being too serious about property and earnings. The change in his mind if he changes it, should be a change in his ethos about property and desert. The truth which he will come to will be not some particular fact about a particular situation but one of a very general and diffuse character.

Finally, two words about 'fittingness'. We say a punishment may 'fit' a crime. Now mercy can be noble. What *facts* will make it so? I don't say there aren't any—but mercy at least is not an obligation in the particular case. It is always supererogatory; otherwise it would be justice, not mercy. Professor Chisholm's account leaves no room to this. Mercy would have to be *required* in an overriding way, to have the right to override the fittingness of punishment.

Second, and more generally, the very plastic concept of fittingness does not seem to me to bear the strain that he puts upon it—the strain of justifying a supposedly precise and formal account of duty and right and wrong action. It is as if he took a piece of plasticine and shaped it *ad hoc* into a variety of shapes, to join description of states of affairs and action, and said: Look, they are linked by fittingness.

I have a suspicion that he has been too ambitious, that his account of 'overriding' is valuable and could be seen to be applicable in some narrowly restricted field.

Comment: 'Reasons, Requirements and Practical Conflicts'

BY J. RAZ

Professor Chisholm is obviously right in stating at the beginning of his illuminating paper that many of the more important problems of practical reason concern the ways in which the demands of practical reason may intersect and conflict. I find myself in complete sympathy with what I take to be his main thesis, namely that practical reason can give rise to diametrically conflicting demands and that talk of diametrically conflicting demands does not always lead to contradictions, for a conflict of demands results from a difference in the grounds for the demands. I further agree that such conflicts are often resolved when we consider the demands of the conjunction of the states of affairs giving rise to the conflicting demands, for we may find that one demand overrides the other or that they cancel each other.

Having expressed my sympathy with Professor Chisholm's main thesis let me also confess that I was not convinced by his implicit claim that the principles of the logic of requirement he expounded today go a long way towards solving the main problems of practical reason. I shall comment very briefly on three subjects:

A:　Types of conflict of practical reason.
B:　Reasons for action and the Logic of Requirement.
C:　Types of overriding.

A:　TYPES OF CONFLICT OF PRACTICAL REASON

The key terms in Professor Chisholm's theory are 'requirement', 'ought' and 'duty'. The meaning he assigns to these terms is only remotely related to their meaning in ordinary English discourse. Though the point is never made by Professor Chisholm, I take it that he is completely unperturbed by this fact. His aim must have been merely to define a set of technical concepts with the help of which one would be able to talk intelligibly about conflicts of practical reason. In this I believe that he was successful.

But the scant attention he paid to the logic of ordinary discourse means that his success is very partial and incomplete. A comprehensive theory may very well include a set of technical concepts providing a framework for precise and clear discourse. But to show that they fulfil their function one must, firstly, analyse the logic of ordinary discourse on matters involving conflict of reasons and, secondly, show that the proposed conceptual framework can be used for the same purposes. We must be convinced that it either reflects the basic features of ordinary discourse or that it can usefully replace it. To the extent that Professor Chisholm refrains from dealing with these matters he leaves important problems unsolved, including some which are essential for any attempt to pass judgement on his theory. All that I can hope to do here is to make a few unsystematic remarks in an attempt somewhat to clarify the nature of the problems involved.

1. *Some problems about ordinary discourse:* There are conflicts of rules and of principles. Conflicts of rights, of duties and of reasons, etc. To deal with the problems of conflicts in practical reason one must explain the nature of each of these cases of conflict and the relations between them. I believe that all these kinds of conflict can ultimately be explained by reference to conflicting 'ought'-statements, of the type 'x ought to A in C' and 'x ought to B in C' where it is impossible for x to do both A and B in C. Conflicting 'ought'-statements can both be correct. An 'ought'-statement is correct if there are reasons for the agent to perform the act in those circumstances. Since there can be conflicting reasons there can be correct though conflicting 'ought'-statements. It must be admitted that there is an air of paradox in the statement that it may be true both that I ought to keep my promise and that I ought to break it. The

apparent paradox can be explained away as the product of pragmatic implicatures. Because of the pragmatical requirement that the speaker should not hold back relevant information my saying to John, you ought to keep your promise, has the pragmatic implicature that I do not believe in any reasons overriding those for keeping the promise. The same, of course, is true of John, and therefore, if he tells me that on the contrary he ought to break his promise, there is a genuine conflict of opinions for we are both stating our views on the balance of reasons. But this is so because of the pragmatic implicatures, not because of the meaning of 'ought'.

2. *The importance of partial conflicts:*   It is not my purpose here to solve any of the problems I mentioned. I merely intend to indicate some of the more important problems that a theory which, like Professor Chisholm's theory, is designed to solve the problems of conflict in practical reason must tackle. Let me mention yet another type of conflict disregarded by Professor Chisholm.

If there are reasons for x to do A in circumstances C and if at the same time there are reasons for x to do B in C and if x cannot do both A and B in C then x is faced with a case of a diametrical conflict. Professor Chisholm's is a theory of diametrical conflicts. My characterization of a diametrical conflict is incomplete for it leaves unexplained the nature of the factors because of which x cannot do both A and B in C. Professor Chisholm's explanations are incomplete for the same reason: nowhere does he explain what he means by the incompatibility of actions. I do not wish to enlarge on this theme but let me note in passing that Professor Chisholm comes near to mentioning the problem in his comment on his third axiom saying that $pRq \supset \sim N[(p\&q)$ does not obtain]. This principle, he says, 'is reflected in the principle that "ought" implies "can" '. He is of course right, all the more so because he was careful not to say that his axiom *reflects* the principle that 'ought' implies 'can'. Clearly that my doing A is not logically incompatible with my doing B does not entail that I can do both. We do need, however, a fuller explication of the principle that 'ought' implies 'can' in order to be able to characterize the nature of diametrical conflicts which are the only type of conflict with which Professor Chisholm is concerned. So long as Professor Chisholm's logic can explain only those conflicts which are due to logical incompatibility it remains impotent for it is unable to deal with the majority and the most troublesome cases of diametrical conflicts.

However important is the problem of diametrical conflicts, it must be admitted that non-diametrical partial conflicts are much more common, and one may well wonder whether Professor Chisholm's logic as it is does in any way illuminate their nature.

If an agent has reasons to do A and reasons to do B and if his doing one of those acts will affect any aspect of his ability to perform the other act then he is confronted with a practical problem of (at least) a partial conflict. To make my meaning more precise let me introduce examples of three types of partial conflicts of practical reasons and contrast them with the clear case of diametrical conflict in which I have reason both to keep an appointment and to help a man injured in an accident but cannot do both.

(*a*) Assume an agent has both a reason to perform a generic act A in circumstances of type C and a reason to perform a generic act B in C^1. There is no assumed incompatibility between the two generic acts and a person can usually do both. Usually, but not always. In certain circumstances it is impossible to perform both and sometimes conditions C and C^1 obtain in conjunction with further factors making it impossible for the agent to do both A and B. One can usually both tell the truth and keep one's word, but sometimes they prove to be incompatible and a choice has to be made. In such cases one's reasons to do A in C partially conflict with one's reasons to do B in C^1 because in certain circumstances there is a diametrical conflict between the reasons for A and those for B.

(*b*) In order to introduce the second type of partial conflict we have to distinguish between various generic acts by the

CPR

degree of their specificity. Kicking a ball is a more specific act than lecturing which is more specific than teaching. Acting fairly or to everyone's benefit are highly unspecific acts. Saying 'Hello' or drinking a cup of tea are highly specific acts. In general the specificity of an act is in reverse to the number of heterogeneous acts the doing of which on different occasions counts as doing the action in question. Unspecific acts are acts which can be done by doing any of a large variety of other acts.

A reason for performing A partially conflicts with a reason for performing B if some ways of doing B, though not incompatible with doing A, are incompatible with some ways of doing A. In other words if there is an act B^1 by which B can be done and which is incompatible with the doing of A^1 which is a way of doing A. To the extent that a reason for an act is also a reason for any act by which it can be done, the second type of partial conflict can also be characterized in terms of diametrical conflict: A reason for A conflicts with a reason for B if A can be done by A^1 and B by B^1 and the reasons for A^1 and for B^1 conflict diametrically.

(c)   The third type of partial conflict concerns cases where there are reasons to achieve two goals and where the full realization of one goal though compatible with the realization of the second goal to a certain extent is incompatible with its realization in the highest degree. A government having reasons both to secure growth and to maximize equality is confronted with a typical case of partial conflict of both the second and the third types. It is not difficult to see that this type of partial conflict can also be characterized by reference to cases of diametrical conflict which it engenders.

B: REASONS FOR ACTION AND THE LOGIC OF REQUIREMENT

I mentioned some of the problems of conflict of practical reason not dealt with by Professor Chisholm merely to correct the impression of the great simplicity of this philosophical field which might be created by his paper. As I have already said I find much to agree with in his treatment of diametrical conflicts of practical reasons, which is the problem with which he is most directly concerned. His reluctance to interpret his key term R, nevertheless must make one postpone judgement until some further clarification is provided.

1. *Reasons for action and 'requirements'*. We mention both facts and rules and principles as reasons: 'You should give him the book because you said you will.' 'You should not lie to him because one should not deceive people.' It may be tempting to say that the first item in an R-relation is a fact which is a reason, and that some true R-statements are statements of rules and principles. If this interpretation is correct it raises a few questions which I am sure Professor Chisholm could easily answer in his reply. Can we apply this interpretation to R-statements in which the state of affairs required is not one of an agent performing an act or refraining from one? Can it be applied to the following of his examples: 'A curve may demand a certain completion and seem to reject all others?'

The fact that an act would realize or promote some value or that it is good or bad in itself is a reason for action: 'This tax law should be adopted because it will increase equality.' Are values appropriate items for the R-relation? 'Deceiving is wrong because it is incompatible with human dignity or with regarding people as ends in themselves.' Should we say that human dignity requires that one will not deceive? If malice is wrong in itself what is it that requires that we shall not act with malice?

2. *Professor Chisholm's principle of non-contradiction*. This seems to be an appropriate name for T3: $pRq \supset \sim (pR \sim q)$. I have no objection to this principle, but it should be clear that its application is far from straightforward. Imagine that I witness one man shoot another from a passing car. This, let us assume, requires both that I attend to the injuries of the victim and that I shall pursue his attacker, but doing one of these acts entails the non-performance of the other. Is not this a case of one state of affairs requiring both p and not–p? Of course, Professor

Chisholm will be able to deal with this and similar examples with relative ease. My point is that to defend his theory he must employ an elaborate theory of identity of states of affairs which might well be counter-intuitive and counter-productive. What would normally be regarded as the same state of affairs differently described will turn out to be two different states of affairs. Furthermore, he will have to employ some elaborate theory of the completeness of reasons. If p appears to require both q and not–q it must be that it is really p and r, and not p by itself, which requires either q or not–q. I would be grateful if Professor Chisholm would elaborate on this point.

3. *The special case of interpersonal conflicts.* Some conflicts of practical reason are interpersonal. This is the case whenever one person has a duty the performance of which will make it impossible for another person to discharge his obligations. Should this affect the considerations of the first person, and if so in what way? Such conflicts call for a special consideration which is not provided by Professor Chisholm. His logic applies to interpersonal conflicts for according to it it is possible that p requires s (i.e. that x will do A) and that q requires t (i.e. that y will do B) whereas it is necessarily true that not (s and t). This means that if (p and q) requires s and does not require t then the requirement for t is overridden by that for s. If we accept that if pRs and s entails not t then $pR \sim t$ it would follow from T4 that if pRs and qRt and $N(s$ and t does not obtain) then 'either not $[(p\&q)R\,s]$ or not $[(p\&q)\,R\,t]$' is a theorem. This means that in every interpersonal conflict at least one requirement overrides the other. This result shows that because Professor Chisholm has not confined his logic to personal conflicts A3 $pRq \supset \sim N$ ($p\&q$ does not obtain) is wider in certain respects than the principle that 'ought' implies 'can' and cannot be justified by it. The result that in every interpersonal conflict at least one requirement overrides the other can be justified, if at all, which I doubt, only by assuming that every interpersonal conflict generates a personal conflict. If the performance of a duty of mine will prevent somebody from discharging a duty then I

have a conflicting duty not to perform the act. I wonder whether Professor Chisholm does maintain this. The fact that he defined (in D8) a *prima facie* duty to refrain from acting in a way which precludes taking the duty of another as a ground for my duty to refrain makes one wonder whether he really intended his logic to apply to interpersonal conflicts at all.

4. *The plausibility of T5.* Professor Chisholm's fifth theorem (which is derived from A7 by substitution) reads: $pRq \supset [(p\&s)Rq \ v \ (p\&\sim s)Rq]$. This means that if both $\sim[(p\&s)Rq]$ and $\sim[(p\&\sim s)Rq]$ then it is not the case that pRq. Since it is necessary that either s obtains or that $\sim s$ obtains the theorem means that there is no requirement which is necessarily overridden. This would have been plausible enough but for the fact that 'an overriding may itself be overridden.' Let us assume that the following is the case:

(1) pRq
(2) sRu
(3) $\sim sRv$
(4) $N[(q\&v)$ does not obtain] & $N[(p\&u)$ does not obtain]

I do not think that the conjunction of these statements is necessarily false. It does, however, amount to a conflict of requirements. Let us, therefore, further assume that the conflicts are resolved in the following way: the requirement for q that would be imposed by p would be overridden both by s and by $\sim s$. But the requirement for q that would be imposed by the conjunction of $p\&t$ would be overridden only by $\sim s$. It would not be overridden by s. If this is the case then the following is true:

(5) $\sim[(p\&s)Rq]$
(6) $\sim[(p\&\sim s)Rq]$
(7) $[(p\&s)\&t]Rq$

The conjunction of (1), (5) and (6), however, contradicts T5. Do we have any reason for concluding that the conjunction is necessarily false? If the fact that the requirement for q that would be imposed by p would always be overridden (as shown by (5) and (6)) would have meant that it is necessary that it is not the case that q ought to obtain (cf. D4), then we should have accepted the conclusion. But since (7) shows that this is not the case, because the overriding of the requirement for q may itself be overridden, we have no reason to accept the conclusion. It may well be a necessary truth that:

(8) $[N\sim(\text{it ought to be that } q \text{ obtains})] \supset \sim(pRq)$

But, it seems to me false that q is not required by p if that requirement is necessarily overridden. I would, therefore, suggest that T5 and with it A7 must be either rejected or modified at least if we wish to preserve Professor Chisholm's other assumptions.

It might be useful to illustrate the sort of situation I have in mind by an example. I am not confident that I have a good example but let me lay the following one:

Promising John that I shall kill him (p) requires killing him (q). John is either sane (s) or insane ($\sim s$). Both impose requirements (different in each case) which are incompatible with killing him and override that requirement, in so far as it is imposed by my promise. But if John has an incurable and very painful illness (t) the overriding is overridden. So that in these circumstances I am required to do what I promised. (This may not be the case if John is insane. His sanity may be essential for the requirement to stick.) It is worth noting that his illness in itself (t) certainly does not require killing him. It is only my promise that does so. The illness is only relevant for the overriding to be overridden. Therefore, it is not open for Professor Chisholm to say that in the cases I have in mind it is always t that requires q and never p. He could, of course, maintain that p does not require q at all and it is only the conjunction of p and t that requires q. The example I have chosen was meant to show that by doing so he would contradict sound moral beliefs. If this example fails to do so, others will no doubt succeed.

C: TYPES OF 'OVERRIDING'

Professor Chisholm's explanation of the notion of overriding makes clear how one can talk of practical conflicts being resolved. It does nothing to explain how they are resolved. To the extent that it suggests that all cases of overriding are essentially alike it is grossly misleading. I shall briefly survey several cases of conflict and of overriding in order to show the different considerations involved. Some of my examples will demonstrate how widely Professor Chisholm's concept differs from the ordinary one. Before I start I wish to mention one important case of such discrepancy. If pRs and qRt and s entails not t, then if $(p\&q)R(svt)$ but $\sim[(p\&q)Rs]$ and $\sim[(p\&s)Rt]$ then according to Professor Chisholm both requirements are overridden, whereas ordinarily we would say that none of them is overridden.

  1. I promised John to make him a gift of my dog on the first of July. Therefore, I have a reason to do so. On the first of June John released me from my promise and I no longer have a reason to give him my dog. This is not a case of conflict nor does Professor Chisholm claim that it is. Yet it is a case of overriding in his logic. There is, of course, nothing wrong in stretching the concept of overriding to cover cases where no conflict exists. It may, however, be thought somewhat unfortunate that such cases should be drastically separated from others which seem to resemble them. Imagine, e.g., that John did not release me from my promise but that my dog died on the first of June. $p\&r$ does not require q, but this is no longer a case of overriding since $p\&r$ is incompatible with q. Professor Chisholm's requirement of compatibility in the definition of 'would be overridden' does not seem adequate to its task.

  2. John, who had invited me to a dinner party greets me with a wanton and humiliating insult when I arrive. His invitation and my acceptance of it are reasons for me to behave politely and not to give offence. His subsequent insult is reason for making clear what I think of his behaviour. This is incompatible with polite behaviour, but the nature of his insult is such that I have no longer any reason for behaving politely. The requirement to be polite is not merely outweighed it is completely cancelled out. If I behave politely I will not be doing something

which I have at any rate some reason to do, for now I have none at all.

3. My daughter is getting married and setting up an independent household. I have reason to give her a dish-washer and a washing machine. Both will save her time and work. I can give her either of them but not both. I should give her the washing machine because it will save more of her time and energy. The reasons for giving her a washing machine override those for giving her a dish-washer, but they do not cancel them out. I still have reason to give her a dish-washer, even though it is overridden. In this respect this example differs from the previous one.

4. I have reason to to provide my daughter with a washing machine but I have also reason to pay her university fees. I cannot do both. The latter reason overrides but does not cancel the former one. In this respect this case resembles the previous one. But the calculation is different. Both the washing machine and the dish-washer serve the same goal—making life more comfortable. A university education will serve my daughter in a different way than having a washing machine. It will broaden her horizon and enable her to acquire a profession and with it economic independence. My present choice involves judgement concerning the relative importance of different values, whereas my previous choice involved merely an estimate of the relative utility of two courses of action with respect to one value.

5. Gordon, an employee of a large financial concern, is offered a deal by which he can make a considerable sum of money by forging one document. He needs the money very badly and therefore has a reason to accept the offer. He is uncertain as to the moral merit of the case. Forgery and breach of faith are usually wrong but he is aware of a powerful argument purporting to establish that in the circumstances the forgery will not be morally reprehensible at all. He turns down the offer, not because he believes that the act would be morally wrong and the moral considerations outweigh the self-interested ones, but because he thinks that he cannot trust his judgement. He is

afraid that the temptation is such that it will affect his judgement and therefore he refuses to consider the pros and cons and
acts in his normal way. I should make it clear that Gordon did
not assess the risk that the temptation will affect his judgement
and did not add this likelihood of making a mistake to his
calculations. He considered the possibility of doing so and dismissed it because he found that he could not trust himself to
evaluate the likelihood of a mistake due to temptation. This is
a case of a conflict of reasons and yet it differs fundamentally
from the previous cases mentioned. Gordon has decided to act
as he did not because he believed that the reasons for his action
outweigh the reasons against it, but because he believed that he
has reason to refrain from fully considering the merit of the
case. Later on he may conclude that on the merits he should
have accepted the offer and yet continue to believe that he was
right in refusing to assess the various factors involved. He acted
on a reason for action of a special kind which I shall call an
exclusionary reason for it is a reason for disregarding other
reasons which do apply to the case. I do believe that Gordon's
reasoning may very well have been valid. But more important
is the fact that people do act, rightly or wrongly, on exclusionary reasons and that the theory of practical reason is at fault for
not recognizing their presence, let alone their importance.

6. While serving in the army Jeremy is ordered by his com-
manding officer to appropriate and use a van belonging to a
certain tradesman. He, therefore, has reason to obey the order.
His friend urges him to consider his action carefully. Maybe
that the loss to the tradesman outweighs the utility to the war
effort of following the order and that it also outweighs the danger
to Jeremy of disregarding it. If this is so, he contends, the
general effects of disobeying on the army's morale and discipline
will be on the whole beneficial. Jeremy, however, refuses to
engage in this reasoning. An authoritative order, he argues, is
an exclusionary reason. It is a reason to perform the act required
and to disregard countervailing reasons. He admits that it
does not exclude all countervailing reasons. If he were to be

commanded to perform a moral atrocity he would refuse. Exclusionary reasons do not usually exclude all contrary considerations. But his, he thinks, is an ordinary case and the exclusionary reason should prevail. Without commenting on the merit of this particular case let me say that Jeremy is right in thinking that the concept of an authority in practical reason entails that its authoritative directions are exclusionary reasons for action. Many explanations of the concept failed by disregarding this.

7. I agree with Professor Chisholm that whenever one has a duty to do *A* it is required that one shall do *A*, or as I prefer to put it, one has a reason for doing *A*. But Professor Chisholm maintains that the contrary is equally true: whenever one has a reason to do *A* (it is required that he should do *A*) he has a duty to do *A*. This makes it impossible for him to deal with the problem of supererogation. Michael has reason to use his earnings for the benefit of his family. He also has reason to donate two-thirds of it to Oxfam. Assume that he does not donate the money. Some will say that he acts wrongly for the money would produce much better results if donated to Oxfam. Others will maintain that he did nothing wrong in not donating the money. The latter may be mistaken but it would be odd to maintain that they are committed either to factual mistakes or to contradiction. Is their position coherent? Assume that they accept that donating the money to Oxfam will do more good than spending it on one's family. They maintain that the donation would have been an act of supererogation and yet that Michael did nothing wrong. They are precluded from saying that the needs of one's family are more weighty reasons than the more pressing needs of other people for this would mean that had Michael donated the money he would have acted on the lesser reason. And yet they are equally precluded from saying that the reasons for the donation are more weighty for they maintain that Michael did nothing wrong in not acting on these reasons.

The way out of this dilemma is through the notion of an exclusionary permission. As Professor Chisholm has mentioned in passing, sometimes saying that an act is permitted is simply saying that there are no reasons for avoiding it. But the notion has several other uses and one of them is that of the exclusionary permission. Saying that I have an exclusionary permission to do an act does not entail that there are no reasons for not doing it but it does entail that there are reasons which entitle me to disregard, to exclude from my considerations some reasons for not doing it. Exclusionary permissions differ from exclusionary reasons in that they do not require that I shall disregard the excluded reasons. They merely entitle me to do so. I do wrong when I do not disregard reasons excluded by exclusionary reasons, whereas I am not doing any wrong when I consider reasons I am permitted to disregard, indeed I may even be acting virtuously.

Those who treat supererogation in the way described above believe that people have an exclusionary permission to disregard certain very weighty reasons but that they act virtuously if they do not do so. Michael did nothing wrong in resolving the conflict of reasons the way he did but not because he acted on the more weighty reason but because he had an exclusionary permission to disregard it. The reasons for asserting such exclusionary permission probably involve belief in a certain autonomy of the individual *vis-à-vis* the needs of other individuals, but this is a different story.

I have mentioned some points which call for clarification. I have also challenged Professor Chisholm on four issues: A3 and interpersonal conflicts, the plausibility of T5, his last condition in the definition of overriding and the promised dog and the problem of supererogation. My main purpose, however, has been to indicate some of the complexity of the problems of conflict of practical reasons and in particular to commend to you the notions of exclusionary reasons and exclusionary permissions.

Comment: 'What does Chisholm require of us?'

BY J. W. N. WATKINS

Professor Chisholm says that his requirement-relation 'is like the relations of logic' (p. 5). But *which* logical relation is it like? Not the relation of logical implication; for that obeys the following principle: if a conclusion *q* is logically implied by premiss *p*, then it is logically implied by any augmented premiss *p&x*, whatever *x* may be (and even if *x* is inconsistent with *p*). I will follow Popper in referring to this as 'the principle of the augmentation of premisses'.[1] It is a conspicuous feature of Chisholm's requirement-relation that it does not obey anything like the principle of the augmentation of premisses: it can easily happen that *p* requires *q* but *p&r* does *not* require *q*.

Chisholm suggests that there is a strong analogy between his requirement-relation and a confirmation-relation (which he interprets as a probability-function). The analogy is a good one, at least with respect to augmentation of premisses. For probability logic allows that the probability of a statement *a* may be maximal relative to a premiss *b*, but minimal relative to the augmented premiss *b&c* (where *b* and *c* are consistent with each other): we can have both $p(a,b) = 1$ and $p(a,b\&c) = 0$.[2]

An advantage of probability logic over classical logic is, of course, that it enables us to relate statements to one another where neither is a logical consequence of the other. But there is a price to be paid for this increased flexibility: we may not

[1] Proposition *3.41 of Russell and Whitehead's *Principia Mathematica* (vol. i, p. 113) expresses the content of this principle, but it is not there dignified by a special name. So far as I know it was Popper who first singled it out and christened it. See his 'On rules of detachment and so-called inductive logic' in *The Problem of Inductive Logic*, ed. I. Lakatos (North–Holland, Amsterdam, 1968), pp. 130–9. The present comment is a straight application of the anti-inductive argument of that paper to Chisholm's 'logic of requirement'.

[2] Popper has provided a neat example: 'Let *a* be the statement that a number drawn from an infinite collection of natural numbers is odd and *b* the statement that the number drawn is prime, and let [*c*] be the information that the number drawn is the number 2' (op cit., p. 132).

'detach' or assert a conclusion which is highly probable, given certain asserted premises; for these premises might be augmented in a way that rendered the conclusion highly improbable. Given evidence b, and given that a hypothesis a is highly probable relative to b, we may *not* conclude that a is highly probable *tout court*. We may not conclude from:

(1) b
(2) $p(a,b) \geqslant 1-\varepsilon$

(where ε is some arbitrarily small fraction) to:

∴ (3) $p(a) \geqslant 1-\varepsilon$

For there may be—(indeed, there always *will* be unless $p(a,b) = 1$)[3]—some statement x (perhaps a *true* statement x) such that $p(a,b\&x) = 0$.

Now in Chisholm's 'logic of requirement', so far as I understand it, the principle of the augmentation of premises is rejected, but *a rule of detachment is retained*. Recasting the three types of argument which he gives on p. 2 in his terms (and using his definition D2 for 'overridden') we get:

(A) (1) p
     (2) p requires s
∴   (3) s is required.
(B) (1) $p\&q$
     (2) $p\&q$ requires $\sim s$
∴   (3) $\sim s$ is required.
(C) (1) $p\&q \& r$
     (2) $p\&q \& r$ does not require s
∴   (3) s is not required.

Here, three different conclusions, the first inconsistent with the second and third, are respectively drawn (asserted, detached) from a series of increasingly augmented sets of premises. Chisholm says that 'each of the arguments is a valid logical argument' and also that 'one may consistently affirm the premises *and conclusions* [my italics] of all three arguments'

[3] See Popper, op. cit., p. 135.

(p. 3). But how can one consistently affirm both '*q* is required' and '*q* is not required'? Unpacking these conclusions into the language of *prima facie* duties (p. 13) does nothing to remove the inconsistency: they become respectively: '*S* has a *prima facie* duty to perform *A*', '*S* has a *prima facie* duty *not* to perform *A*' and '*S* does *not* have a *prima facie* duty to perform *A*'.

If Chisholm had been writing about confirmation instead of about moral rules, he might have claimed that from the premiss: '*a* is highly probable, given *b*; moreover, *b* is true' we are entitled to draw the conclusion: '*a*'s *prima facie* probability is high.' And he might have added that if the probability of *a*, given *b*&*c*, is low, and if *c* comes to be accepted as well as *b*, then *a*'s high *prima facie* probability has been 'overridden' or 'defeated'.[4]

With the hope of retaining something like a rule of detachment, some confirmation theorists have introduced, as a surrogate for the principle of the augmentation of premisses, the notion of *total evidence*. Their idea might be put like this. Suppose that hypothesis *a* is highly probable, given evidence *b*; and suppose that *b* comprises *all* the available evidence; then there is no premiss *x*, not logically implied by *b*, with which *b* might be *justifiably* or *legitimately* augmented. Hence *a*, to the best of our knowledge, *is* highly probable.

Something like this idea of total evidence plays an important role in Chisholm's system. He reports approvingly, and correctly, that Bolzano called the probability of a proposition relative to total evidence its *absolute* probability; and Chisholm regards the distinction between '*prima facie* duty' and 'duty proper' as analogous to Bolzano's distinction between relational probability and absolute probability (p. 14): if *p* requires *q* and if, moreover, 'a survey of all of the relevant *a posteriori* evidence' reveals no *x* such that *p*&*x* either does not require *q* or requires ~*q*, then *q* is not merely required but 'ought to

---

[4] See the paragraph on p. 10 that concludes with the sentence: 'We do not say, in such cases, that one confirmation has been "overridden" or "defeated", in virtue of another, but we could.'

exist' (p. 16)—what had been a *prima facie* duty becomes a *duty*.

I consider that Bolzano's use of the term 'absolute probability' was unfortunate. For 'total evidence' is an essentially *relative* concept: it refers to all the evidence *known to a certain person at a certain time*. So we would have to say that 'the' absolute probability of a proposition may be high for *A* and low for *B*, or high for *A* on Monday but low for him on Tuesday. (This sort of variability is avoided in Popper's construal of absolute probability as the probability of a proposition 'relative', not to *all* evidence, but to *no* evidence, to zero or tautological information.)[5]

The notion of total evidence is obviously an idealized concept: no one could *spell out* all the evidence now available to him. But Chisholm mitigates this difficulty by speaking, as we saw, of all the *relevant* evidence. But a serious difficulty remains.[6] Suppose that *p* represents one piece of relevant information known to *A*, and *r* another. And suppose that *p&r* requires *q*. Now try to formulate the assumption that *p&r* constitutes *all* the relevant information known to *A*. Call this assumption *s*. Now *s* is a *highly relevant* piece of information: without it, *q* merely prescribes a *prima facie* duty; with it, *q* prescribes a 'duty proper'. So *s* was false: *p&r* did *not* include *s* and did *not*, therefore, constitute all the relevant information known to *A*.

And even if 'total relevant information' were a coherent notion it would not do the job it was intended to do. There is no valid inference in probability logic of the form:

(1) *b*.
(2) *b* is the total relevant information.
(3) $p(a,b) \geq 1-\varepsilon$.
∴ (4) $p(a) \geq 1-\varepsilon$.

Nor could there be any valid inference of an analogous pattern

---

[5] K. R. Popper, *The Logic of Scientific Discovery* (1959), p. 318.

[6] Once again I am applying a point made by Popper in the work cited in footnote 1; see pp. 137–8.

in a 'logic of requirement'. The essential point remains: where there is no principle of the augmentation of premisses, there can be no detachment.

The answer to the question posed in my title seems to be this. In Chisholm's sense of 'require', a great deal may be required of us: we may have ever so many *prima facie* duties. But in the sense of 'require' whereby to say that I am *required* to do a certain thing means that I jolly well ought to *do* it, it turns out that *nothing* could actually be required of us: nothing could be asserted to be a duty *tout court*.

Reply to Comments

BY RODERICK CHISHOLM

I cannot do justice to all of the many points raised by Professor Anscombe and Mr. Raz. In what follows I shall restrict myself to eight general points.

1. Both Professor Anscombe and Mr. Raz wonder whether my account is adequate to the fact that there are certain actions which are supererogatory. I would think that in general, if we equate the supererogatory with non-obligatory well-doing, then the concept of supererogation fits very nicely into an ethics of requirement. Where p is some good state of affairs, we can distinguish 'it ought to be that p obtains' from 'S ought to bring it about that p obtains' ('It ought to be that S brings it about that p obtains'). Can't we say, then, that S's bringing it about that p obtains is *supererogatory* if and only if (i) it ought to be that p obtains but (ii) it is not the case that S ought to bring it about that p obtains? (Perhaps we should add 'and it is not the case that S ought not to bring it about that p obtains.') Thus if it ought to be that the poor are fed and if I'm not obligated to feed them (and not obligated not to feed them), then if I do feed them, my act is supererogatory.

Professor Anscombe, however, proposes a rather difficult example. 'Mercy can be noble,' she writes. 'What *facts* will make it so? I don't say there aren't any—but mercy at least is not an obligation in the particular case. It is always supererogatory; otherwise it would be justice, not mercy. Professor Chisholm's account leaves no room for this. Mercy would have to be *required* in an overriding way, to have the right to override the fittingness of punishment.'

The vocabulary of requirement and fittingness is a natural one to use in this situation. Thus St. Anselm wrote: 'When Thou dost punish the wicked, it is just, since it agrees with their deserts; and when though dost spare the wicked, it is also just, since it befits thy goodness.'[1] But the example is difficult because it is not entirely clear what the moral principles are that it presupposes. 'Mercy at least is not an obligation in the particular case.' Just how are we to take the situation?

We may assume that someone A has performed a sinful act and that A's performance of that sinful act requires that A be punished. We may also assume that there is some other person B who is such that his act of mercy in withholding punishment from A is supererogatory. I would suppose that, if B's act of mercy in withholding punishment is supererogatory, then it is not the case that B ought to punish A and it is also not the case that B ought not to punish A. If my account of supererogation is correct, there is a certain good which B's act brings about but which is such that 'in the particular case' it is not B's obligation to bring it about. What would this good be? One possibility is this: that someone, *someone or other*, ought to show mercy toward A. Another is this: that *now and then B* ought to show some mercy, or he ought to show mercy toward *some person or other*. In any of these cases, we could say that B's act of mercy toward A is supererogatory. What happens, then, to the requirement that A be punished? Perhaps we could say that B's act of mercy overrides it.

2. I said that 'the incontinent man may be said, in the following

[1] *Proslogium*, Chapter 10.

DPR

sense, to "do what he knows he ought not to do". His act is one such that his information and moral principles imply that it ought not to be performed; but he restricts his view to only a part of the relevant situation, making use only of enough of his information to be able to draw the conclusion that the act is not one which ought not to be performed.'

Professor Anscombe writes: 'Certainly ignorance of particular facts in a situation is sometimes operative in *akrasia*, but what makes it that as opposed to counter-voluntariness (what Aristotle called *akourion*) is that the ignorance is voluntary, e.g. careless; or even chosen, as when one has the attitude: "I don't want to know about that because I might have to think or act differently if I did." . . .'

I think I may not have made myself sufficiently clear on this point. Akrasia, to be sure, is voluntary ignorance. What I had wanted to suggest was this: the fact that requirements may be overridden and that these overridings may themselves be overridden provides the incontinent man with a number of innocent-seeming ways in which he may keep himself in ignorance and thereby feel justified in doing what he wants to do. Suppose that there obtain states of affairs, *p*, *r*, and *s* of this sort: (i) *p* requires *q*; (ii) it is not the case that the conjunction, *p* and *r*, requires not-*q*; but (iii) it is the case that the conjunction, *p* and *r* and *s*, requires not-*q*. If the incontinent man wants it to be the case that the tempting act *q* is one that he ought to perform, then in contemplating his course of action, he may voluntarily restrict his vision to *p*. Or if he is willing to think of *q* as something that is permitted but not itself a duty, then he may extend his vision to *r*. But if he does not want to think of *q* as being something he ought *not* to perform, then he will not go on to consider *s* or, at any rate, he will not go on to consider the conjunction, *p* and *r* and *s*. He may, however, consider each of the conjuncts separately and then tell himself 'And I have considered each of the relevant pieces of information . . .'. But if he has considered each of the parts without considering the whole, he has left himself in ignorance.

3. Professor Anscombe thinks that my puzzle about the *a priori* is a muddle. I would say that a proposition is *a priori* if it is necessarily the case that anyone who understands that proposition knows that it is necessarily true. This concept has a long and respectable tradition. Thus Leibniz wrote, of the propositions that Locke called maxims or axioms: 'You will find a hundred places that the Scholastics have said that these propositions are evident *ex terminis*, as soon as the terms are understood, so that they were persuaded that the force of conviction was grounded in the knowledge of the terms, i.e. in the connection of their ideas.'[2] (Leibniz excluded the proposition expressed by 'I exist' from the class of axioms or maxims on the ground that, although it is 'an immediate truth, ... it is not a necessary proposition whose necessity is seen in the immediate agreement of ideas. ...') I take it that St. Thomas was also referring to such propositions when he said that certain premisses 'are manifest through themselves'.[3]

Surely there *is* ground for puzzlement if it is the case both (1) that there are certain propositions which are *a priori* in the sense I have described (propositions which are such that necessarily if you understand them then you see that they are true) and (2) that we do seem to make mistakes with respect to *a priori* propositions. We *do* make mistakes in our sums, as Professor Anscombe says. How can this be, if the particular logical and mathematical propositions with which we are concerned, are *a priori*? It seems to me that this fact *does* call for an explanation.

What happens, then, when we make mistakes in our sums? Sometimes, perhaps, there has been a slip of memory: we mistakenly thought we had carried the 2; or we passed over some figure having thought that we included it; or we inadvertently included something twice. ... But sometimes, it must be admitted, we just seem to get the *a priori* proposition wrong. In my haste I may say to myself '7 and 5 are 11' and then the

<hr/>

[2] *New Essays Concerning Human Understanding*, Book IV, ch. 17.
[3] *Commentary on the Posterior Analytics*, Lectio 4, No. 10.

result will come out wrong. But when I utter this formula to myself and then apply it to the column of figures, am I really contemplating the proposition that 7 added to 5 is equal to 11? It's not clear to me that I am. It seems to me rather that I have simply contemplated what Brentano called a 'surrogate' for the proposition and that, had I really contemplated the proposition itself then, if it is *a priori*, I would not have gotten it wrong.

The foregoing, at least, is an attempt to explain how it is that we seem to get certain *a priori* propositions wrong—the ones that we seem to get wrong when we make mistakes in arithmetic. And in my paper I attempted to explain how it is that we seem to get certain other *a priori* propositions wrong—those having to do with ethics. It may well be that the explanations can be improved upon. Unlike Professor Anscombe, however, I think that the facts do call for an explanation.

4. I think that Mr. Raz has misunderstood me on two points. The first is that he takes the expression '*S* is required to perform *A*' as I understand it to mean the same as '*S* has a reason for performing *A*'. But I would say that, although the first of these two expressions implies the second, the second does not imply the first. If I have an irrepressible desire to buy a car but have no money and if you have money and I know how to get it, then I may have a reason to rob you; but, I would say, there is nothing in the situation that *requires* my robbing you.

Mr. Raz has many important and suggestive things to say about having reasons. But much of his discussion, if I am not mistaken, is quite compatible with what I have tried to say about requirement.

5. The second point on which Mr. Raz has misunderstood me concerns my interpretation of 'state of affairs'. As Professor Anscombe recognizes, I understand this expression in such a way that, despite the identity of the evening star with the morning star, that state of affairs which is Socrates viewing the evening star is *not* identical with that state of affairs which is Socrates viewing the morning star. (Indeed I would propose the following criterion of identity for states of affairs: a state of

affairs *p* is identical with a state of affairs *q* provided it is impossible for anyone to believe that *p* occurs without thereby believing that *q* occurs, and it is impossible for anyone to believe that *q* occurs without thereby believing that *p* occurs. Or one might define '*p* entails *q*' as 'It is impossible for anyone to believe that *p* occurs without believing that *q* occurs,' and then cite mutual entailment as a criterion of identity.)[4] But Mr. Raz's discussion shows that he takes me to be using 'state of affairs' in the way in which other philosophers use the term 'event'.

Thus he cites this example: 'Imagine that I witness one man shoot another from a passing car. This, let us assume, requires both that I attend to the injuries of the victim and that I shall pursue his attacker, but doing one of these acts entails the non-performance of the other. Is not this a case of one state of affairs requiring both *p* and not-*p* ?' Suppose we equate *r* with the state of affairs expressed by 'I witness one man shoot another from a passing car', we equate *p* with 'I attend to the injuries of the victim', and we equate *q* with 'I pursue his attacker'. I am inclined to disagree with Mr. Raz's three suggestions, namely (1) that *r* requires *p*, (2) that *r* requires *s*, and (3) that *s* entails not-*p*. I would say that *r* by itself does not require *p*; we must add something to *r* to get a larger situation that requires *p*. But something *different* must be added to *r* to get a requirement for *q*. And *p* and *s* as they stand are not incompatible; it is only by adding something to the one or to the other that we create an impossible situation.

6. In discussing types of overriding, Mr. Raz calls attention to an important distinction I had ignored. Suppose: (i) *p* is such that, when it obtains, it would require *q*; (ii) *p* does obtain; and (iii) *q* is, or becomes impossible. Mr. Raz proposes an example we might put this way: (*p*) I promise a friend to give him my dog (alive) tomorrow; but (*r*) my dog dies between now and tomorrow. Obviously in such a case I am no longer bound by

---

[4] I have tried to set forth my views on states of affairs and their relations to events and propositions in 'Events and Propositions', *Nous*, Vol. IV (1970), pp. 15–24, and 'States of Affairs Again', *Nous*, Vol. V (1971), pp. 179–89.

the requirement imposed by p. But given my definition of 'overriding' (D2), one cannot say, in this situation, that r overrides the requirement for q imposed by p. For the third condition of the definiens is not satisfied, since (we may assume) the conjunction of p and r is incompatible with q.

Let us say that, in such a case, the requirement for q is *nullified*. This concept might best be defined, in the following way, by appealing to temporalized physical possibility:

D10   The requirement for q, that is imposed by p, is nullified at t by s =Df (i) pRq, (*ii*) s occurs at t, and (iii) it is physically impossible that, if s occur at t, then q occur at t or after t.

(We might remind ourselves that 'if John's sitting occurs at t then John's not sitting occurs after t' does not describe a state of affairs that is impossible.)

One important difference between nullifying and overriding would be this. If I am required to perform a certain action A and if the requirement is overriden but not nullified, then I am subject to conflicting requirements and am required therefore to choose between them. But if the requirement that I perform A is nullified but not overriden, I am not thereby subject to conflicting requirements. (It may well be, of course, that the nullification of a requirement, along with the circumstances under which it occurs, creates a new requirement. If I cannot deliver the dog to my friend, then an explanation at least is called for—unless of course the friend is also dead.)

One may ask: 'What if the requirement that you bring about q is nullified and you don't *know* that it is? In such a case aren't you still required to bring about q?' I would say that, from the fact that the requirement that I bring about q is one that has been nullified, it follows that I am no longer required to bring about q. But in all likelihood anything requiring a man to bring about q also requires him to try or to endeavor to bring about q. And so it may well be, that if I don't know that the requirement to bring about q is one that has been nullified, then I am still required to try or to endeavor to bring about q.

7. I had said that, whenever a person is subject to conflicting requirements, at least one of the requirements is overridden and therefore that, although there may be conflicts of '*prima facie* duties', there are no conflicts of 'absolute duties'. Mr. Raz points out correctly that this does not help in connection with interpersonal conflicts. What if you and I have duties which are such that it is impossible for both of them to be fulfilled: I can perform my duty if and only if you cannot perform yours ? If this is in fact the case then there *is* a genuine conflict of absolute duties. But I wonder whether it is in fact the case. Might it not be rather that there are certain actions A and B, which are such that my duty is to perform A if and only if you do not perform B, and your duty is to perform B if and only if I do not perform A ?

8. Mr. Raz asks: 'Are values appropriate items for the R-relation ? . . . If malice is wrong in itself what is it that requires that we shall not act with malice ?'

One might, of course, attempt to *define* value in terms of the requirement-relation. One might say, for example, that the good is that which everything requires. Or, perhaps more plausibly, that a state of affairs is intrinsically good if it is such that (i) something requires that it occur and (ii) if anything requires that it occur then that thing indefeasibly requires that it occur. (See (D5).) Then a state of affairs might be said to be intrinsically bad if it is such that (i) something requires that it not occur and (ii) if anything requires that it not occur then that thing indefeasibly requires that it not occur. Thus if malice is intrinsically bad, then among the things that require that it not occur, and therefore indefeasibly require that it not occur, is one's knowledge that others can be affected by one's acts.

But if we do not thus attempt to define value in terms of requirement, then couldn't we say simply that the fact that a given state of affairs is good imposes a requirement that it occur, and the fact that a given state of affairs is bad imposes a requirement that it not occur ?[5]

---

[5] Mr. Raz notes that my assumptions have the consequence 'that there is no requirement which is necessarily overridden' and he

J. W. N. Watkins raises a number of important questions about the analogy I had drawn between the concepts of the theory of requirement and those of the theory of confirmation. The questions concern what Popper calls 'the principle of the augmentation of premisses' and what Bolzano had called 'absolute probability'. I believe that Watkins has misunderstood me with respect to the principle of the augmentation of premisses and that he is mistaken with respect to absolute probability.

Watkins formulates the principle of the augmentation of premisses as follows: 'if a conclusion q is logically implied by premiss p, then it is logically implied by any augmented premiss $p\&x$, whatever x may be (and even if x is inconsistent with p).' He then notes correctly that in the sense in which I have understood the concept of requirement, 'it can easily happen that p requires q but $p\&r$ does *not* require q.' And then he draws the conclusion that the requirement relation 'does not obey anything like the principle of the augmentation of premisses.' This conclusion is, of course, correct if we take it to mean that the result of replacing 'logically implied' by 'required' in the above statement of the principle of the augmentation of premisses would be false. But Watkins' conclusion is incorrect if one takes it to mean, as evidently he does, that 'in Chisholm's logic of requirement . . . the principle of the augmentation of premisses is rejected.' For I am as certain as Watkins is, that the principle of the augmentation of premisses is true.

This misunderstanding of what I had tried to say lends Watkins to misinterpret the three types of argument I had

suggests that this consequence is counter-intuitive. But I am not convinced that there are plausible counter-examples. Mr. Raz attempts to construct a counter-example by assuming (i) that my promising to kill John requires my killing John, and then noting (ii) that this requirement would be overridden by the assumption that John is sane and also by the assumption that John is not sane. But I do not believe that (i) is true. For even if it is true, as I have suggested, that my making a promise requires my keeping that promise, this requirement could be overridden by the fact that *what* I have promised is that I kill John.

presented at the beginning of my paper. He reformulates the three conclusions, respectively, as (A) '*S* is required', (B) '*S* is required', and (C) '*S* is not required', and he then says, of these three conclusions, that the first is inconsistent with the second and third. But the conclusions, as I had formulated them, were (A) '*S* has a duty to perform *A*', (B) '*S* has a duty not to perform *A*', and (C) 'The requirement, imposed by *p*, that *s* perform *A* has been overridden.' These three conclusions, as I had said, are consistent with each other. (To remove the appearance of inconsistency, I went on to suggest that, in the first two conclusions the expression 'a duty' be replaced by 'a *prima facie* duty'.) If, as Watkins proposes, we reformulate the conclusions using the term 'requires', then we should have, not what he has given us, but (A) 'There is something that requires *s*', (B) 'There is something that requires not *s*', and (C) '*p* is such that, even if it requires *s*, it is entailed by a wider state of affairs that occurs and does not require *s*'.

The application of probability theory is similar. It can easily happen that *p* confirms *q* but that *p*&*r* does not confirm *q* (or that *q* is probable in relation to *p* but not probable in relation to *p*&*r*). Hence the result of replacing 'logically implied' by 'confirmed' in the statement of the principle of the augmentation of premises would be false. But from this it does not follow that, in order to apply the theory of probability, one must give up the principle of the augmentation of premises.

Suppose that *p* confirms *q* and that *p*&*r* does not confirm *q*. Then we may 'detach' the two conclusions. 'There is something that confirms *q*' and 'There is something that does not confirm *q*' and we may add, quite consistently, that the second something entails the first. Or, if we are applying the theory of probability in a particular case, then we may have arguments analagous to the three arguments with which I had begun:

(A) (1) *p* is evident for *S* at *t*

(2) *p* confirms *q*

∴ (3) Something confirms *q* for *S* at *t*

(B)   (1) *r* is evident for *S* at *t*
       (2) *r* confirms not *q*
∴   (3) Something confirms not *q* for *S* at *t*
(C)   (1) *w*, as well as *p*, is evident for *S* at *t*
       (2) *w*&*p* does not confirm *q*
∴   (3) *p* is such that, even if it confirms *q* for *S* at *t*, it is part of a
       wider body of evidence that does not confirm *q* for *S* at *t*.

From 'There is something that requires *S* to perform *A*', we
cannot infer that *S* has an absolute duty to perform *A* (that
S ought to perform *A*). We must also know that this something
occurs and that there occurs no wider state of affairs which
entails that something and which does not require *S* to perform
A. And, analogously, from 'There is something that confirms *q*
for *S* at *t*,' we may not infer that *q* is more probable than not for
S at *t*. We must know, not only that this something is evident
for *S* at *t* and that it confirms *q*, but also that there is no proposition *r* which is such that *r* entails that something, *r* is also
evident for *S* at *t*, and *r* does not confirm *q*.

We can draw an analogy, then, between '*prima facie* duty'
and 'absolute duty', on the one hand, and '*prima facie* probable'
and 'absolutely probable', on the other:

A is a *prima facie* duty for *S* if there occurs an *x* such that *x*
requires *S* to perform *A*; and *A* is an *absolute* duty for *S* if there
occurs an *x* such that *x* requires *S* to perform *A* and there occurs
no *y* such that *x*&*y* does not require *S* to perform *A*.

p is *prima facie probable* for *S* if there is a *q* such that *q* is evident
to *S* and *p* is probable in relation to *q* (*q* confirms *p*); and *p*
is *absolutely probable* for *S* if there is a *q* such that *q* is evident
to *S* and *p* is probable in relation to *q*, and if there is no *r* such
that *r* is evident to *S* and *p* is not probable in relation to *p*&*r*.

If a proposition is thus absolutely probable for a subject *S*,
then it is probable in relation to the totality of propositions that
are evident to *S*.[6] Watkins notes, quite correctly, that these
concepts should be fixed to a definite time, for what is absolutely

----

[6] But it should be noted that, in the above definition, 'absolute
probability' is not *defined* in terms of total knowledge, or total evidence.

probable for S at one time may not be absolutely probable for him at other times. A reference to a definite time x should thus be assumed to be implicit in the formulae above. Watkins feels, therefore, that Bolzano's term 'absolute' is misleading in this use. The term does not matter, of course, as long as we are careful to distinguish the concepts expressed by the following three expressions:

(i) 'p is probable in relation to q'; (ii) 'q is evident to S at t and p is probable in relation to q'; and (iii) 'q is evident to S at t, and for every r, if r is evident for S at t, then p is probable in relation to $q\&r$'.

When the latter concept is applicable, then we may say that p is probable in relation to the *total evidence* of S at t—or, alternatively put, to the totality of propositions that S knows at t to be true. I had said that it is in this third sense of probability that it is correct to say the probability should be taken as the 'guide of life'. This thesis might be expressed in the following rule:

'Base your decisions at any given time, not only upon those propositions you know to be true at that time, but also upon those propositions which are probable in relation to the totality of propositions you know to be true at that time.'

But Watkins, like Popper, has doubts about the practical applicability of any such rule. Such a rule, of course, would be inapplicable if scepticism is true—if there is nothing that we know, or if there is nothing that we know that we know. I think it may be agreed, however, that such scepticism is absurd. In the paper to which Watkins refers, Popper had argued that the following considerations show that our rule cannot possibly be

The definition here given may also be found in my *Theory of Knowledge* (Prentice-Hall, Inc.: Englewood Cliffs, N.J., 1966), p. 9n. I have discussed these concepts in more detail in 'On the Nature of Empirical Evidence' in Roderick M. Chisholm and Robert J. Swartz, eds., *Empirical Knowledge* (Prentice-Hall, Inc.: Englewood Cliffs, N.J., 1973). It should also be noted (I think Watkins may have misunderstood me with respect to this point) that the concepts of absolute probability and of total knowledge, or total evidence, are not involved in my definition of 'absolute duty'.

put into practice: '. . . if *b* is my total knowledge, then I must know this fact before I can use the rule; but if I *know* that *b* is my total knowledge, then *b* was *not* my total knowledge, because my total knowledge was actually *b* plus the knowledge that *b* is my total knowledge.'[7] But is it true that, in order to apply the rule formulated above, I must know with respect to some proposition or set of propositions *b* that *b* is my total knowledge ? I do not think that it is.

Let *p* be the proposition that I have never been on the moon. We may concede, for purposes of argument, that perhaps I do not now know that *p* is true. But I do have a certain body of evidence *e* which is such that *p* is highly probable in relation to *e*. I do not now know what my total knowledge is and, as Popper's argument suggests, it may be impossible for me to know what it is. But I do now know the following general proposition about my total knowledge: that *p* is highly probable, not only in relation to *e*, but in relation to the conjunction of *e* and any other propositions that I now know to be true. And if I can know this general proposition about my total knowledge, then I can also know that *p* is highly probable in relation to my total knowledge—even though I do not know precisely *what* my total knowledge is.

Can one seriously maintain that, in addition to that set of propositions *e* which constitute my evidence for believing that I have never been on the moon, there may yet be, for all I know, a certain further proposition *i* which is such that (1) I know *i* to be true and (2) in relation to *e&i* the proposition that I have never been on the moon is *not* highly probable ? Such a thesis, surely, is totally absurd.

Consider, then, the following type of inference:

(1) *b* is known by *S* at *t*

(2) For every *x*, if *x* is known by *S* at *t*, then $p\,(a,bx) \geqslant I-\epsilon$

∴ (3) $p\,(a) \geqslant I-\epsilon$

[7] K. R. Popper, 'On Rules of Detachment and so-called Inductive Logic', in I. Lakatos, ed., *The Problem of Inductive Logic* (North–Holland: Amsterdam, 1968), pp. 130–9. The quotation appears on p. 137.

If we read the expression $p(a)$ as 'the absolute probability that a has for S at t', then, if I am not mistaken, we may say, of such an inference, that the premisses may be known to be true by S at t, that they logically imply the conclusion, and therefore that, in accordance with the principle of the augmentation of premisses, S may detach the conclusion and affirm that it is true, no matter how the premisses might be further augmented.

II / Choice, Orderings and Morality

Amartya Sen

I INTRODUCTION

As my starting point I shall take David Gauthier's somewhat liberal rewording of a question of Plato: 'Do you really want to convince us that the dictates of morality are in all circumstances coincident with those of rational self-interest or not?'[1] Whether or not youthful Plato was being thus led up the garden path, a generation of the theory of games seems to have made it exceedingly difficult to respond to the question in the affirmative. Gauthier's own answer derives from a study of 'the Prisoners' Dilemma' in which individual rationality seems to lead to collective ill.[2] I think this game is interesting to examine

[1] D. P. Gauthier, *Morality and Rational Self-Interest* (Prentice-Hall: Englewood Cliffs, N.J., 1970), p. 2. Plato's own question seems to have been somewhat less specific and more mysterious: 'Do you really want to convince us that right is in all circumstances better than wrong or not?' (quoted by Gauthier, p. 1, from the translation by H. D. P. Lee of *The Republic*, p. 357).

[2] 'The Prisoners' Dilemma' is presented in R. D. Luce and H. Raiffa, *Games and Decisions* (Wiley: New York, 1958), ch. 5. An interpretation of Rousseau's distinction between 'the general will' and 'the will of all' in terms of the Prisoners' Dilemma can be found in W. G. Runciman and A. K. Sen, 'Games, Justice and the General Will', *Mind*, LXXIV (October 1965), and whether the idea of optimality breaks down in a Prisoners' Dilemma-type situation has been investigated by A. Rapoport, *Two-Person Game Theory* (Michigan, 1966), and J. Watkins, 'Imperfect Rationality', in R. Borger and F. Cioffi, eds., *Explanation in the Behavioural Sciences* (C.U.P.: Cambridge, 1970).

in this context and I shall propose to do so, but first I wish to comment on a preliminary question.

Rationality, as a concept, would seem to belong to the relationship between choices and preferences, and a typical question will take the form: *'Given* your preference, was it rational for you to choose the actions you have chosen?'[3] There is no immediate reason why it should discriminate between one type of preference and another. On the other hand, it seems hardly perplexing to ask: 'While your actions follow rationally from your preferences, will you not agree that these are nasty preferences and your actions weren't morally justifiable?' Morality would seem to require a judgement among preferences whereas rationality would not. Thus viewed, the assertion that the dictates of morality need not coincide with those of rationality might appear to be trivial.

This straightforward disposal of the problem is, however, unjustified for two separate reasons. First, in a situation where the outcome depends on other people's actions in addition to one's own, there is no clear translation from one's preferences over outcomes to actions to be chosen by him. The choice of rational action depends then on the actions of others, and ultimately on the preferences of others. On the other hand, many models of morality would specify certain actions as immoral (or unfair or unjust) given the preferences of all the people involved. Thus rational action and moral action may both be defined on the set of preferences of all and in this context the question of the correspondence of rationality and morality has some substance to it.

Second, one of the interests in games like the Prisoners' Dilemma lies in the fact that the usual postulates of rational behaviour (even after taking into account the preferences of others) yields a situation that is inferior for all. Thus the concept of individual rationality becomes very difficult to define and an attempt to escape from this problem through the use of

[3] Cf. K. J. Arrow, 'Rational Choice Functions and Orderings', *Economica*, New Series, Vol. 28 (1959).

the notion of collective—as opposed to individual—rationality would involve ideas that relate to the concept of morality.

In the next section the Prisoners' Dilemma is examined in the light of these observations. In Section 3 two variants of the Prisoners' Dilemma are introduced and in this context the idea of a moral ranking of preference orderings is studied. Developing this idea further, in Section 4 a model of morality is proposed and some of its uses examined.

2   THE PRISONERS' DILEMMA, RATIONALITY AND MORALITY

There are, so the story runs, two prisoners to be tried, each known to be guilty of a major crime (jointly committed), but the prosecution does not have enough evidence to prove this. What the prosecution does have is proof of a joint minor crime. So each prisoner is asked separately whether he will confess or not. If both do, then they will be tried for the major crime but get a reduced sentence, say 10 years. If neither does then they will be tried for the minor crime and will get 2 years each. If one does and the other does not, then the pillar of society goes free and the other gets the full penalty of 20 years. Given this choice, each argues that if the other does confess it is better for him to confess also and if the other does not then again it is better that he confesses. So each decides to confess and led by reason they go to prison for 10 years each whereas they would have got only 2 years each if they each refused to confess. That's the dilemma.

Notationally, let a_1 and a_0 stand respectively for prisoner A confessing and not doing it, and similarly b_1 and b_0 for prisoner B confessing and not doing it. The preference orderings of A and B (in descending order) are respectively:

A: $a_1b_0, a_0b_0, a_1b_1, a_0b_1.$
B: $a_0b_1, a_0b_0, a_1b_1, a_1b_0.$

For A and B respectively a_1 and b_1 are strictly dominant strate-

gies and a_1b_1 will be the outcome, but both prefer a_0b_0 to a_1b_1.
They would be both better off with a mutual non-confession
contract, but it would be in the interest of each to break it
unless there is enforcement. Rousseau's much-researched-on
statement on the necessity of being 'forced to be free' seems to
be shockingly relevant.[4] But in the absence of enforcement, they
are both worse off despite strictly 'rational' behaviour.

In what sense is confession rational? In the absence of a contract neither prisoner can influence the other prisoner's action
and given the other prisoner's action—no matter what—it is
better for each to confess. That individual rationality may produce a situation that is collectively worse is known in other
contexts also, but this case brings out the conflict very sharply
indeed.

What about morality? We would seem to get a lead from
Kant's dictum: 'Act always on such a maxim as thou canst at
the same time will to be a universal law.'[5] Certainly neither
prisoner would like that confessing becomes a universal practice, and the only universal law that each prisoner would like
is that everyone should refuse to confess, since a_0b_0 is superior
to a_1b_1. Thus non-confessing would seem to satisfy Kant's
'moral law.'[6] It satisfies Sidgwick's 'principle of equity' as well
which would require that 'whatever action any of us judges to
be right for himself, he implicitly judges to be right for all
similar persons in similar circumstances.'[7]

What about Rawls' concepts of fairness and justice?[8] In the
primordial equality of the 'original position', each would have

[4] Runciman and Sen, p. 556.

[5] I. Kant, *Fundamental Principles of the Metaphysics of Ethics*,
translated by T. K. Abbott, 3rd edition (Longmans: London, 1907),
p. 66.

[6] In this simple case, it also satisfies the somewhat more rustic
'golden rule' of the Gospel: 'Do unto others as ye would that others
should do unto you.'

[7] H. Sidgwick, *The Method of Ethics* (Macmillan: London, 1907),
p. 379.

[8] J. Rawls, 'Justice as Fairness', *Philosophical Review*, Vol. 67
(1958); also his *A Theory of Justice* (Harvard: Cambridge, Mass.,
1972).

EPR

clearly preferred that neither should confess. It certainly improves the position of the worst-off person since it improves the position of each.[9] Since $a_0 b_0$ is the only outcome that is Pareto-superior[10] to the individualistic outcome, it is possible to derive a principle in favour of non-confession from the Pareto principle also.

And Hare ?[11] His—as Hare takes a lot of pains to explain—is not a system of morality but one of the language of morals. But recommending non-confession would seem to satisfy Hare's two 'rules of moral reasoning': 'When we are trying, in a concrete case, to decide what we ought to do, what we are looking for (as I have already said) is an action to which we can commit ourselves (prescriptivity) but which we are at the same time prepared to accept as exemplifying a principle of action to be prescribed for others in like circumstances (universalizability).'[12] Again the choice would seem to fall between $a_0 b_0$ and $a_1 b_1$, and each would prefer the rule of non-confession.

Suppes' 'grading principle' of justice will support this too and it is easily checked that non-confession is a 'justice-saturated strategy' for each.[13] Also Harsanyi's 'ethical preferences' must demand that each should prefer non-confession to confession

[9] In a critique of the Runciman–Sen paper referred to earlier, John Smyth argues that 'there is no reason to suppose that the general will does will the *just* resolution of conflicting interests' ('The Prisoners' Dilemma II', *Mind*, LXXXI (July 1972)). He points out that 'there is every reason for supposing that "just", like good in G. E. Moore's scheme of things, is a unique predicate that cannot be identified with any particular set of things—conduct, contracts, rules, or whatever' (p. 430). Even without entering into a debate as to whether this is the case or not, it should be explained that we were referring to the particular theory of justice of Rawls—as we did say and as Smyth quotes us saying—and in that framework it is clear that non-confession would correspond to a just solution.

[10] V. Pareto, *Manuale di Economia Politica* (Societa Editrice Libraria: Milano, 1906).

[11] R. M. Hare, *The Language of Morals* (Clarendon Press: Oxford, 1952); *Freedom and Reason* (Clarendon Press: Oxford, 1963); *Essays on the Moral Concepts* (Macmillan: London, 1972).

[12] Hare, *Freedom and Reason*, pp. 89–90.

[13] P. Suppes, 'Some Formal Models of Grading Principles', *Synthese*, Vol. 6 (1966); reprinted in his *Studies in the Methodology and Foundations of Science* (Dordrecht, 1969).

though their actual preferences—Harsanyi calls them 'subjective preferences'—might go in favour of confession.[14]

We can discuss moral models (or principles of moral reasoning) put forward by others, but we have already covered a broad spectrum and it is indeed easy to see that it will be difficult to find a moral argument in favour of confession by the prisoners. The conflict between moral (or just) action in any of these models and rational behaviour in the usual sense is, therefore, obvious in this case. It is, however, significant that if all pursued dictates of morality rather than rationally pursuing their own self-interests, all would have been better off. This isn't really very surprising. Sacrificing some individual gain—given the action of others—for the sake of a rule of good behaviour by all which ultimately makes everyone better off is indeed one of the most talked-of aspects of morality. But it is interesting to enquire in this context whether morality can be expressed in the form of choice between preference patterns rather than between actions. We take up this question in the next section.

3 PREFERENCE TYPES, MORALITY AND WELFARE

Consider a variation of the preference orderings of the two prisoners:

A: $a_0b_0, a_1b_0, a_1b_1, a_0b_1.$
B: $a_0b_0, a_0b_1, a_1b_1, a_1b_0.$

In this case each prisoner would prefer to confess if he felt that the other would do that and let him down, but would not confess if he thought that the other would not. In this variant of the Prisoners' Dilemma there are two equilibrium points, viz. a_0b_0 and a_1b_1, and what the outcome would be would depend on how each prisoner expects the other to behave. The interesting difference between this game—I shall call it the Assurance

[14] J. C. Harsanyi, 'Cardinal Welfare, Individualistic Ethics and Interpersonal Comparisons of Utility', *Journal of Political Economy* Vol. 63 (1955). See also P. K. Pattanaik, 'Risk, Impersonability and the Social Welfare Functions', *Journal of Political Economy*, Vol. 76 (1968).

Game—and the Prisoners' Dilemma is that a contract of mutual non-confession does not need any enforcement in the Assurance Game whereas it is the crux of the matter in the Prisoners' Dilemma.[15] Each prisoner will do the right thing if it is simply assured that the other is doing it too and there is no constant temptation to break the contract.

The preferences in the Prisoners' Dilemma and in the Assurance Game will be called here PD-preferences and AG-preferences respectively for the sake of brevity. It is of interest to note that not only is it the case that acting according to the AG-preferences makes it possible to avoid social inoptimality in terms of AG-preferences, it makes it possible to avoid social inoptimality in terms of PD-preferences as well. That is if everyone behaved *as if* they had AG-preferences and had the assurance of similar good behaviour by others, they would be better off even if they actually had PD-preferences.

Even the requirement of assurance does not arise if the individual preferences were the following:

A: $a_0b_0, a_0b_1, a_1b_0, a_1b_1.$
B: $a_0b_0, a_1b_0, a_0b_1, a_1b_1.$

Here a_0 and b_0 are strictly dominant strategies for A and B respectively and each would appear to be adamant on not letting the other person down. Calling these preferences OR-preferences, meaning other-regarding preferences, it is clear that if both behaved *as if* they had OR-preferences they would definitely be better off even in terms of PD-preferences compared with what would happen under individually rational behaviour under PD-preferences.

Under AG-preferences and OR-preferences a_0b_0 is clearly the best outcome for all and under PD-preferences it is the only outcome better for both than the non-cooperative solution of the PD-game. AG-preferences guarantee that this optimum

[15] A. K. Sen, 'Isolation, Assurance and the Social Rate of Discount', *Quarterly Journal of Economics*, Vol. 81 (1967), and 'A Game-Theoretic Analysis of Theories of Collectivism in Allocation', in T. Majumdar, ed., *Growth and Choice* (Oxford University Press: London, 1969).

will be reached given 'assurance', OR-preferences guarantee the optimum unconditionally, while PD-preferences guarantee that this outcome will never be reached except through an enforceable contract. In so far as morality has got something to do with reaching social optimality, it is tempting to rank the three pairs of preferences in a moral order: OR-preferences, AG-preferences, PD-preferences, and society may evolve traditions by which preferences of the OR-type are praised most, AG-type preferences next, and PD-type preferences least of all. Since for each pair the two members are exactly symmetrical except for the substitution of 'you' for 'me' and vice versa (they are isomorphic to each other), we can treat this as a ranking of three orderings over the possible outcomes. Moral rankings of this kind would seem to correspond closely to the possibility of securing mutual benefits through individual rationality calculus.

The fact that by acting as if one's preferences were of the OR-type mutual benefits could be obtained in terms of PD-preferences or AG-preferences as well, raises the further question of the relation between welfare and preferences. It is common to identify individual preferences as reflection of individual welfare, and—from the end of observations—to treat welfare as a numerical representation of preferences revealed by individual choices.[16] If social pressures are generated to persuade people to act according to, say, OR-preferences, while their true interests correspond to PD-preferences, a dichotomy between revealed preferences and welfare would seem to be necessary.[17]

[16] This assumption is very widely used in welfare economics as well as in studies of consumers' behaviour. A critical evaluation of this approach in some detail is presented in a forthcoming paper ('Behaviour and the Concept of Preference', *Economica*, Vol. XL, 1973).

[17] While this is not the occasion to go into practical debates on modes of behaviour, the controversy in China on the possible use of non-material incentives for running the collectives and communes was closely related to the issue under discussion and even to the particular contrast between PD-preferences on the one hand and AG- and OR-preferences on the other. During the 'Great Leap Forward' period (1958–60), there was a strong attempt to move away from incentive payments towards distribution of a substantial part of the total income

Social inoptimality might be avoidable only by a moral code of behaviour that drives a wedge between preferences and welfare.

An analytical aspect of this whole question is the relevance of ordering the possible orderings of outcomes. Rather than expressing moral views in terms of one ordering of outcomes, it may be necessary to express them through a ranking of the possible *orderings* of outcomes. In the next section this question is examined.

4 ORDERING THE ORDERINGS

Let X be the set of all possible outcomes and π be the set of all possible orderings of the elements of X. A moral view can be defined as a quasi-ordering Q of the elements of π. (A quasi-ordering is a ranking relation that is reflective and transitive but not necessarily complete, as indeed a moral view need not be.)

What does a moral quasi-ordering Q stand for? Various interpretations are possible. It might take the form of a moral desire to have one preference pattern over outcomes rather than another, i.e. for $R^1, R^2 \varepsilon \pi$, if $R^1 Q R^2$ but not $R^2 Q R^1$, the person concerned would have morally *preferred* to have R^1

on some criterion of needs ('the supply portion')—sometimes as much as 80 to 90 per cent (see C. Hoffman, *Work Incentive Practices and Policies in the People's Republic of China, 1953–1965* (Albany, N.Y., 1967)). Interpreting a_0 as working hard oneself, a_1 as not working hard, b_0 as others working hard and b_1 as others not working hard, the PD-preferences may well be typical results of *individualistic* calculus in a system without material incentives (cf. my 'Labour Allocation in a Cooperative', *Review of Economic Stuaies*, Vol. 33 (1969)). There seems to have been a vigorous controversy in China on the subject and also moral argumentation relating to contrasts broadly corresponding to the dichotomy between PD-preferences and AG- or OR-preferences, and an aspect of the 'cultural revolution', which followed the 'Great Leap Forward' and the problems generated then, seems to have been closely connected with this type of issue. See C. Riskin, 'Homo Economicus vs. Homo Sinicus: A Discussion of Work Motivation in China', Conference on New Perspectives for the Study of Contemporary China, Montreal, 1971.

preference ordering rather than R^2 over X. Or else Q may correspond to one's ranking in terms of praiseworthiness, i.e. R^1 deserving more praise than R^2.

Are there any advantages in viewing the problem in this way rather than in terms of a more traditional framework? There would seem to be some. In some models a contrast between moral orderings and actual orderings is not permitted at all and the failure to pursue a moral course—a commonly recognized phenomenon—is quite firmly put on what seems to me to be the rather slender shoulders of *akrasia* ('the weakness of will') In models that do permit such a distinction (e.g. Harsanyi's) there is a zero-one contrast between the actual ordering and one moral (or 'ethical') ordering. In the model prepared here there can be gradations of morality, e.g. one can say—if one wishes to—that AG-preferences are morally superior to PD-preferences and OR-preferences morally superior to AG-preferences. The 'moral-non-moral' zero-one distinction is frequently not robust enough to permit the expression of our thoughts.

Furthermore, the problem of *akrasia* itself, on which some ethical theories depend heavily,[18] becomes much easier to understand once the all-or-none distinction of moral and non-moral behaviour is dropped. There may be a sequence of preference orderings of outcomes ranked by this person in moral terms. He might wish to have a different preference ordering R from the one he does have and might try to move towards higher ranked members of π. But what preference one has is not entirely in one's control. There is nothing particularly schizophrenic in saying: 'I wish I had a vegetarians' tastes, for I disapprove of the killing of animals, but I find vegetarian food so revolting that I can't bear to eat it, so I do eat meat.'[19] This person's attempt at shifting his preferences

[18] See, for example, R. M. Hare, *The Language of Morals*, pp. 169–70, and *Freedom and Reason*, pp. 77–80.

[19] In terms of the classification used in my paper 'The Nature and Classes of Prescriptive Judgments', *Philosophical Quarterly*, Vol. 17 (1967), this would be a 'non-compulsive' value judgement.

in the vegetarian direction is clearly a moral exercise given his disapproval of killing, but should he fail to make it, it might be a bit glib to describe it as a 'weakness of will'. But it is a case of a failure to do something which the man in question would regard as morally superior (on the grounds of its following from an ordering that he morally prefers).

This model may be of some relevance also in resolving the problem of the impossibility of the 'Paretian liberal' which I have tried to discuss elsewhere.[20] There are two persons A and B, the latter a prude and the former anything but one. There is a book, say, *Lady Chatterly's Lover* (henceforth *LCL*) to which A is pro and B is anti. A would like best that both read it, next best that B alone reads it ('stuffy B's horizon needs broadening more than mine'), next best that he himself reads it, and worst of all nobody reads it. For B, the best alternative is that nobody reads it, next best that he himself does so alone ('poor A is more vulnerable than me'), next best that A alone reads it and the worst of all that both read it. There is only one copy of the book. A liberal who believes in the Paretian criterion of social improvement ('if everybody prefers x to y, then x is socially better than y') faces the following dilemma:

If the choice is between B alone reading *LCL* and nobody reading it, I should think that it is better that he doesn't, since he himself doesn't wish to and as a liberal I shouldn't let A's desire that B reads *LCL* interfere with this. If the choice is between nobody reading it and A reading it, I think A should read it, since A wants to and I shouldn't let B's desire to stop A from doing it interfere with this. If the choice is between A reading it and B reading it, as a believer in the unanimity rule (the Pareto principle) I must support B's reading it since both prefer that to A's reading it. So—let's see—it is better that B reads it rather than A, better still that nobody reads it (rather than B does), even better that A reads it (rather than none), still better that B reads it (rather than A), . . .∞

[20] A. K. Sen, 'The Impossibility of a Paretian Liberal', *Journal of Political Economy*, Vol. 78 (1970), and *Collective Choice and Social Welfare* (Oliver & Boyd: London, 1971), chs. 6 and 6*.

In this triple every alternative seems worse than another; there is an intransitivity—in fact there is no best element, which is an even stronger result than intransitivity for a finite set.[21] So there is a conflict in this and one must choose between the unanimity rule (the Pareto principle) and the liberal principle as interpreted here. Consider now a liberal who is ready to stick his neck out in favour of *A* reading it (since he clearly wants to) and *B* not (since he does not). If he is an outsider, then there is no immediate problem and he simply overrides some preferences on grounds of their 'nosiness'. But if he is *A* or *B*, how can he justify his decision? He himself 'prefers' that *B* reads it rather than *A*, so how can he say that *A* 'should' read it rather than *B*? The answer lies in his evaluation of his own preference. Suppose we are concerned with *A*. He can now argue:

I do prefer that prude *B* reads it; it will do him a lot of good. But he does not want to. And I am liberal enough to believe that if he does not want to then he should not. So given his preference, I should not really prefer that he should read the book. I must rank my preferences, and my preference that he reads it is of a lower moral order than what my preference would be if I took his views into account.

Similarly a liberal *B* would be able to escape from depriving *A* from reading *LCL* and reading it himself by prefering a more moral preference ordering (incorporating liberal values) to the one he actually expressed. Both the arguments turn on a ranking of preference orderings.

It can be seen that in terms of the basic preference structure the Paretian Liberal paradox has the same ordering as the Prisoners' Dilemma.[22] Putting a_1 and a_0 respectively for *A*'s

[21] This problem arises not only in this example, but completely generally; see Theorems 6*1 and 6*2 in my *Collective Choice and Social Welfare*, pp. 87–8. For some internal inconsistencies in liberalism itself, see A. Gibbard, 'Is the Libertarian Claim Consistent?' (mimeographed), Dept. of Philosophy, Chicago University, 1972.

[22] Pointed out in Ben Fine's 'Individual Liberalism in a Paretian Society' (mimeographed), London School of Economics, 1972.

reading *LCL* and his not reading it, and putting b_0 and b_1 respectively for B's reading the book and his not reading it, we get exactly the PD-preferences. Left to themselves a_1b_1 will happen, i.e. A the non-prude will read it and B the prude will not. This is Pareto inferior to a_0b_0, i.e. A the non-prude not reading it and B the prude reading it. In the Prisoners' Dilemma the individualistic outcome a_1b_1 was criticized on Paretian grounds (and related ones). Here the liberal accepts a_1b_1 and criticizes the use of the Paretian criterion. Where does the difference lie? Undoubtedly in the differential moral status of the respective preference orderings in the two cases. In the original Prisoners' Dilemma example the preference for a_0b_0 over a_1b_1 (shared by PD-, AG- and OR-preferences) is not dominated by some other ordering on any obvious moral grounds, whereas in the liberal paradox it clearly is ranked lower by a liberal than a preference ordering incorporating liberal values. The difference lies in the ordering of the preference orderings.

5   CONCLUDING REMARKS

Games of the type of the Prisoners' Dilemma bring out a conflict between individual rationality and social optimality. From this a contrast between rational behaviour and morality can be derived in terms of the usual models of moral reasoning.

It is, however, significant that some simple variations of the preference pattern in the Prisoners' Dilemma make morality and rational behaviour perfectly consistent. More interestingly, if people behave *as if* they have these modified preferences (AG- or OR-preferences in our example), they end up being better off even in terms of their unmodified preferences (PD-preferences). On the practical side this raises important questions about cultural orientation of behaviour (an illustration of this problem was given in terms of work motivation in rural China) and on the analytical side this causes difficulties for the usual treatment of individual welfare orderings as identical with revealed preferences (common, for example, in welfare economics).

In this context a broader question on the framework of moral judgements was also examined. It is possible to define a moral ordering not directly on the space of outcomes (or actions) but on that of the orderings of outcomes (or actions). I have tried to demonstrate that there are advantages in such a framework.

Comment: 'Self-interest and Morality'

BY J. W. N. WATKINS

Sen claims that the Prisoners' Dilemma reveals an obvious and clear-cut divergence between the dictates of rational self-interest and the dictates of morality—or, at least, of any morality that satisfies both a principle of fairness and the Pareto-principle.[1] This claim is highly plausible; nevertheless, I shall resist it (in Section I). After pointing out that certain variations in the prisoners' rankings of the outcomes would, respectively, render the collectively best outcome either likely or even certain, Sen further claims that the primary task, in moral reasoning, is to rank alternative *rankings* of outcomes in a meta-ranking. I shall also resist this claim (in Section II).

I

By 'dictates of morality' I mean the implications of a man's moral outlook for what he should *do* in given situations. It is to be expected that a person with a strong moral outlook will rank various alternative states of society differently than would an amoral person guided solely by self-interest. But that is not our question. Our question is whether his moral outlook will lead him to *act* differently. Like Sen, I will consider only one kind of situation, that exemplified by the Prisoners' Dilemma.

[1] What the Pareto-principle (in its stronger form) says, essentially, is that if some or all of the people concerned prefer x to y while none of them prefers y to x, then x is socially preferable to y.

To simplify the discussion I will operate exclusively with two pure types of actor. I will call them the Egoist and the Moralist. They are equally intelligent and rational, and they have similar preferences (both prefer Mozart to pop, Jane Austen to porn, or whatever). There is just one big difference between them: the Egoist in all his actions is trying to satisfy optimally just his preferences, whereas the Moralist gives equal weight to the preferences of people who would be significantly affected by his action (or inaction).[2] Our Egoist may be quite an amiable fellow with considerable sympathy with other people's feelings. He would prefer to step round, rather than on, another's gouty toe. But we must not endow him with so much sympathy as to turn him into a crypto-Moralist. For example, any sympathy felt by him for a poker-opponent who is losing heavily must not be so lively as to disturb his aim of maximizing his own winnings.

In a society where some people have power over others it seems rather likely that someone in a position of power would act differently if he were a Moralist than if he were an Egoist. But Game Theory, in which the Prisoners' Dilemma arises, assumes that the players are essentially equal. No player exercises any *control* over another player. The police, in the Prisoners' Dilemma, set the conditions of the game, but only the prisoners play it, and *they* are equals. (I suggested on another occasion that, except that there are only two of them, the situation confronting the prisoners is formally analogous to that confronting the individuals in a Hobbesian state of nature[3]— which is a paradigm of a human condition where no one is in any way beholden to anyone.) Given conditions of non-coercion and equality, it is no longer so obvious that a Moralist will act differently, other things being equal, than an Egoist would. After all, the Egoist, in trying to do as well as he can for himself,

[2] This is in line with Hare: 'For the essence of morality is to treat the interests of others as of equal weight with one's own.' (R. M. Hare, *Applications of Moral Philosophy* (Macmillan: London, 1972), p. 115.)

[3] J. W. N. Watkins, 'Imperfect Rationality' in R. Borger and F. Cioffi, eds., *Explanation in the Behavioural Sciences* (Cambridge University Press: Cambridge, 1970), § 5.2.

has to take very careful account of the people with whom he is competing, co-operating, or otherwise interacting. True, he takes other people's preferences into account in a very different spirit from that in which a Moralist takes them into account. Still, he does attend to them (if he is rational, as Game Theory assumes) very closely. I think that it is significant that Game Theory, although it imputes a kind of ruthless egoism to the players, has turned out to have considerable ethical suggestiveness (for instance, in connection with fair arbitration), just because it assumes equality and rationality.

But this brings us to the Prisoners' Dilemma and to Sen's claim that 'the conflict between moral (or just) action . . . and rational behaviour in the usual sense is . . . obvious in this case' (p. 59).

I will take over Sen's notation, where a_1 stands for 'A confesses', a_0 for 'A does not confess', b_1 for 'B confesses' and b_0 for 'B does not confess'. The four possible outcomes, expressed negatively in prison years, may be represented thus:

	b_0	b_1
a_0	$-2, -2$	$-20, 0$
a_1	$0, -20$	$-10, -10$

In each pair the figure on the left represents A's 'payoff', that on the right B's.

Just how A would rank these four collective outcomes if he were a Moralist we will consider in a moment. That he would rank them differently than he would if he were an Egoist is not in dispute. The question is whether his different, and moral, ranking of them would lead him to *act* differently; and the answer to this is not so obvious. As Sen rightly says, 'in a situation where the outcome depends on other people's actions in addition to one's own, there is no clear translation from one's preferences over outcomes to actions to be chosen by him' (p. 55). To discover whether, within the set-up of the Prisoners' Dilemma, Moralism and Egoism dictate different *actions* requires a detailed investigation. Sen did not undertake this. I will. The results will turn out to be rather counter-intuitive. Various assumptions are possible about the amount of information one prisoner has about the other. It will turn out that, under most of these assumptions, even if *both* prisoners were Moralists, they would be in a dilemma about how to act analogous to the dilemma of two Egoists. Under one limiting assumption the dilemma gets resolved in the right way. But under an alternative assumption it gets resolved in the *wrong* way. Instead of a systematic divergence, we shall find a considerable *convergence* between the dictates of morality and the dictates of self-interest. Moreover it will turn out that, judged by a criterion of collective utility, Moralism has no clear-cut advantage over Egoism.

Now to the details. Let prisoner A be a moralist. (How he came to be involved in a serious crime need not concern us. Indeed, the reader is asked to forget the sordid, and strictly irrelevant, details of this specific version of the game. What matters is its formal structure.) How he will rank the outcomes is, I think, clear enough. He will regard both a_1b_0 and a_0b_1 as bad because so grossly *unfair*. Since they are equally unfair he is free to discriminate between them on extra-moral grounds. He therefore ranks a_0b_1 (which gives him twenty years in prison) last, and a_1b_0 next to last. As to the two equally fair outcomes, he obviously prefers a_0b_0 as Pareto-superior to a_1b_1. Thus his ranking (in descending order) will be: a_0b_0, a_1b_1, a_1b_0, a_0b_1. (Notice that this ranking is different both from Sen's AG-ranking and his OR-ranking. I will revert to this in Section II.)

But does he act differently from the way he would if he were acting out of self-interest? Let us consider the problem that faces A under various assumptions as to his knowledge about B.

1. Suppose that A does not know whether B is an Egoist or a Moralist. (In this imaginary society everyone *is* either an Egoist or a Moralist.) Then the fact that A regards a_0b_0 as the best outcome by no means dictates that he should choose a_0. In this

case, A faces a painful dilemma: a_0 will lead either to the *best* or (if B chooses b_1) to the *worst* outcome. Choosing a_0 involves a major gamble. Choosing a_1 involves only a minor gamble but guarantees that the morally best outcome will *not* be achieved. I will call this horrid choice a type-(1) dilemma.

2. Suppose that A knows that B is a fellow Moralist who, however, does not know that A is a Moralist. Then A knows that B is facing a type-(1) dilemma: there is a serious risk that B will play safe with b_1, and A may still prefer to defend against that risk with a_1. I will call A's dilemma here a type-(2) dilemma.

3. Suppose that A knows that B is a Moralist who knows that he, A, is a Moralist; but A also knows that B does not know that A knows him, B, to be a Moralist. Then A knows that B is facing a type-(2) dilemma and hence that he, B, may prefer to play defensively with b_1. Then A's dilemma is still unresolved (though his temptation to gamble on a_0 has no doubt grown stronger as we proceeded from case (1) to case (3).)

4. Suppose that A and B are both Moralists who know that the other is a Moralist *and* that the other knows him to be a Moralist. Now at last the dilemma is resolved, and in the right way: A can choose a_0 knowing that B will choose b_0.

Case (4) constitutes a clear success for Moralism. But now consider a different case which, however, is like (4) in not being infected by uncertainty due to lack of information about the other player: A is again a Moralist who knows all that he needs to know about B for him (A) to make a rational choice.

5. Suppose that A is a Moralist who knows B to be an Egoist. Now the orthodox game-theoretical view, which Sen accepts, is that a rational agent acting from pure self-interest is bound to choose a dominant strategy if one is available to him, as it is here. (I will shortly question this view; but the result we are about to obtain will not be disturbed.) This means that B is bound to choose b_1. Suppose that A accepts the orthodox view, and hence regards b_1 as certain. Then A must choose a_1 to secure the second best and avoid the worst outcome. In this

case, the a_1b_1 outcome seems inevitable. Here, the Moralist's dilemma *is* resolved, but in the wrong way.

Let us now make A an Egoist, like B. Is it true that two Egoist prisoners are likewise condemned to the a_1b_1 outcome? The orthodox view implies that the so-called 'Prisoners' Dilemma' is not really a *dilemma* at all (for self-interested prisoners). Against this I have argued elsewhere,[4] with acknowledgements to Rapoport, that the Prisoners' Dilemma does confront [Egoist] prisoners with a genuine dilemma, that it represents one kind of situation (there are others) where the idea of acting rationally (in the sense of acting in an optimizing way according to the logic of the situation) breaks down. Since this argument is relevant to the present discussion I will reproduce it here.

The argument gains plausibility as the a_1b_1 outcome is worsened, and the a_0b_0 outcome improved, relative to a_1b_0 and a_0b_1. (The criterion of identity for this 'game' is just the *order* of the pay-offs; so long as this is preserved, changes in the amounts of the pay-offs do not alter the game from a game–theoretical point of view.) So as a preliminary step I will revise the outcomes as follows: if one prisoner confesses and the other does not, the first gets one year in prison, the second 20 years; if both confess, both get 18 years; if neither confesses, both get 2 years. Thus we get this revised matrix:

	b_0	b_1
a_0	$-2, -2$	$-20, -1$
a_1	$-1, -20$	$-18, -18$

As before, a_1 dominates a_0 and b_1 dominates b_0.

6. Suppose now that A and B are both rational Egoists. Prisoner A begins by reasoning as follows. 'If B chooses b_0, I do better with a_1 than with a_0; and if B chooses b_1, I again do better with a_1 than with a_0. In short, whatever B does, I do better with a_1. So I must obviously choose a_1.'

At this early stage A is still looking at a_1b_0 as a hopeful

4 Op. cit., pp. 202–6.

possibility. But now he reflects that B is, after all, just as self-interested and rational as himself; and this surely means that B, likewise, will obviously choose b_1. The immediate effect of this realization is simply to reinforce A's previous conclusion: 'If B is sure to choose b_1 I must certainly *not* choose a_0, for that would give me the worst pay-off of all.'

So far so good; or rather, so bad: for it now seems to A that they are heading inevitably for 18 years; although 18 years is not so bad as 20 years, it *is* very bad. Presumably B too is bleakly resigned to a similar fate.

'But dammit,' A exclaims to himself, 'we *don't* have to resign ourselves to 18 years. We have been offered the chance of 2 years. Let us grab it. We have only to swerve from our present collision courses. B must surely see this too.'

So A veers towards a_0. But now he has second thoughts. What if B outsmarts me with b_1? 20 years! And suppose he doesn't: then I can outsmart with a_1. One year!'

So A veers back towards a_1. But not for long. He sees all too well that if B is likewise veering towards b_1, they are back at square one, heading for 18 years. 'But dammit,' A exclaims . . .

I am claiming, not that rational self-interest does dictate a_0 for A and b_0 for B, but only that it does not dictate a_1 and b_1: the prisoners *are* in a dilemma; there is no determinate solution to their optimization-problem.

I will round off this part of the discussion by reconsidering the mixed case of an Egoist up against a Moralist.

7. Suppose that B is an Egoist who knows that A is a Moralist who knows that B is an Egoist. Then B might reason as follows: 'For A the best outcome is a_0b_0. So A would dearly like to choose a_0. Good. I will choose b_1 and stand a good chance of getting a_0b_1, my best outcome. But wait: A will presumably anticipate this choice of mine; and this will oblige him to choose a_1, since a_1b_1 is his second-best outcome, while a_0b_1 is his worst outcome. But this only makes it all the more essential for me to stick to b_1: it would be disastrous for me to choose b_0 against his a_1.'

FPR

Case (7) is case (5) again, but considered now from the Egoist's point of view. If B's reasoning here is correct, as it seems to me to be, that supports the conclusion provisionally reached under (5), namely that our Moralist A would be obliged to choose a_1 if he knew that he was up against an Egoist B.

Thus we arrive at the remarkable, and rather disconcerting, conclusion that the prospect of a happy (that is, a_0b_0) solution of the Prisoners' Dilemma is even less hopeful when one of the prisoners is a Moralist than when both are Egoists. How can this be?

I think that the answer lies in the equality and symmetry of the prisoners' situations when both are Egoists. Just because both can depend on the other instinctively plumping for his dominant 'strategy', each can see very well where they are heading (18 years) and each can see that if both swerve on to the opposite course they will serve their interests much better (2 years). (True, each can also see that if only *he* swerves, he will get 20 years; yet if neither of them swerves . . . this is the dilemma.)

In the other case there is no such symmetry: the Egoist knows that his thinking is not being duplicated by the other prisoner. Now he is up against someone who rates 18 years for both as the *second-best* outcome.

The results of our survey seem to me to be rather interesting, in a discouraging sort of way. The orthodox game-theoretical view that two rational Egoist prisoners are bound to end up in a_1b_1 is certainly plausible; and given this view, it is again plausible to attribute this poor collective performance to their egoism: if only A had not selfishly preferred a_1b_0 to a_0b_0 and B had not preferred a_0b_1 to a_0b_0, if only each had tried to satisfy the other's interest equally with his own, then, presumably, they would have achieved a_0b_0?

Instead, it has turned out that the honours, with regard to collective benefit, are pretty even between Egoism and Moralism (a Moralist being someone who tries to satisfy others' interests equally with his own). In those cases—(1) to (3)—where a Moralist lacks a relevant piece of information about the other prisoner, he is faced by a dilemma which he may resolve in either way. In those cases—(4) to (7)—where both prisoners know all they need to know about each other, Moralism scores one success: if both prisoners are Moralists, then their dilemma is resolved in the right way and a_0b_0 is assured. Egoism cannot match this result: if both prisoners are Egoists, there is only the *possibility* that each will emerge from his dilemma in a way that achieves a_0b_0. The outcome of their situation is indeterminate. But this Moralist success is offset by a failure. Replacing one of two Egoist prisoners by a Moralist *worsens* their situation: its outcome is now determinate, but in the wrong way: a_1b_1 is now assured.

II

I turn now to Sen's suggestion that the primary task for a moral agent is not to get results, but to lick his preferences into a good shape (the idea being that, if everybody did this, good results would follow of themselves).

It seems to me (though I will not argue this here) that a moral agent's first concern should be to get results (reduction of suffering, removal of injustices, and so on): he should be essentially outward-looking. I am against ethical views that give morality an introverted twist—for instance, the view that to act rightly is to act from the right motive. (Someone who, conceding that a politician, say, has done well, says: 'Yes, but what was his *motive*?' is, to my mind, asking a morally irrelevant psycho-analytical question which, psycho-analysis has taught us, may be very difficult to answer.)

Sen's suggestion seems to me to come rather close to this. It seems to imply that to act rightly is to act from the right preference-ordering. And this would tend to give morality an introverted twist: the primary question for a moral agent would no longer be: 'What changes in the human world around me ought I to try to bring about?' But: 'How ought I to order my preferences?' But two things lead me to suspect that Sen is really on my side here. First, he does not actually demand that we order our preferences aright, but only that we *act* as if we had done so: a kind of collective utility-promoting pose is asked of us. Second, the *only* justification that I can discern for what he calls OR-preferences is that they have been so rigged as to ensure the right result (a_0b_0) in the Prisoners' Dilemma.

Let me spell out the contrast between OR-preferences and the way our Moralist assesses the various outcomes. (I should mention that, after hearing Sen's reply to the first version of this paper, I now think that I am unfair to him in what follows. He was not really advocating OR-preferences for their own sake. Rather, in comparing them favourably with AG- and PD-preferences, he was illustrating his idea that moral philosophy may function as a meta-level ordering of alternative orderings of preferences over outcomes. However, my criticism of OR-preferences can stand as a contribution at this meta-level.)

As I conceived him, the Moralist has personal preferences, just like other people. He (in the person of Prisoner A) ranks a_0b_0 as morally preferable to a_1b_0, not because he personally prefers two years in prison to one, but because, giving B's similar preferences parity with his own, he sees that a_0b_0 is fair and will satisfy their respective interests best.

Our Moralist ranked a_1b_1 as second-best and a_0b_1 as worst. In Sen's OR-preferences, this is reversed: A ranks a_0b_1 as second-best and a_1b_1 as worst. Frankly, I find this sub-ordering absurd, from the points of view both of morality and of self-interest. Why on earth should A 'prefer' the outcome that is (i) grossly *unfair* and (ii) gives him the *worst* pay-off? Does being moral mean being such a glutton for self-punishment that one actually *welcomes* a glaring injustice to oneself? (One can see why Sen does not expect us actually to *have* these preferences, but only to act as if we had them.)

I admit that a morally good man might spend some moral

effort in trying to reorganize his preference-system, especially if he had a disposition (e.g. pederasty) whose indulgence he regarded as harmful to other people. But as I envisage him, his main moral effort goes, not into self-reform, but into trying to act upon the world around him in a way that takes equal account of other people's preferences. This conception is essentially dualistic: it is perfectly possible that someone would personally *prefer* to do one thing but decides, more or less regretfully after taking other people's preferences into account, that he *ought* to do another. Sen claims that his approach is helpful in connection with 'the problem of *akrasia*' (p. 63), but on my dualistic view there is nothing philosophically problematic about *akrasia*: 'weakness of will' or 'backsliding' is rather to be expected when people who can see well enough what they ought to do find that it is not at all what they would personally prefer to do.

This brings us back to the main question: do the dictates of morality, as here conceived, systematically diverge from those of self-interest? Those philosophers who conceive moral conduct as conduct inspired by a purely moral motive have a vested interest in an affirmative answer: otherwise people might be doing the right thing for the wrong reason, and where then would morality lie? For my part, I am not interested in analysing the motives of a man who is acting well, and I have no wish that people should be under continuous temptation to act wrongly so that they will be the more praiseworthy when, by an effort of self-abnegation, they succeed in acting rightly. For me, the more overlap there is between prudence and morality, between leading a happy life and leading a good life, the better. The Prisoners' Dilemma appeared to Sen and others, with good reason, to drive a wedge between prudence and morality: it appeared to be a paradigm of a situation where prudence dictates one course and morality the opposite course. So I am rather gratified to have found that this appearance is misleading.

Reply to Comments

BY AMARTYA SEN

I

Watkins begins with the statement that 'Sen claims that the Prisoners' Dilemma reveals an obvious and clear-cut divergence between the dictates of rational self-interest and the dictates of morality—or, at least, of any morality that satisfies both a principle of fairness and the Pareto-principle', and proceeds to argue against this claim. This is not quite what I did claim, my contention—as far as this particular point is concerned—being only that 'games of the type of the Prisoners' Dilemma bring out a conflict between individual rationality and social optimality,' and that 'from this a contrast between rational behaviour and morality can be derived in terms of the usual models of moral reasoning.' The 'usual models' covered were those of Sidgwick, Rawls, Hare and Suppes, and since these models do not exhaust all interpretations of morality satisfying 'both a principle of fairness and the Pareto-principle', the quoted claim was neither made nor implied. Furthermore, the main point of my paper was not concerned with the conflict between morality and rational self-interest in the Prisoners' Dilemma, but with claiming certain advantages for defining 'a moral ordering not directly on the space of outcomes (or actions) but on that of the orderings of outcomes (or actions).' The Prisoners' Dilemma served only as an illustration.

II

However, Watkins' analysis of the Prisoners' Dilemma is interesting in itself and I shall try to give it the careful scrutiny that it deserves. I shall argue that Watkins has not really established, as he claims, 'that the honours, with regard to collective benefit, are pretty even between Egoism and Moralism', defining a Moralist as 'someone who tries to satisfy others' interests equally with his own'.

Watkins summarizes his findings related to the different cases thus:

In those cases—(1) to (3)—where a Moralist lacks a relevant piece of information about the other prisoner, he is faced by a dilemma which he may resolve in either way. In those cases—(4) to (7)—where both prisoners know all they need to know about each other, Moralism scores one success: if both prisoners are Moralists, then their dilemma is resolved in the right way and a_0b_0 is assured. Egoism cannot match this result: if both prisoners are Egoists, there is only the *possibility* that each will emerge from his dilemma in a way that achieves a_0b_0. The outcome of their situation is indeterminate. But this Moralist success is offset by a failure. Replacing one of the two Egoist prisoners by a Moralist *worsens* their situation: its outcome is now determinate, but in the wrong way: a_1b_1 is now assured.

First note that even if we accept each of the statements on the individual cases, it is not easy to conclude, as Watkins does, that the honours are 'even.' The responsibility for the failure in the case with one Egoist and one Moralist is put on the shoulders of moralism. Why so? It is, of course, true that we can arrive at this case by 'replacing one of the two Egoist prisoners by a Moralist', but we can equally easily arrive at it by replacing one of the two Moralist prisoners by an Egoist! The success in the case of two Moralists in contrast with the case of two Egoists, conceded by Watkins, is *not* 'offset' by presenting the spectacle of sure-fire failure in the case in which there is one of each type.

III

Next, I would like to dispute Watkins' reading of the individual cases, in particular the last two. The possibility of the emergence of the 'right' solution a_0b_0 in the case of two Egoists is demonstrated by Watkins by an argument that crucially involves the symmetry of the two prisoners' situations. Indeed, as he puts it himself: 'I think that the answer lies in the equality and symmetry of the prisoners' situations when both are Egoists.'

Watkins' analysis of this particular case is both interesting and important, but surely it is a mistake to concentrate on the equality and symmetry in the stories that usually go with the formal presentation of the Prisoners' Dilemma. As long as the orderings of the outcomes remain the same, the actual prison sentences can be varied in any way we like, making the position of the two prisoners quite asymmetrical as far as the magnitude of prison sentences are concerned. For example, if we replace the four pairs $(-2, -2)$, $(0, -20)$, $(-20, 0)$ and $(-10, -10)$ in the original pay-off matrix by $(-2, -1)$, $(0, -12)$, $(-20, 0)$, and $(-10, -11)$, we shall still have the same dilemma. But it will certainly make it difficult to assume that each Egoist presumes that his thinking is being 'duplicated' by the other.

Furthermore, the type of egoistic reasoning outlined by Watkins essentially makes each prisoner assume—at least temporarily—that the other prisoner's action will be a *function* of his own action and will in fact coincide with it. A does it implicitly when Watkins induces him to exclaim: 'But dammit, we *don't* have to resign ourselves to 18 years. We have been offered the chance of 2 years. Let us grab it. We have only to swerve from our present collision courses. B must surely see this too.' It is precisely because B's choice cannot be assumed by A to be a mirror-reflection of his own choice that the dilemma of the prisoners is supposed to arise. 'Let us grab it' is a hollow slogan in this non-co-operative game.

IV

I turn now to Watkins' last case—the Moralist facing the Egoist. His argument that in this case all is lost and a_1b_1 will emerge is based on his assumption—made at the beginning of his paper—that the Moralist puts a_1b_0 and a_0b_1 below both

a_0b_0 and a_1b_1. Given this fact, the Moralist responds to the Egoist's b_1 by choosing a_1.

But is it clear that the Moralist must prefer a_1b_1 to a_0b_1? This is an important question not only for its relevance to Watkins' case (7), but also because this is crucial to Watkins' criticism of the OR-preferences proposed in my paper. The latter is an important element in his critique, presented in Part II of his paper, of my analysis of viewing morality as a ranking of rankings, and Watkins argues: 'my criticism of OR-preferences can stand as a contribution at this meta-level'.

Watkins poses the following rhetorical question for a Moralist preferring the OR-preferences: 'Does being moral mean being such a glutton for self-punishment that one actually welcomes a glaring injustice to oneself?' But no such gluttony need be involved. Consider Watkins' revised pay-off matrix in terms of which he analyses these cases. a_1b_1 produces (–18, –18), i.e. 18 years in prison for each, while a_0b_1 produces (–20, –1), i.e. 20 years for the Moralist and one year for the other. There is nothing extraordinary for a Moralist to prefer (–20, –1) to (–18, –18). Indeed, if these were utility numbers, as in game theory they are meant to be, then a Utilitarian Moralist must accept the superiority of a_0b_1 over a_1b_1, since the former yields – 21 as opposed to – 36 yielded by the latter. Utilitarianism is a rather narrow approach to morality, but it is easy to identify other interpretations of morality which share with utilitarianism the preference for a_0b_1 over a_1b_1.

One can, of course, choose utility numbers such that a Utilitarian need not have this part of the OR-preferences (as he must with Watkins' own matrix).[1] 'Moralists' may or may not in fact have OR-preferences, but what is definitely wrong

---

[1] The utility sum maximization yields the ranking: a_0b_0 best, a_0b_1 tied to a_1b_0 next, and a_1b_0 worst. This is also the result of applying the Watkins matrix to the Watkins definition of a Moralist as 'someone who tries to satisfy others' interests equally with his own'. In the OR-preference specified in my paper we have the ranking: a_0b_0, a_0b_1, a_1b_0, a_1b_1. The only difference lies in the tying of a_0b_1 with a_1b_0 in the former. The superiority of a_0b_1 over a_1b_1 is common to both ranking.

is the view that a Moralist has to be 'a glutton for self-punishment' to prefer $a_0 b_1$ to $a_1 b_1$, and also that in case (7) $a_1 b_1$ is bound to emerge.

V

These are my main disagreements with Watkins. I am, of course, somewhat disappointed that he chose to focus his attention on a relatively narrow aspect of my paper. Regarding the main point that I tried to put forward, viz. the advantages of viewing morality as a ranking of rankings, Watkins says little. He also seems to identify my position with the 'suggestion that the primary task for a moral agent is not to get results, but to lick his preferences into good shape'. This is not my position. In my paper I had in fact tried to show the link between preferences and outcomes and had analysed the advantages of acting according to *as if* preferences—different from the real ones—precisely from the point of view of achievement of results. Watkins seems to concede this later when he is led 'to suspect that Sen is really on my side here'.

These issues are, in any case, only marginally touched in Watkins' engaging paper; his main concern is an analysis of the comparative advantages of 'moralism' and 'egoism' in the Prisoners' Dilemma. The thrust of Watkins' paper lies in the claimed demonstration that the honours are 'pretty even' between 'moralism' and 'egoism'. I have already explained why I do not believe that such a demonstration has been provided.

III / Practical *vs.* Theoretical Reason—An Ambiguous Legacy

Jaakko Hintikka

The interrelations of theoretical and practical reason pose a multiplicity of problems which are of considerable urgency both for theoretical and for practical purposes. In order to cover as many of these repercussions within the purview of my discussion, I shall keep my definition of 'practical reason' as wide as possible, even at the cost of some vagueness. By practical reason I shall simply mean reason in so far as it is occupied with human action, human doing and making, and with the results of such action. I shall mainly consider certain problems concerning the relationships between practical and theoretical reason from a historical point of view. These historical questions will lead us to important systematic problems. In this paper, I shall touch on these systematic problems only in so far as they arise out of historical material and can be discussed by reference to it. I envisage the task of my paper as providing materials and impulses for deeper systematical discussions.

One of the most striking features of the history of the two types of knowledge (reason), theoretical and practical, is that they are almost inextricably intertwined. This inseparability is the main thesis of my paper. Perhaps the best large-scale example of the inseparability is the tradition which is somewhat in eclipse in these days in philosophy and which may perhaps be called the tradition of genuine knowledge as maker's knowledge.[1] 'Maker's knowledge' is here supposed to cover also 'doer's knowledge', for no distinction between *poiesis* and *praxis* is intended. The underlying idea of this tradition may be said to be the idea that we can obtain and possess certain especially valuable kinds of *theoretical* knowledge only of what we ourselves have brought about, are bringing about, or can bring about. It emphasizes thus certain theoretical uses of practical reason, we may perhaps say. A few quotations illustrate this tradition and its different ramifications. A medieval exponent of this idea of 'genuine knowledge as maker's knowledge' is Maimonides who writes:

There is a great difference between the knowledge which the producer of a thing possesses concerning it, and the knowledge which other persons possess concerning the same thing. Suppose a thing is produced in accordance with the knowledge of the producer, the producer was then guided by his knowledge in the act of producing the thing. Other people, however, who examine this work and acquire a knowledge of the whole of it, depend for that knowledge on the work itself. For instance, an artisan makes a box in which weights move with the running of water, and thus indicate how many hours have passed. . . . His knowledge is not the result of observing the movements as they are actually going on; but, on the contrary, the movements are produced in accordance with his knowledge. But another person who looks at that instrument will receive fresh knowledge at every movement he perceives. The longer he looks on, the more knowledge does he acquire; he will gradually increase his knowledge till he fully understands the machinery. If an infinite number of movements were assumed for the instrument, he would never be able to complete his knowledge. Besides, he cannot know any of the movements before they take place, since he only knows them from their actual occurrence.[2]

This quotation illustrates several features of the idea of

[1] I have earlier surveyed it briefly in 'Tieto on valtaa', in Jaakko Hintikka, *Tieto on valtaa ja muita aatehistoriallisia esseitä* (WSOY: Porvoo, 1969), pp. 19–34.

[2] *Guide for the Perplexed*, Part III, ch. XXI (p. 295 of the Friedländer translation, Routledge and Kegan Paul: London, 1904). The passage is also remarkable in that it contains—albeit implicitly—the earliest comparison of the world to a clockwork known to me.

'maker's knowledge'. First, behind it lurks apparently the idea that only the maker of a complex mechanism knows it because only he can know its purpose. This assumption is among the more dated aspects of the tradition of maker's knowledge. It seems to have as one of its antecedents the Aristotelian idea that the defining characteristic of any entity is its peculiar function or product.[3]

Second, in speaking of an infinite mechanism Maimonides has in mind God's knowledge of the universe, which he moves on to consider after the quoted passage. The idea of genuine knowledge as maker's knowledge is hence here being applied *ad maiorem gloriam Dei*. In fact, Maimonides' explicit conclusion is that 'it is impossible for us in contradistinction to God to know that which will take place in future, or that which is infinite'.

The ambivalence of the idea is illustrated by its use by Francis Bacon to advertise the importance of human scientific knowledge. 'Human knowledge and human power meet in one; for where cause is not known the effect cannot be produced.' 'The true and lawful goal of sciences is simply this, that human life be endowed with new discoveries and powers.' The idea of 'knowledge as power' which is here expressed by Bacon is but a different application of the assumption we found in Maimonides. What distinguishes the two is mainly Bacon's optimism with respect to human knowledge, that is, human power. It must in fact be admitted that in many respects pessimistic conclusions from the same principle should have been as close at hand in Bacon's time as the optimistic ones. No wonder we find such Renaissance sceptics as Sanchez inferring in so many words the insignificance of human knowledge from the insignificance of human power over nature. It is a sobering thought that the leading idea of the intellectual background of modern applied science and scientific technology can be traced

[3] I am not quite sure that this applies to Maimonides, although it certainly applies to many other early versions of the idea of 'maker's knowledge'. In Part III, ch. XIII, Maimonides writes that 'it was not a final cause that determined the existence of all things, but only God's will'.

back to sceptical and theological principles calculated to extol the
superiority of the Divine practical reason over the human one.

Other ambiguities in the idea of genuine knowledge as
maker's knowledge are in evidence within the realm of human
knowledge. A glimpse of them is seen in as hardheaded a
thinker as Hobbes, for whom the superior knowledge connected
with a maker's 'practical reason' is demonstrative knowledge.
'The science of every subject is derived from a precognition of
the causes, generation, and construction of the same. . . .
Geometry therefore is demonstrable, for the lines and figures
from which we reason are drawn and described by ourselves;
and civil philosophy is demonstrable, because we make the
commonwealth ourselves. But because of natural bodies we do
not know the construction, but seek it from the effects, there
lies no demonstration of what the causes be we seek for, but
only of what they may be.' (See *English Works*, Vol. 7, p. 184.) A
modern political scientist is undoubtedly envious of Hobbes' conviction that 'civil philosophy' can reach the same demonstrative
certainty as geometry, in contrast to the non-demonstrative
uncertainties of our sciences of nature. Be this as it may,
the serious implication of Hobbes' view is that even within
the realm of human reason the idea of genuine knowledge as
maker's knowledge can be put to uses almost diametrically
opposite to those technological ones Francis Bacon was busy
propagating. In fact, the most straightforward application of the
idea is to use it to argue for the superiority of the knowledge we
have in the field of history and other humanities over the
knowledge we have of nature. One of the most outspoken
defenders of this view was undoubtedly Giambattista Vico
according to whom 'the rule and criterion of truth is to have
made it'.[4] From this principle, he concluded that since the
world of history and society, 'il mondo delle nazioni', is man-
made, our knowledge of it is superior to our knowledge of

---

[4] *Opere* (Laterza ed.), I, p. 136 (quoted by Fisch and Bergin in the
introduction of their translation of Vico's *Autobiography* (Cornell
University Press: Ithaca, N.Y., 1944), p. 38.

'il mondo della natura'. 'Whoever reflects on this cannot but marvel that philosophers should have bent all their energies to the study of the world of nature, which, since God made it, He alone knows; and that they should have neglected the study of the world of nations, or civil world, which, since men had made it, men could come to know.'[5]

It is important to realize, however, that even in Vico we do not have a distinction between two kinds of knowledge but a difference in degree. Hobbes bracketed political science with geometry, and likewise Vico sought to apply his methodological ideas to the realm of mathematics and natural science. True to his principles, he for instance advocated the synthetic (constructive) methods of traditional geometry and disparaged the analytic (algebraic and non-constructive) methods of Cartesian geometry.[6]

These Vichian ideas provoke several different kinds of comments. First, the absence of a sharp methodological difference between humanistic studies and natural sciences in Vico— however great a difference in degree he may have postulated between them—makes their respective status subject to be influenced by experience, especially by the relative success or failure of man's attempts to control his physical environment or his historical destiny. From this point of view, modern experience may be said to demonstrate how little truly intentional action there is even among the phenomena studied in Vico's 'New Science'—that is, in language, culture, history, literature, and politics. Man's mastery over his physical environment has opened a much larger scope for maker's knowledge than the most rudimentary control he exercises over his society or his culture.

This point is not unrelated to a third ambiguity in the idea

---

[5] Vico, *Scienza Nuova*, §331 (tr. by Bergin and Fisch as *The New Science of Giambattista Vico* (Cornell University Press: Ithaca, N.Y., 1948).

[6] Cf. Giambattista Vico, *On the Study Methods of Our Time*, tr. by E. Gianturco (Bobbs-Merrill Co.: Indianapolis, 1965), pp. xxiii–xxvi, 21–30.

of genuine knowledge as maker's knowledge. It concerns the scope of this kind of privileged knowledge. Here the famous contrast between Vico and Descartes may turn out to be a difference of degree rather than a difference in kind—at least when viewed in a suitable light. A. N. Whitehead claimed to have found in Descartes 'the implicit assumption that the mind can only know that which it has itself produced and retains in some sense within itself' (*The Concept of Nature*, Ann Arbor ed., p. 32). Sartre's famous essay on Cartesian freedom is predicated on the attribution of essentially the same presupposition to Descartes. It is not easy to see how these claims are to be reconciled with the kind of knowledge which we according to Descartes have of the physical world and which so offended Vico. Albeit, it is hard not to see something of the Whiteheadian assumption operative in Descartes' discussion of those first and foremost sources of certainty which Descartes finds in the operations of the human mind itself. After all, man's conscious thoughts are as fully of his own making and as fully under his own control as anything one can think of—or so it seems. This interpretation of a Cartesian man as constituting himself through his thinking is supported by the 'performative' analysis of the Cartesian *cogito* for which I have argued earlier.[7] It can also be supported by a juxtaposition of the Cartesian doctrine of man's essence being thinking with the Aristotelian doctrine, elsewhere appealed to by Descartes in so many words, that each thing's essential nature equals its immediate cause.[8]

But if this perspective on Descartes is acceptable, his great antagonist Giambattista Vico is seen to differ from him in the last analysis only by being bolder—or perhaps less critical. For Vico, the scope of epistemologically relevant maker's knowledge is not restricted to human thoughts, plans, decisions, intentions,

[7] '*Cogito Ergo Sum:* Inference or Performance?', *Philosophical Review*, Vol. 71 (1962), pp. 3–32.

[8] 'Reply to the Fourth Set of Objections', Vol. II, p. 112 of the Haldane and Ross translation (Cambridge University Press: Cambridge, 1931).

hopes, and wishes but comprises also their concrete manifestations and results in the realm of culture and society.

Here we may perhaps have a moral for contemporary topical discussions of that paradigm use of practical reason which has sometimes been called 'practical knowledge' or 'intentional knowledge'. This type of knowledge is very closely related to what I have called the idea of maker's knowledge. Miss Anscombe, who has given us some of the most interesting recent discussions of the subject, quotes with approval Aquinas' account of practical knowledge: Practical knowledge is 'the cause of what it understands'.[9] This is strongly reminiscent of maker's knowledge, especially when contrasted by Aquinas to 'speculative' knowledge which 'is derived from the objects known'. Christopher Olsen has in fact argued at some length and with some cogency that the characteristic feature of our knowledge of our intentions is that it is a species of maker's knowledge.[10]

This observation alone does not solve the conceptual problems concerning intentional or practical knowledge. It nevertheless helps us to obtain something of a perspective on such knowledge. One thing we can now see especially clearly is the danger of falling into the Cartesian trap. It seems to me that although Miss Anscombe has not fallen prey to this danger, some of her readers have been misled by the fact that she introduces the idea of knowledge of intentions through examples of one's knowledge of the position of one's limbs and of the place of one's pain. (These are not necessarily examples of intentional knowledge, but they are said to be instances of 'knowledge without observation' under which knowledge of our intentional actions also falls.) These examples are not very happy samples of practical knowledge (maker's knowledge) for a reason similar to the reason why the Cartesian realm of maker's knowledge was pathologically narrow. One simply has to grant to Vico that

[9] G. E. M. Anscombe, *Intention* (Basil Blackwell: Oxford, 1957), p. 87.
[10] *Philosophical Quarterly*, Vol. 19 (1969), pp. 324–36.

an objectively existing painting or poem can be the product of
an act which is as truly creative (and as truly free, Sartre would
add) as the movements of my arms or legs. Without imputing
the mistake to any particular philosopher, I am tempted to
suggest that the use of such paradigms reflects either an
intellectual timidity or else radical pessimism *vis-à-vis* philosophers' chances to understand people's creative activities within
his own culture (and within other cultures, for that matter).

What is even more important philosophically, the use of
one's thoughts or movements of one's limbs as conceptual
paradigms of the objects of intentional knowledge would not do
justice to the nature of such knowledge. It could easily create
the impression that a special kind of direct agency or causation
is needed of the objects of intentional knowledge. This is
definitely not required, it seems to me. The product of my
intentional activity of which I can have 'maker's knowledge'
can be connected with my own action by an arbitrarily long
causal chain provided that this chain is known to me. On the
other hand, a man can play the role of a merely causal factor
without thereby gaining practical or intentional knowledge of
its outcome, viz. when he is ignorant of the rest of the causal
connections. This point was already made vigorously by John
Locke in his criticism of Filmer as applied to the socially
important case of parenthood. Human race is often perpetrated,
Locke observes, 'against the Consent and Will of the Begetter.
And indeed even those who desire Children, are but occasions
of their being, and . . . do little more towards their making, than
Ducalion and his Wife in the Fable did towards the making of
Mankind, by throwing Pebbles over their Heads' (*Two Treatises*,
§54). In brief, according to Locke, God 'is *King* because he is
indeed Maker of us all, which no Parents can pretend to be of
their Children' (ibid., §§52 and 53).

The movements-of-limbs example is misleading because it
does not bring out this important connection between maker's
knowledge or practical knowledge and one's theoretical knowledge of causal dependencies. The only processes involved in this

misleading example are psychophysical ones whose causal mechanisms are largely unknown, at very least to the great majority of human agents. Hence precisely the wrong impression is easily created by it. At best, it may be used to represent the first minimal step in the chain of events leading to the desired result, for presumably some sort of psychophysical activity is always needed to initiate the chain. But even this statement, though unexceptionable, embodies a wrong emphasis, for a man can start a chain of events of the relevant sort not so much by carrying out certain bodily movements as sending out suitable messages. What is being emitted is then information rather than ordinary physical influence.

Our insight into an essential connection between practical and theoretical knowledge establishes an important link with history. In a historical perspective, Vico is speaking of the same sort of practical knowledge as Francis Bacon. By increasing man's knowledge of causal dependencies Baconian science has increased his chances of obtaining maker's knowledge of nature in a sense which Vico would be hard put to deny. Any concept of 'practical knowledge' which is restricted to culture or society as contrasted to (say) technology is thus historically inaccurate.

I suspect that the recent preoccupation of several philosophers with one's knowledge of such things as one's pain and the position of one's limbs is at least partly due to a truly Cartesian reason, viz. to a quest of certainty, that is, a quest of knowledge in a sufficiently honorific sense of the word. As soon as physical paraphernalia are needed, the possibility of something's going wrong is opened, such philosophers seem to have thought. One of Miss Anscombe's examples of knowledge without observation is knowing what one is writing on a chalkboard with one's eyes closed. As Miss Anscombe herself points out, this knowledge is not certain if it is thought of as knowledge of the actual outcome, for this may fail to match the intention. (I may have mistaken a stone for a piece of chalk.) Thus there is a temptation to try to trace the chain of causes back to those early stages where no unreliable foreign implements were employed and where accordingly nothing could have gone wrong. I do not see, however, that the factual certainty of one's control of one's limbs is any greater than the certainty one can have of suitable purely physical causal connections. If anything, the former certainty can sometimes be smaller than the latter, and is not in any way absolute. The slips between the cup and the lip need not always be more numerous than those between the lip and the intention, one may perhaps say. I cannot unfortunately take time out here and criticize the alleged incorrigibility of our knowledge of the position of our limbs or of our mental states such as pains, as I would have to do in order to defend my position adequately. Suffice it here to evoke such *prima facie* counter-examples as the proverbial professor who means A but says B (and who writes down C when the answer is D), Freudian as well as non-Freudian slips of tongue, and the difficulty of practising skills of dexterity and co-ordination. (In one sense, it is easy to aim an accurate gun correctly in that there are no external obstacles to doing so, though in another sense it may be a very difficult feat indeed. Perhaps we should take our clue in this matter from the etymology of the verb 'to intend'.)

In order to avoid misunderstanding, it must be emphasized that practical knowledge certainly is not exhausted by that theoretical knowledge of causal connections which lead up to the desired result, although it may comprise such knowledge as an element. Although I cannot here discuss adequately the nature of such practical knowledge or maker's knowledge, it may nevertheless be pointed out that at the very least the co-occurrence of active awareness of the requisite causal connections with a conceptual framework for judging the outcome of action is required. This outcome may or may not be successful, but one of the most characteristic features of intentional action is that the agent must be able to tell ahead of time (among other things) what counts as success and what not. An especially important element here seems to be this double requirement of awareness of knowledge: it has to comprise *both* knowledge of the causal connections *and* the knowledge needed to judge the outcome. The latter is in some cases due to the agent's knowledge of the nature of the outcome, including its mode of operation. In other cases, it may be due to his decision, that is, to his having imposed on himself aims of a certain sort. Typically, both elements are present.

One of the most interesting variants of the tradition of 'maker's knowledge' in effect suggests that we can have *a priori* knowledge of things only through imposing this kind of anticipatory framework on them.[11] 'Reason has insight only into that which it produces after a plan of its own', says Kant (*Critique of Pure Reason*, B xiii, tr. by Kemp Smith).

The role of this double knowledge of awareness is perhaps perceived best in comparison with other accounts of the nature of practical knowledge. Among many other pertinent things, Miss Anscombe says that when 'events effected by human beings' are called intentional, a special kind of description of these events is being used. 'In fact the term "intentional" has reference to a *form* of description of events' (op. cit., p. 84). This does not solve our problems, however, but rather poses them in a new form. It is notorious that as long as our language is extensional, the mode of description of individuals, predicates, or events is immaterial. Part of the import of Miss Anscombe's remark therefore is the etymologically unsurprising but nevertheless highly significant point that the language of intentions is intentional: substitutivity on the basis of *de facto* identity does not hold in it. But then so is the language of ordinary 'theoretical' knowledge, belief, and expectation. Hence one is naturally led to ask whether the involvement of these notions in the concept of intention might go some way towards explaining the peculiarities of the idea of intentional knowledge. In an intentional production of an outcome a

[11] For a partly historical, partly systematic application of this idea, see 'Quantifiers, Language-Games, and Transcendental Arguments', Chapter V of Jaakko Hintikka, *Logic, Language-Games, and Information* (Clarendon Press: Oxford, 1972).

double creation as it were seems to be taking place. Besides bringing about the result in a purely causal sense (when successful) the agent creates through his knowledge, his beliefs, and his expectations a kind of framework in which the result can be discussed even when the agent is unsuccessful. I do not see why we cannot along these lines try to account for intentional knowledge as a kind of an *informed* maker's knowledge. Perhaps —just perhaps—intentional action is to be understood as being nothing more and nothing less than informed action (doubly informed in the sense I explained earlier). I cannot argue for this suggestion here, but I cannot resist the temptation, either, of reminding you that this is precisely what intentional action should mean in the last analysis historically.[12]

Be this as it may, there are other signs pointing to a greater unity of theoretical and practical knowledge than some recent philosophers have acknowledged. An important *focus* of recent discussions of practical reason and practical reasoning has been the concept of practical syllogism which goes back as far as Aristotle. I find this concept one of Aristotle's less happy inventions, and it seems to me that it has recently created a great deal of unfortunate oversimplification.

In Aristotle, the concept of practical syllogism is best considered against the background of his more comprehensive analysis of the genesis of human action which he carries out under the label of a discussion of deliberation. Aristotle's own description of deliberation is as follows:

'We deliberate not about ends but about means. For a doctor does not deliberate whether he shall heal, nor an orator whether he shall persuade, nor a statesman whether he shall produce law and order, nor does any one deliberate about his end. They

[12] I am told that the term 'intentio' was used for the first time in a theoretical sense in Latin in the translations of Aristotle's writings from Arabic. The two twelfth-century translators, Dominicus Gundisalinus and John of Spain, translated by 'intentio' the Arabic word which apparently had in turn been used to render the original Greek words for form in those cases where this form was present in the soul, that is, literally, where the soul was 'informed'. (I am grateful for this information to Professor Dagfinn Föllesdal.)

assume the end and consider how and by what means it is to be attained; and if it seems to be produced by several means they consider by which it is most easily and best produced, while if it is achieved by one only they consider how it will be achieved by this and by what means *this* will be achieved, till they come to the first cause, which in the order of discovery is last. . . . And if we come on an impossibility, we give up the search, e.g. if we need money and this cannot be got; but if a thing appears possible we try to do it. By 'possible' things I mean things that might be brought about by our own efforts; and these in a sense include things that can be brought about by the efforts of our friends, since the moving principle is in ourselves. The subject of investigation is sometimes the instruments, sometimes the use of them; and similarly in the other cases—sometimes the means, sometimes the mode of using it or the means of bringing it about.' (*Nic. Eth.*, III, 3, 1112b12–20, 24–31, tr. by W. D. Ross.)

Deliberation thus results in decision which initiates the step-by-step realization of the aim. In this process, the same intermediate steps which were contemplated in the opposite order in the deliberation are put into effect one by one.

Practical syllogism is best seen as the first step in the reverse process. It is a minimal step, and presumably the first step, in putting the decision into effect. In it the contemplation of an end and the realization that it can be reached through something which is in one's power are combined to yield an action as its 'conclusion'. As Aristotle puts it, what happens in a practical syllogism 'seems parallel to the case of thinking and inferring about the immovable objects of science. There the end is the truth seen (for, when one conceives the two premisses, one at once conceives and comprehends the conclusion), but here the two premisses result in a conclusion which is an action—for example, one conceives that every man ought to walk, one is a man oneself: straightaway one walks' (*De Motu Animalium* 7, 701a–15).

An interesting clue to Aristotle's meaning is given by his

comparison of the process of deliberation with geometrical analysis: 'For the person who deliberates seems to investigate and analyze in the way described as though he were analyzing a geometrical construction [or proof, *diagramma*] . . . and what is last in the order of analysis seems to be first in the order of becoming' (*Nic. Eth.* III, 3, 1112b21–24).

If a historical reminder is needed of the inseparability of theoretical and practical reason, it is hard to think of a more ironical one than this Aristotelian analogy. For precisely the same geometrical analysis was to be the main methodological paradigm of the first great modern scientists.[13] In Newton this paradigm is emphasized in so many words, but it is scarcely any less conspicuous in Galileo or in Descartes. It offers in fact a useful but neglected systematic model of scientific explanation. It is thus instructive indeed to find precisely the same conceptual model at the bottom of both the most typical operation of practical reason and one of the first and foremost methodological ideas of modern natural science.

Even apart from this historical perspective, Aristotle's comparison shows that the links between the different successive means to an end are assumed by Aristotle to be of the sort studied in the theoretical sciences.

The crucial oversimplification in Aristotle's account of deliberation, however, is the assumption that we can analyse deliberation in terms of linear (i.e. not branching) sequences of ends-and-means. Some of Aristotle's formulations go even further and envisage only one chain of means (intermediate ends) connecting the ultimate end with what we can ourselves do. This is wildly oversimplified, for normally the desired end can be brought about in several different ways. In one passage Aristotle recognizes the problem and says that 'if it [the end] seems to be produced by several means they [the agents] consider by which it is most easily and best produced' (*Nic. Eth.* III, 3,

---

[13] See 'Kant and the Tradition of Analysis', ch. IX of *Logic, Language-Games, and Information* (note 11 above), and the literature referred to there.

1112b16–17). This innocent-looking admission is in reality extremely damaging for Aristotle's purposes in several respects. First, the 'good and ease' Aristotle mentions do not easily fit into his conceptual framework, for this framework seems to be predicated on the idea that values always enter into it as ends. For instance, values are apparently supposed to enter into his discussion of deliberation through ends and the rest of Aristotle's deliberative paraphernalia is in so many words said to consist of means (presumably a hierarchy of means).[14]

In Aristotle's account of practical syllogism, the same feature is in evidence in his idea that the major premise of such a syllogism deals with 'the good' while the minor premise deals with 'the possible'.[15] How differences in value between different competing minor premises could enter into such a picture, remains a mystery.

In his discussion of *akrasia* in the *Nicomachean Ethics* VII, 3, Aristotle seems to assume that only one minor premise can actualize at a time. This is scarcely compatible with the comparison between different ways of bringing about a desired end which we saw Aristotle mentioning, and in any case it would amount to a serious flaw in Aristotle's account of the genesis of human action into which comparisons between different, equally practicable means to the same end frequently enter.

One can put essentially the same point in slightly different terms. If Aristotle had consistently allowed comparisons

[14] Cf. the first sentence of our first quotation above from *Nic. Eth.* III, 3.

[15] *De Motu Animalium* 7, 701a23–30. It is not perhaps immediately obvious that the 'two kinds of premisses' Aristotle mentions here are the major and the minor premiss. That they are can nevertheless be seen in two ways: (i) A comparison with *Nic. Eth.* III, 3,1112b27 strongly suggests that the premisses 'of the possible' are minor premisses. (ii) Otherwise, there is no continuity in Aristotle's argument in *De Motu Animalium* 7. Aristotle wants to say that we occasionally suppress the *minor* premiss of a practical syllogism. 'What we do without reflection, we do quickly.' For this purpose, he needs precisely the distinction between the major and the minor premiss, not any old distinction between different kinds of premisses. On my interpretation, the former is just what is made at the crucial passage in terms of 'the good' and 'the possible'.

between different means to the same end, as he ought to have done and as he at least once did, it would have spoiled the account he in fact gives of a practical syllogism. According to this account, an action results 'immediately' when the major premiss and the minor premiss are at the same time actualized in the soul. This is implausible as soon as a comparison is needed either between different minor premisses or between different longer sequences of means where the realization of sequences is what is involved in the practical syllogism in question.

Modern theorists of practical syllogism have occasionally recognized that something is amiss here. Their remedies have not been very successful, however. Some of them have made the minor premiss of a practical syllogism into a *necessary* condition of the end with which the major premise deals. Then we have a model of human action which is formally unobjectionable. It should be obvious, however, that this course destroys the value of a practical syllogism as a model of intentional action, for it should be obvious that the means through which we in fact realize our ends seldom, if ever, embody necessary conditions of these ends. I do not see that any appeal to *ceteris paribus* clauses or to relative necessity is likely to make a difference here, either.

This line of thought is analogous to the mistake of those interpreters of the Greek geometrical analysis who have it to consist (in the case of theoretical analysis) of a series of deductive inferences which start from the desidered theorem. A closer examination of both the mathematical practice and the pronouncements of the theorists of the method prove this view to be misleading, however.[16]

Other recent philosophers seem to put down the difficulty I pointed out in Aristotle merely as an indication of a difference between theoretical syllogisms and practical ones, of which the latter are not supposed to be 'apodeictic'.[17] Much

[16] See my forthcoming paper (with Unto Remes) on the Greek concept of geometrical analysis.

[17] Cf. Anscombe, *Intention* (note 9 above), pp. 58–9.

more is involved here, however, than just a difference between theoretical and practical syllogisms. Aristotle is overlooking an important structural feature of human decision-making.

In the parallel problems dealt with in Antiquity under the heading of geometrical analysis, the number of solutions (one, more than one, none) and their conditions were studied in the part of a problem which was known in Antiquity as *diorismos*. Neither the theory nor the practice of *diorismos* yields any solution to the problems that beset Aristotelian theory of deliberation, however.

Nor is the presence of several parallel sequences of means to the same end the only respect in which Aristotle's accounts of deliberation and practical syllogism are oversimplified. There is no realistic hope of dealing with deliberation in terms of several linear sequences of means, either. In order to see the difficulties involved here, we may ask: What sorts of entities are the members of these sequences supposed to be? It is clear that we can hope to get away with *linear* sequences only if the members of these sequences are *states of affairs* (specified by propositions). The dependencies between events, processes, particular tools or implements, or other similar entities of a non-propositional type are likely to be too many-faceted to enable us to capture them in linear sequences of means to an end.

It is doubtful whether Aristotle can be said to have held consistently that the different means to an end have to be thought of (at least for the purpose of his account of deliberation) as states of affairs. Some statements of his square quite well with this reading. Others seem to violate it outright. For instance, even in the passage quoted above from *Nic. Eth.* III, 3, instruments rather than their use appeared as a class of means.

But even if we can give Aristotle the benefit of doubt and think of the successive means to an end which are involved in deliberation according to Aristotle as states of affairs, his problems are not yet over. For even if we can in principle describe the realization of the end by means of a succession of states, it is obvious that the point of the description remains to spell out the multivariate causal or functional dependencies between different non-propositional factors of the situation. Aristotle's own analogy with geometrical analysis serves us well here. Although superficial analysts of Greek geometrical analysis still often discuss it in terms of a sequence of *propositions* connecting the desired theorem or construction with axioms, postulates, or previously established results, it is amply clear—especially from actual mathematical practice—that the gist of the famous procedure was to study step by step the interdependencies of the different geometrical entities—lines, circles, points, etc.—involved in the figure which represents the desired theorem or construction.[18] When Descartes and others began to represent these interdependencies systematically in algebraic terms, *analytic* geometry came about. (Here we can see where the name came from.) What is being analysed in geometrical analysis, in brief, is not the inferential step from axioms and earlier theorems to the desired new theorem, but the figure—better, the geometrical configuration—with which the theorem deals. In such analysis, dependencies between more than two terms are constantly present, hence destroying all hope of handling the situation in terms of linear sequences of dependencies between the different entities considered. By analogy, it is safe to say that the same holds of the analyses involved in Aristotelian deliberation.

It may be objected that this fact does not spoil the Aristotelian idea of deliberation, as little as it spoils Greek geometrical analysis. Of course it does not destroy the idea, but it does two other things. First, it introduces an additional uncertainty into the situation of deliberation. It suggests that deliberation can be successful only if it takes into account enough of the entities relevant to the interdependencies dealt with in deliberation. It has, so to speak, cast its net so wide as to include all the entities through which all the relevant chains of inter-

[18] See notes 16 and 13 above.

dependencies, including roundabout ones, pass in the situation in question. This is analogous to the highly interesting fact that a geometrical analysis can be sucessful only if enough of the relevant geometrical entities are considered, in other words, only if enough 'auxiliary constructions' have been carried out in the figure. I have argued elsewhere that this kind of uncertainty is inevitably present in all applications of non-trivial knowledge even when the laws that govern the situation are known.[19] I have also shown that in a sense there cannot in general be any mechanically applicable (i.e. recursive) criterion as to when enough 'auxiliary constructions' have been carried out, although in certain particular theories (including, as it happens, elementary geometry) there can be. This kind of uncertainty is therefore inevitably present in Aristotelian deliberation in general. It leads to the almost paradoxical and highly significant result that the procedure by means of which we humans according to Aristotle reach our decisions is not itself decidable (i.e. effective or recursive).

For another thing, the presence of ramified dependencies which cannot be summed up in linear sequences of means to an end has striking consequences for the notion of practical syllogism. Practical syllogism was supposed to be an account of how knowledge of an end and awareness of a means to it which is under one's control combine to yield an action calculated to realize that end. If instead of just one means one has to keep an eye on several simultaneously or sequentially existing factors a certain configuration of which is the 'means' dealt with in the minor premiss of the practical syllogism, an Aristotelian practical syllogism loses its plausibility. Aristotle assumes that the presence of the two premisses in the soul is somehow—for what psychological reasons, we shall not examine here—sufficient to bring about the action. If the 'minor premiss' says that the means of the desired end consist of keeping the lever A at a certain position with one's right hand

[19] See 'Kant Vindicated', ch. VIII of *Logic, Language-Games, and Information* (note 11 above).

while controlling factor x by turning a knob with his left hand at the same time as a friend of his sees to it that another factor y is not changed by turning another knob, it is not only implausible but ridiculous to say that the agent's mind instantaneously clicks and that he 'straightaway' performs the trick or that he 'straightaway' tries to do it. In general, it seems to me that the whole plausibility of practical syllogism as an account of the actual genesis of human action depends on its being couched in oversimplified terms—to employ logicians' jargon, in terms of propositional logic and/or monadic predicate logic, not even in terms of the full first order logic.

The credentials of the idea of Aristotelian practical syllogism as an embodiment of a special kind of practical cognition are thus seen to rest on oversimplifications. Moreover, there is no reason to think that deliberation in the Aristotelian sense of the word can be disentangled from obviously theoretical uses of reason. On the contrary, those very analogies between geometrical analysis and deliberation which have been brought to light and utilized in the arguments just concluded themselves offer effective illustrations of the inseparability of practical and theoretical reason.

Some of the most important conceptualizations which in the past have been employed to support a distinction between practical and theoretical reason are thus seen to be inadequate or else to fail to uphold any sharp distinction. It also seems to me that a different choice of the ideas to be examined would have yielded the same result, although I would not like to claim any sweeping systematical conclusions yet at this stage of discussion concerning the relation of the two. If there is a general moral to be drawn from my discussion, it probably concerns in the first place those *soi-disant* humanists of today who are in effect cutting themselves loose from much of the most truly humanistic heritage in philosophy—especially from the emphasis on man's creative accomplishments and on their connection with his power—by trying to enforce an oversimplified distinction between different kinds or different uses of reason.

Comment:

BY J. L. MACKIE

The main thesis of Professor Hintikka's paper is that practical and theoretical reason are inseparable. Since I agree with this thesis, I shall comment only on two subsidiary matters. One of these is the concept of genuine knowledge as maker's knowledge. Hintikka has not himself endorsed this, but he has very interestingly shown how the concept has been influential, in several divergent ways, in the history of thought. The other is the practical syllogism, which Hintikka regards as 'one of Aristotle's less happy inventions'.

I MAKER'S KNOWLEDGE

The notion that there is a special sort of knowledge that we can appropriately call maker's knowledge, and that is superior to any other sort of knowledge, is, I think, mistaken. Making something—that is, bringing it about that something exists—does not in itself give the maker any knowledge of what he has made; the belief that it does seems to arise from the confusion of at least six distinct points or suggestions.

1. If the maker makes something intentionally, he must know what he is making or has made; but that is merely because it would not count as intentionally making an X unless he knew that it was an X he was making. It is not that the intentionally-making produces the knowledge, but that the knowledge is a prerequisite for the making being described as the intentional making of an X.

2. There is, nevertheless, a special kind of making which could be described as intentional, or, to mark the difference between this and the merely verbal point made in 1, as intelligent. The craftsman who, say, hammers a brass bowl into shape by hand knows what he is doing, knows more or less how each operation he performs will affect his material, and

sees from moment to moment how the job is coming along. What he does is guided by knowledge of all these sorts. In this kind of making knowledge of several sorts is thus embedded, and this kind of making necessarily involves knowledge of some correct description of the product. Anyone who makes something intelligently, in this sense, will necessarily make it intentionally in the sense of 1 above under *some* description. But what he makes may be open to many other equally correct descriptions of which the intelligent maker is unaware.

3. It is true that a person has a specially direct knowledge of his own intentions and indeed of his conscious thoughts in general. But it would be a mistake to try to explain either this as a species of maker's knowledge or maker's knowledge as a species of this. Making in general does not yield authoritative knowledge of the product, so it cannot be simply because we have in some sense made our thoughts and intentions that we are directly aware of them. But equally, knowledge of the product cannot be subsumed under knowledge of intentions. I know in this special way that I am intending to make an X. But it is only in so far as I succeed in carrying out my intentions that I am actually making an X, and my knowledge whether, or how far, I am succeeding is not of any specially direct sort, but is ordinary observational, empirical, knowledge.

4. Practical knowledge in another sense is knowing how to do or how to make something. This may involve no theoretical knowledge, in which case knowing how consists simply in being able to do or to make whatever it may be; or it may involve theoretical knowledge of the kinds used in the intelligent making of 2 above. In either case, if one both intends to make an X and knows how to make an X, then given favourable circumstances (materials, instruments, and forces) one will make an X. But this conjunction of intending and knowing how will not give the maker any specially direct knowledge of the product like that which he has of his intentions. If his knowing how is of the non-theoretical variety, this conjunction will ensure at most that he makes an X, not even that he knows

at all that he is making one or has made one. If his knowing how includes a theoretical element, then indeed he will know that the processes he is performing are appropriate to produce an X, but his consequential knowledge that he is producing an X rests partly on empirical and observational premises, and can be no more direct or authoritative than his knowledge of these.

5. If we accept the notion of a thing's essence as its immediate cause or as its internal causal mechanism—these two are not sharply distinguishable—we may expect that an intelligent maker of something will know that thing's essence. This is not quite correct, however. You can certainly put a clock together from a prefabricated kit, carefully following the instructions supplied; you will then have made a clock intentionally and at least to some extent intelligently, but you might still not understand how it works. What would ensure that you knew its essence would be your having designed the clock, and not merely having put it together in a subordinately intelligent way. But even the maker who is also a designer has no exclusive knowledge of the essence of what he makes: he is not the only one who can *know* its essence. You can find out how a clock works by taking it to bits rather than by putting it together.

We can concede, however, that the man who has acquired, in whatever way, a knowledge of a thing's essence is at least a potential maker of such a thing: if provided with the right materials, instruments, and forces, he could make one. There is a weakened sense of 'maker's knowledge' in which it is the knowledge possessed by such a potential maker. Hintikka, for example, identifies the underlying idea of the tradition of maker's knowledge, with 'the idea that we can obtain and possess certain especially valuable kinds of theoretical knowledge only of what we ourselves have brought about, are bringing about, *or can bring about*' (my italics). Such *potential* maker's knowledge can indeed be equated with knowledge of the thing's essence. But now the making depends on the knowing, not the knowing on the making. In this sense Newton and anyone who has a moderate grasp of the Newtonian theory has maker's knowledge of solar systems that work simply by inertia and gravitation. It is, indeed, almost laughably easy to make a Newtonian solar system, and it is surprising that having made one should have been taken, in the eighteenth century, as any significant illustration of the wisdom (as opposed to the power) of God.

6. There is a hint, in the passage Hintikka quotes from Maimonides, of Hume's problem of induction. There is indeed a difficulty about *a posteriori* knowledge of any universal law, and it is clear that such knowledge would at best be fallible. But if God *enacts* the laws of nature, brings them into existence by *fiat*, then he can know them infallibly despite their universality. A human legislator can similarly have infallible knowledge of a law, though universal in form, which he himself lays down, at least until the courts start reinterpreting it. But what the human legislator knows *a priori* is only a prescriptive universal, a requirement that all Xs should do such and such or should be treated in such and such a way. The divine legislator is regarded as being able to achieve the same *a priori* knowledge-by-*fiat* of descriptive universals, of the ways in which things will actually behave—a very different matter. And there is also only a remote analogy between the divine legislator's knowledge of these laws of working and the (potential) maker's knowledge in 5 above. The ordinary potential maker's knowledge, though prior to the making, is posterior to the independently existing laws of working of his materials and instruments; the notion that laws of working may be known by being themselves made by *fiat* is something quite different.

Having distinguished these six points, we can consider how some of them bear separately upon the ambiguities that Hintikka has found in the application of this notion of maker's knowledge, in particular the question whether maker's knowledge is peculiar to God, as Maimonides thought, or whether men can share it, and, if they can, whether they should expect to achieve it primarily in the realms of physical science and technology, as Bacon and Descartes thought, or primarily in the social and cultural realm, as Hobbes and Vico thought, or in both.

It is clear that only God could have 6, *a priori* knowledge-by-*fiat* of a universal law of working. On this, then, Maimonides is at least negatively right. There is indeed a Leibnizian (and, with a twist, Kantian) view that 'Thought legislates universally; it reveals the wider universe of the eternally possible; and prior to all experience can determine the fundamental conditions to which that experience must conform' (Kemp Smith, *Commentary to Kant's Critique of Pure Reason*, xxxii). That is, by thinking men can participate in a sort of legislation that yields descriptive laws. But neither the Leibnizian nor the Kantian version of this thesis can be defended. On the other hand, men can know the prescriptive rules of institutions they set up—and this variety of knowledge is restricted to the socio-cultural realm—but institutions may well not actually work in accordance with their prescriptive rules, and they obviously do not work only in accordance with these. What happens in a game of cricket or of chess may conform to the rules but is not determined by them.

Knowledge of 'essences', the potential maker's knowledge, my 5, is within men's scope, and has been widely achieved in the biological as well as the physical sciences. There is no reason in principle why we should not achieve it also in the social sciences, but in fact we have acquired very little of it there. But since this sort of knowledge has only a slight connection with actual making this is not surprising: the fact that social institutions are to some extent human products does not make them peculiarly knowable, just because they are not the products of intelligent manufacture or design, but arise from the interaction of many diverse and conflicting intentions. Hobbes and Vico were mistakenly optimistic, as the later course of social science has shown.

The sort of knowledge possessed by an actual intelligent maker, my 2, is again something that men, justifying some of

Bacon's optimism, have achieved in the realms of physical technology and biological technology—roughly, farming—and there is some risk of their achieving it also in the sphere of genetic engineering. It has not been achieved in the social sphere. The deliberate construction or reconstruction of societies has never yet worked out as planned, and there are fairly good reasons why success in this field is unlikely—one being the lack of maker's knowledge of kind 5. But it is not clear whether the success or the failure of such attempts is the more to be feared.

I have been speaking of *maker*'s knowledge. But Hintikka took this as covering also *doer*'s knowledge, and it may be asked whether my strictures apply also to it. (This point was raised in the discussion by Dr. Müller.) For example, does someone not know that he is singing a certain air even if he has recently become deaf? I should say that my comments under 3 do apply also to this sort of case. For example, someone who cannot sing in tune may think that he is singing a certain air when he is not. This need not stop us from saying that someone who in fact is singing a certain air knows that he is: knowledge need not be infallible. But it does show that such doer's knowledge is not of any specially guaranteed sort. Someone who normally can sing in tune, and knows this, either because he can hear himself singing or because other people tell him so, still knows that he is singing a certain air even after he has suddenly become deaf, though something might have suddenly gone wrong with his vocal cords, or with his control over them, at the same time. But this knowledge that he is actually singing the air, and not merely trying to do so, is no more direct, no less inferential, than our ordinary knowledge about many other things. Roughly, he knows in the admittedly direct way in which we know about our intentions and other conscious thoughts that he is trying to sing this air; but only the inductive or analogical knowledge that when he tries to sing an air, he usually does so, will back up his belief that he is now singing this air.

(In the discussion Professor Anscombe disputed the propriety of saying that someone who actually is singing is trying to sing, and knows this. This is an example of a Wittgensteinian thesis which H. P. Grice has, I believe, shown to be mistaken: conditions which must be fulfilled if an utterance is to have the sort of conversational point it normally has are wrongly taken to be part of its meaning or to be prerequisites for its having a truth-value: if someone is singing, successfully and without impediments, there is no point in *saying* also that he is trying to sing, but he may be doing just what someone who is normally described as trying to sing does, as well as actually producing the notes. But even if Wittgenstein's thesis about 'trying' were conceded, my case can still be made out in other terms. There is something, whatever we call it, that the intending singer knows about himself both in the normal situation and when he has become deaf, and whether or not his vocal cords have gone wrong; but there are only ordinary empirical links between this something and his actual production of the desired air.)

2 PRACTICAL SYLLOGISM

Hintikka has criticized the practical syllogism on the ground that its linearity is an over-simplification which invalidates it both as an analysis of the rationality of deliberation and as an account of the actual genesis of human action. I think he is right about this. But can we begin to repair its faults?

First, we could take account of there being more than one known means to a desired end: then a still much simplified analysis would look like this:

(1) I *prima facie* want to bring about A.

(2) A will come about if B occurs in context C, and C is present.

(3) B will come about if D is performed in context E, and E is present.

(4) I can perform D.

(5) A will also come about if F occurs in context G, and G is present.

(6) F will come about if H is performed in context $\mathcal{J}$, and $\mathcal{J}$ is present.

(7) I can perform H.

(8) So I can bring about A either by performing D or by performing H.

(9) I can see no other way open to me of bringing about A.

(10) The cost of bringing about A *via* D and B is x—arising from the effort involved in performing D and from the side effects of D and B as well as of A.

(11) The cost of bringing about A *via* H and F is y—arising from the effort involved in performing H and from the side effects of H, F, and A.

(12) Cost y is less than x, and is outweighed by the advantage to me of A.

(13) Therefore it is reasonable for me to perform H.

Although, as Hintikka insists, the relevant causal relations and interactions will in fact be very complex, the practical problem can be *treated* as one of alternative almost-linear sequences, each consisting of some performance of the agent and its results against a background of relatively fixed circumstances. Given the circumstances or contexts C and E, the performing of D will bring about the occurrence of B, and this will bring about A, and so on.

Though still, of course, terribly simple, this sort of analysis begins to represent the considerations which in some circumstances make a certain choice of action reasonable. But it is much more doubtful whether it ever represents the actual psychological genesis of human action.

One respect in which this analysis is still oversimplified is that it provides for only one agent, who makes his choice against a background of facts and causal relations only, not one which includes other agents and other choices. As soon as we relax this restriction, we are plunged into the sort of situation studied by the theory of games. But even so, if we can make some assumptions about the purposes, information, and intelligence of the other agents it may be possible to determine what course of action is reasonable either in the sense of being that which gives one the highest expectation of advantage or in the sense of being that which gives one the surest guarantee against serious disadvantage or loss.

But how are we to interpret this reasoning? Is it, or is it not, peculiarly practical? One interpretation would include the fact that the agent has such and such desires or preferences or values, such and such a degree of risk-aversion, and the like, among the premises. The reasoning could then be seen as a way of working out an answer to a *theoretical* question, namely 'What possible course of action is most in accord with these preferences (etc.) and this risk-aversion, given that the facts, especially the causal facts, are thus?' Practical reasoning, so interpreted, would be only a sub-class of theoretical reasoning. It would be a selected fragment of theoretical reasoning, marked off by this form of question, which brings together such things as preferences, possibility, and causal relations, which together are specially relevant to action.

But there is another possible interpretation of such reasoning which makes it more distinctively practical. (This was put forward by Professor Anscombe in the discussion.) Instead of a *premiss* stating that the agent has such and such wishes, preferences, and so on, these wishes are rather something in the background that gives point to the reasoning; the premises are the statements about facts, possibilities, and causal relations; and the conclusion is an action or a decision to act—'So I shall do such and such'.

Now it seems undeniable that there is a kind of thinking which may lead up to decisions and actions of which this second interpretation of practical syllogisms (or their more complex developments) provides a more truthful description or idealization than the first interpretation would. Nevertheless, Hintikka's thesis of the inseparability of practical and theoretical reason can still be defended in two ways in this connection. First, some of the subordinate parts of a piece of practical reasoning, thus interpreted, will be theoretical—e.g. A is the only available means to B, and A in the circumstances would lead to *C*, so I can get *B* only by also bringing about *C*. Secondly, if one wants to assess a piece of practical reasoning as a whole, to characterize it as valid or invalid, the most natural way will be to consider the validity of the corresponding piece of theoretical reasoning which would be yielded by reconstructing the practical argument in the form required for our first interpretation. In other words, a piece of practical reasoning can be called valid just when a related piece of theoretical reasoning validly establishes the truth of a conclusion of the form 'This course of action is most in accord with these preferences, values, etc., given that the facts, especially the causal facts, are thus.'

IV / Reason and Violence: A Fragment of the Ideology of Liberal Intellectuals

Roy Edgley

THE ANTITHESIS BETWEEN REASON AND VIOLENCE: SOME CONTEMPORARY EXAMPLES

I want to consider a version of the idea that violence is contrary to reason, or to put in another way what may seem to be the same point, that reason and violence are antithetical or mutually exclusive. Like many philosophical doctrines, this idea, in all its stark unqualified simplicity, runs counter to common sense; yet it's widespread and deeply entrenched, especially among those involved in certain current issues, whether on one side or another. On one side, the antithesis between reason and violence is taken to show that violence is to be rejected: this is part of the ideology of many liberal intellectuals. On another side, the antithesis between reason and violence is taken to show that reason is to be rejected: this is part of a romantic ideology. I propose to say little about violence and more about reason. For however much at the social level one admires reason and deplores violence, philosophically it's reason that is the chief trouble-maker. It's a common misconception of reason, shared by both sides in this dispute, that generates, or at least supports, the antithesis.

I shall take some examples of the use of this antithesis in the discussion of current affairs, and then move on to another example, my chief target—namely, an abstract and philo-sophical deployment of the antithesis. This conjunction of examples will show how discussion of practical social problems may be infected with a kind of confusion that is in a widely acknowledged sense philosophical. My argument will therefore suggest how philosophy can be relevant to current issues and need not leave everything as it is.

All of my examples come from that side of the dispute where I locate the ideology of liberal intellectuals, the side, that is, which, valuing reason, uses the antithesis to deplore violence. My selectivity is discrimination but not prejudice. I've said that it's a misconception of reason that generates the antithesis. That aspect of the misconception that can be described more generally as an alienation of reason is common to many kinds of intellectuals. Intellectuals generally, being themselves reasoners, or what Ezra Pound irreverently calls 'ergoteurs,' have tended narcissistically not only to exalt reason and, if philosophers, to subject it to close and detailed, not to say loving, scrutiny, but also to see at the centre of the concept, as paradigmatic of reason, their own professionally favoured subject, other matters being thus excluded from its scope. Both Platonistic rationalists and empiricists have alienated reason in this way. But in modern times at least, it's intellectuals of the liberal sort, those most closely related to the empiricist tradition, which revives and flourishes when spectacular advances in natural science dazzle philosophers, who are chiefly responsible for and responsive to the particular misconception of reason relevant here; and historically, the romantic reactions that follow such phases denigrate reason under that very misapprehension of it transmitted to them by these liberal intellectuals. The antithesis between reason and violence, whether used to deplore violence or to deplore reason, is in this way a characteristic product of the liberal intellectual ideology.

Examples of the antithesis are not difficult to find these days, when there has been an increase in violence on the part of individuals, such as students and professional people, who belong to classes traditionally thought of as composed of reasonable and responsible citizens. Indeed, one might suppose that it's reason that is chosen as the antithesis of their objectionable violence not only because the objecting is done by liberal intellectuals but also because the people being appealed to are of these traditionally reasonable and responsible classes. But faced seriously with this choice, those who see violence as necessary will reject reason. The alienation of reason is personal and political. What I shall suggest is that it may nevertheless be rooted in the remotest recess of the academic ivory tower, the philosophy of logic.

Here, then, in the first of my examples is a consort of two British politicians, one Tory and one Labour, arguing (in the words of the *Observer* newspaper report of 7 December 1969) 'against the rejection of reason and the cult of violence'. Of Quintin Hogg (now Lord Hailsham again) the report says that he was 'addressing an academic audience at Trinity College, Dublin . . . and he criticized people who tried to use physical action to prevent the tours of the Springbok rugby team or the South African cricketers. . . . Mr. Hogg said he could understand that socialists should do this but not Liberals. "I am in some ways" ', he is reported as saying ' "what used to be called an old-fashioned liberal (with, however, a small 'l'). I believe in the power of reason and persuasion".' For all Hogg's sneer about socialists, however, the report shows that when it comes to reason and violence Labour supporters can be as reasonable and responsible as Liberals and Tories. Indeed, George Thomson was more explicit about the antithesis. According to the report, 'he found much to admire in the new generation . . . but "what I find depressing" ', he said, ' "is their rejection of reason in favour of the romantic violence of Che Guevara" '. Going on to draw further familiar contrasts commonly thought to be related to this antithesis, he called for 'new thinking about new problems', but stipulated that ' "it should be thinking—however fallible and fumbling —and not simply feeling or shouting . . . feeling can become a substitute for thinking" '; and in the words of the report he referred to ' "our democratic socialist philosophy, with its strong ethical and national content, its emphasis on brain rather than blood" '. In this context, the conclusion is irresistible that 'national' is here a misprint for 'rational'.

I've already mentioned the fact that the popularity of the antithesis between reason and violence is due partly to the growth of violence among sectors of society traditionally expected to be more rational than most. In particular, of all our social institutions those most commonly identified with the 'cult of violence' are the universities. We have perhaps by now got so inured to the situation that it may take an effort to realize how severe a shock this identification delivers to the traditional sensibility, with its accumulated images so taken for granted that they have been enshrined in our very language. The first university was in the grove of Academe, and Plato's academy gave us the adjective 'academic'; and both this and the idea of the university as an 'ivory tower' project an image in which the university's institutionalization of reason and objectivity appear as possible only in a place detached from the rough-and-tumble of society, where studious thought and scholarly discussion can proceed without impediment from more violent activities. In these circumstances, the antithesis between reason and violence has a special appeal to liberal intellectuals on the university faculty, who in their turn take it to have a special application to university students. Here, then, in my second example is Lord James of Rusholme, a distinguished education-ist and university vice-chancellor, writing through the medium of *The Guardian* newspaper of 20 October 1969, an 'Open letter to a new student', a letter addressed to all university freshmen at the start of the academic year: '. . . ultimately the universities exist to promote the life of the mind. As soon as their members reject reason, whether by the use of force, or by showing racial prejudice or taking L.S.D., they're lost. Your greatest task will be to reconcile your new liberty with an underlying authority, that of the pursuit of truth. You are joining a community which, with all its imperfections and inadequacies, is based on the assumption that since you are, *ex hypothesi*, pretty intelligent, you will behave rationally most of the time, and if you want to change things, as you well may, you will use rational arguments, and never anything else.'

American universities are even more obvious targets for the liberal use of the antithesis, and my final example at this popular and commonplace level comes from an American source that is no less exalted for being popular and commonplace. I draw the quotation from the book *Academia in Anarchy*, by Buchanan and Devletoglou, where it stands in pride of place as setting the book's theme, admirably matching in message and quality the book's own chapter on violence. In a passage in which the well-known lawyer subversively implies that the law itself is outlaw, President Nixon has said: 'Intimidation and threats remain outlaw weapons in a free society. A fundamental governing principle of any great university is that the rule of reason and not the rule of force prevails.'

It's an oddity, perhaps not incidental, that in these popular appeals by liberals who use the antithesis to deplore violence and recommend rational argument, the antithesis is not itself supported by rational argument. Reasoning with people who already reject reason might, of course, be recognized as futile. But since not many people are capable of rejecting reason all the time, even these might be caught and converted in an off moment; and in any case, there are waverers to be convinced, and even the convinced would have their conviction clarified and strengthened by such an argument. The sheer absence of argument by those who value argument so highly suggests (cynical suspicions and personalities apart) that those who accept the antithesis, whether liberals or not, accept it as too obvious to require argument. It seems to have for them the force of an *a priori* opposition, as if the mere use of these words in stating the opposition were enough: a conceptual matter, if not too obvious for words, at least too obvious for further words. This suspicion is strengthened when one considers how the concept of reason has fared in the hands of those professional exponents of the *a priori*, the philosophers, ancient and modern. I suggest that acceptance of the antithesis between reason and violence among liberal intellectuals has a philosophical rationale, conscious or otherwise, in those conceptual considerations about reason that have impressed, and been made some of them explicit by, philosophers, especially, so far as contemporary liberals are concerned, by those twentieth century philsophers in the empiricist and analytical tradition.

I come now, therefore, to a contemporary philosopher who has both articulated the relevant features of that tradition, and explicitly committed himself, at a philosophical level, to the antithesis between reason and violence: Popper. Popper's views on reason and violence are to be found most compactly in the address 'Utopia and Violence', originally delivered in 1947 but reprinted in 1963 as essay 18 in *Conjectures and Refutations*. Let me quote from this paper some examples of his use of the antithesis. 'I am a rationalist,' he says, 'because I see in the attitude of reasonableness the only alternative to violence'; 'There are many kinds of disagreement in social life which must be decided one way or another. ... There are, in the main, only two possible ways: argument ... and violence'; 'I believe that we can avoid violence only in so far as we practise this attitude of reasonableness when dealing with one another'; 'I choose rationalism because I hate violence'; 'you cannot, by means of argument, convert those who suspect all argument, and who prefer violent decisions to rational decisions'. Popper refers to 'the hope of defeating violence and unreason', and in his peroration he says of 'the true rationalist' that 'Reason is for him the precise opposite of an instrument of power and violence: he sees it as a means whereby these may be tamed'. That this is still Popper's view is shown by a very recent paper, 'Reason or Revolution' (*Archiv. Europ. Social.* XI, 1970), in which he says that 'reason is the only alternative to violence so far discovered'.

REASON AS ARGUMENT AND REASONING: THE THEORETICAL CONCEPTION OF REASON

If we examine these and the other quotations I've given from newspapers, together with the rest of Popper's 'Utopia and Violence' and another essay in which he explicitly defends 'rationalism', namely 'Oracular Philosophy and the Revolt against Reason' (ch. 26 of *The Open Society and Its Enemies*, Vol. II), we find the antithesis between reason and violence aligned with some contrasts that are differently denominated. On the side of violence we find: emotion, passion, and feeling. On the side of reason: argument, thinking, criticism, discussion, talk, language. The popular current attitude that demands 'a dialogue' as the solution of every dispute clearly favours something that can be grouped with these latter items under the general heading of 'reason'.

Of these associated items it is the notion of argument that figures as the central element in Popper's idea of reason. There is in his writing an easy transition from 'reason' to 'argument'. The change is imperceptible; but is, however, of the last consequence. Popper tends, in fact, to identify reason with argument. The temptation to do this is one to which philosophers and intellectuals in general readily succumb; for they are ergoteurs by profession. It's a temptation, moreover, that is constantly present, for obvious reasons, in the field to which Popper has made his most distinguished contribution, the philosophy of science, and this is so whether the philosopher concerned supports or is opposed to Popper on that issue to which the matter is most relevant, the issue of the rationality or otherwise of science. Feyerabend, for instance, now one of Popper's most uncompromising critics, seems to hold that science is less rational than Popper and others have thought, and one of his reasons is that argument is less effective and important in science than Popper implies. In 'Consolations for the Specialist' (*Criticism and the Growth of Knowledge*, eds. Lakatos and Musgrave), Feyerabend refers, in a section called 'The Role of Reason in Science', to 'entirely new reaction patterns' that may occur in the development both of children and of science, and he writes: 'the only function of rational discourse may consist in increasing the mental tension that precedes *and causes* the behavioural outburst. Now—is this not exactly the kind of change we may expect at periods of scientific revolution? Does it not restrict the effectiveness of arguments (except as a causative agent leading to developments very different from what is demanded by their *content*)? Does not the occurrence of such a change show that science which, after all, is part of the evolution of man is not entirely rational and cannot be entirely rational? For if there are events, not necessarily arguments which *cause* us to adopt new standards, will it then not be up to the defenders of the status quo to provide, not just arguments, but also *contrary causes*? And if the old forms of argumentation turn out to be too weak a contrary cause, must they then not either give up, or resort to stronger and more "irrational" means? (It is very difficult, and perhaps entirely impossible, to combat the effects of brainwashing by argument.) Even the most puritanical rationalist will then be forced to leave argument and to use, say, *propaganda* not because some of his arguments have ceased to be *valid*, but because the *psychological conditions* which enable him to effectively argue in this manner and thereby to influence others have disappeared. And what is the use of an argument that leaves people unmoved?' An almost identical passage occurs in 'Against Method' (*Minnesota Studies in the Philosophy of Science*, Vol. 4), in a section significantly entitled not 'The Role of Reason in Science' but 'The Limits of Argument'; and in footnote 27 of that paper he mentions 'K. R. Popper, whose views I have in mind when criticizing the omnipresence of argument' and adds '. . . are irrational changes an essential part of even the most rational enterprise that has been invented by man? Does the historical phenomenon "science" contain ingredients which defy a rational analysis? Can the abstract goal of coming closer to the truth be reached in an entirely rational fashion, or is it perhaps inaccessible to those who decide to rely on argument only?'

In some of the contexts referred to in my earlier quotations, on reason and violence, the role of argument is so peculiar that nobody but a philosopher could swallow it without acute indigestion. Notice, for instance, the oddity of Lord James' advice to the new university student: 'If you want to change things, as you well may, you will use rational arguments, and never anything else.' Clearly Feyerabend is right here. By and large, the only things that can be directly changed by argument alone, rational or otherwise, are people—their thoughts, feelings, attitudes, and behaviour. But if these people are themselves students who follow Lord James' advice, they in their turn will use nothing but rational arguments in order to change things. One gets a picture of Lord James' ideal university as an insane community of ergoteurs arguing incessantly among themselves and with others, but never actually doing anything else in order to bring about the changes they want. They would never, for instance, cast a vote in an election in order to change things, for casting a vote is not arguing, either rationally or irrationally. They would never book a room for a meeting, for booking a room is not arguing. They would never change their surroundings by painting pictures or making music, for these are not arguing. Is it really suggested that someone who stood in front of a blank canvas and tried to change it into a picture simply by arguing would be a paradigm of rationality? Argument may be required at some point or other in these affairs, but argument alone is hardly likely to be effective.

Popper's discussion of reason and violence is restricted to a narrower context than Lord James', a context not of ways of changing things in general but of ways of settling disagreements or disputes between people. But even within this more restricted range of topics, Popper's claim that 'there are, in the main, only two possible ways: argument . . . and violence' is obviously false unless the qualification is given so much weight that the whole alternation becomes highly misleading. The general problem is this: in a dispute, what methods are there of changing people's states of mind in such a way that the dispute is resolved or ended? It's clear that argument and violence are far from exhaustive. One extremely pervasive way, at both the personal and large-scale social level, is by the threat of sanctions, and another is by the actual use of such sanctions. The law uses these methods, and not all its sanctions involve violence. Workers on strike use them and strikes are not necessarily violent. Non-violent civil disobedience is a further example, and boycott another. Neither is any of these in itself argument; but we should note that as methods of trying to bring a dispute to an end their mode of operation is to give one of the parties a reason for doing something he would not otherwise do. Though arguments involve the giving of reasons, reasons can be given to people in other ways than by argument. Another method of trying to resolve a dispute is by demonstration—and I'm not referring to the kind of demonstration after which one can write 'Q.E.D.'. At the level of personal disputes and disagreements Popper's alternatives of argument or violence are even more obviously far from exhaustive. Without wishing to suggest that I'm here making disclosures about my own private life, I list the following as other ways of resolving disputes: keeping quiet; singing a song; making jokes, especially at one's own expense; giving a present; cooking and eating a meal; having a drink; going for a walk; going to bed and forgetting it; going to bed and making love. Some of these some of the time can be done, and I hope I won't be accused of canvassing my merely subjective opinion if I commit myself to the value-judgement that they should be done, both without violence and without being introduced or accompanied by the solemnities of argument and discussion.

Am I here confusing two different things, on the one hand settling or resolving a dispute and on the other merely ending it? Isn't it the case that there is a dispute or disagreement only if there is some question to which two or more people are offering incompatible answers, so that the disagreement is resolved only if the problem in dispute is solved, at least in the eyes of the disputants? If, for instance, you and I disagree and dispute about whether the British and Stormont policy of internment has strengthened the hand of the I.R.A. provisionals in Ireland, I can end the dispute by shooting you dead. You then no longer disagree with me. But neither, of course, do you agree with me. Have I then resolved the disagreement, even though we are still not in agreement? If this is a confusion, it is Popper's: for he regards violence as an alternative method to argument in deciding disagreements.

An argument, then, may come not merely to an end but also to a conclusion; and it's with conclusions of arguments in this sense that ergoteurs are most familiar. In particular, philosophers and logicians have refined a conception of argument (identified with the concept of inference) according to which an argument is a set of propositions distinguishable into premiss(es) and conclusion, between which holds some logical relation, e.g. of implication, such that the truth or probable truth of the conclusion either does or does not follow from the premiss(es). This logician's conception of argument is typical of the anti-psychologism of much twentieth century thinking in and about logic. Popper himself has played a leading part in the campaign against psychologism, and his 'third world' and 'epistemology without a knowing subject' are the latest products of this campaign. But whatever its value as a demarcation device isolating the logician's specialism, the doctrine of anti-psychologism in the philosophy of logic has been a persistent source of confusion on certain crucial topics. In conjunction with another familiar dogma, the doctrine of the logical autonomy of values, it has for instance helped to breed the illusion that reason is value-free, obscuring the facts that the concept of a valid argument is evaluative or normative ('valid' arguments being 'good' or 'legitimate' arguments) and that the concept of argument or inference as the concept of what is being appraised or evaluated is essentially psychological, i.e. it identifies certain activities or states attributable to people. The notion of logic is closely connected with that of reason, and both, like validity, function as terms of appraisal in this context. Thus an argument that is valid can be said to be a *rational, reasonable,* or logical argument, as opposed to an irrational, unreasonable, or illogical one. If the premises of such an argument are true the conclusion is justified, and the conclusion as well as the argument can be said to be *rational* or *reasonable*; and as the argument argues for, rather than against, that conclusion (i.e. in its favour), so the premisses themselves then constitute *reasons,* good or strong or perhaps conclusive, for accepting the conclusion, i.e. for thinking or believing it to be true.[1] The favourable evaluative force of these concepts of reason justifies the liberal claim that what is contrary to reason is unacceptable and to be rejected.

The logician's conception of argument identifies an argument solely in terms of its premiss(es) and conclusion. But such a set of propositions can be regarded as an argument only in the sense of being what somebody could or might argue—and this word 'argue' is here an activity verb, signifying something that people can do. Arguing is producing arguments in the logician's sense, and doing this involves thinking to oneself, or talking to somebody else; and this thinking or talking is what is called *reasoning*. Now it's only reason in the sense of an activity, i.e. as reasoning, the kind of thinking or talking that is arguing, that can be properly regarded as a way, means, or method of doing anything. In other words it's only this notion of reason that can enter into any contrast between reason and violence as ways of doing things. And it's clear that there's something[2] to be said for the view that in this sense reason and violence are exclusive of each other. The *a priori* antithesis between reason and violence is at least plausible as an *a priori* distinction between reasoning and violence: clubbing a victim to the ground is certainly not reasoning with him. Violence, a logician might say, is a contrary

[1] For a fuller account of these matters see my *Reason in Theory and Practice* (Hutchinson, 1969).
[2] But only something. As Keith Graham and others have pointed out to me, an argument may be violent and may in some circumstances constitute an act of violence against someone.

of reason n this sense. Does it follow that violence is contrary to reason?

The favourable evaluative force that I have drawn attention to in some uses of the word 'reason' and its cognates is not transmitted in any straightforward way to the concept of reasoning. For example, a piece of reasoning may be unreasonable or irrational, i.e. contrary to reason, in the sense that the arguments produced are invalid: the reasons offered to support the conclusion may fail to justify it and so may be bad reasons or, as we sometimes say, not reasons at all; and more strongly, the conclusion itself may be contrary to reason in having nothing to be said for it, no reasons in favour of accepting it. It might be thought, however, that though arguments and reasoning, and the conclusions and beliefs we can argue for or against, may be irrational, nevertheless it's only the activity of reasoning and the beliefs and propositions it leads to that stand any chance of being rational and so justified. Among activities, on this view, it's only in that activity of thinking or talking known as reasoning that reason can be exercised, and only on this activity and the beliefs and propositions that can constitute its conclusions that the positive normative force of reason can be brought to bear.

This tendency to associate the value of reason solely with the 'theoretical' items I have mentioned, namely propositions, belief, thinking, and talking, has been characteristic of much philosophy, and some of the linguistic philosophy of the twentieth century has strengthened the tendency by helping to shape a linguistic conception of logic, in which logical relations are supposed to hold in virtue of the linguistic rules governing the use of words and thus essentially between utterances or things that can be said or put into words. Liberalism's Hamlet syndrome, the temperamental inactivism that historically leads it to a preference for words and thought rather than deeds, here finds a philosophical rationale. The theoretical (and linguistic) conception of reason may in this way function as part of the substructure of the ideology of liberal intellectuals.

It remains to be shown that this substructure is a muddle, not to say mystification.

First, it's to be observed that this conception of reason alienates reason not only from violence but from every other human activity or response excluded from the 'theoretical' items I have listed. For instance, human passions, emotions, feelings, and attitudes are excluded: the contrast between reason and passion is another potent part of the philosophical background, and as my examples show is easily associated with the contrast between reason and violence. More relevant here is the exclusion of all human actions and activities other than those of reasoning itself. It is this exclusion, though unrecognized as such, that accounts both for the gap between Popper's alternatives of argument and violence and for Lord James' contention that the only rational way of changing things is by rational argument. Lord James' view follows from the theoretical conception of reason, and this I count as a *reductio ad absurdum* of that conception.

Second, it does not follow that these excluded items are contrary to reason, i.e. irrational or unreasonable, and therefore to be rejected. In particular, though clubbing a victim to the ground is not reasoning with him, it does not follow that violence is contrary to reason. For on our account so far, properly understood, the evaluative contrast between rationality and irrationality, betweeen conforming and being contrary to reason, is applicable only within the range of theoretical items, not outside it. What follows is that violence is neither rational nor irrational; that violence is not unreason but nonreason.

Third, there is in any case a serious muddle in the list of 'theoretical' items reserved for reason's accolade, a muddle involving the inclusion in that list of an item that could be regarded as practical rather than theoretical, namely the activity of reasoning. I've already pointed out that it's only reason in the sense of an activity that can be contrasted with violence as a way of doing things; and I've said that the favourable evaluative force in some uses of the word 'reason' and its cognates is not transmitted straightforwardly to this concept of reasoning. So far, however, I've been content to go along with the idea that a piece of reasoning can be appraised as rational or irrational according to whether the argument is valid or invalid, good or bad, in the logician's sense. But those notions of rationality and irrationality will therefore apply, at least primarily, to the argument in the logician's sense, and though the activity of arguing or reasoning will contain, as what is argued, an identifiable argument in that sense, it does not follow that the rationality or irrationality of the activity of arguing can be understood in the same way. In fact, it's clear that arguments as activities can be appraised in ways for which the logician's criteria are not sufficient and possibly not necessary. Certainly, the fact that an argument in the logician's sense is rational is not sufficient for it to be rational for everybody, or anybody, to produce such an argument or piece of reasoning on any or every occasion. For instance, I may know or think that my daughter has measles, and if my wife questions whether she has I may be able to produce evidence, and thus an argument, giving adequate reasons for my belief. But however rational my argument, and however rational a thing this might be to do in those circumstances, the rationality of the argument in the logician's sense would not make it a rational thing to do in other circumstances, e.g. at a political meeting about Vietnam, or in the middle of a performance of *The Three Sisters*, or when I'm trying to change a blank canvas into a picture. Similarly, though there may be many rational arguments in the logician's sense in favour of the conclusion that my next-door neighbour smokes pot, whether or not it would be reasonable for me to reason out whether he does seems to depend on a variety of other considerations, such as whether the thing would be worth knowing, or useful to know, or just none of my business.

We might respond to these matters by adhering to the theoretical conception of reason but purifying our idea of what is theoretical by eliminating from it the activity of reasoning or arguing. On this purified theoretical conception of reason the only items that could be rational or irrational would be arguments in the logician's sense, and the only items for or against which there could be reasons would be the propositions or beliefs that could form the conclusions of such arguments. At the height of the Enlightenment Hume used a pithy version of this conception ('Reason is the discovery of truth and falsehood') as a weapon against rationalism, and so helped to pave the way for the romantic reaction. Violence on this view could not conform to reason; for though someone might conclude an argument by clubbing his victim to the ground, this act of violence could not be the conclusion of an argument in the logician's sense, i.e. it could not be a true proposition drawn from facts that could figure as premises and thus as reasons supporting that act. But it would also follow that violence could not be contrary to reason either; and any act or activity whatsoever would be similarly excluded from rational appraisal, including the activity of arguing or reasoning.

PRACTICAL REASON, TECHNOLOGICAL AND OTHERWISE

However, Hume realized that some questions about the rationality of action seem to be indistinguishable from questions about the rationality of certain related propositions or beliefs (or judgements, as he called them). In doing something of one description one necessarily does things of other descriptions; and the question whether there are reasons for doing a thing will depend in part at least on what other things one is thereby doing. This is a general condition of which considerations about the effects of one's actions are a special case. Thus one kind of consideration involved in deciding whether there are reasons for doing such-and-such will be whether doing that thing is effective in doing something else, e.g. achieving a purpose that one has. For instance, if I want to kill the greenfly on my roses and know that spraying them with insecticide will kill them then I know how to kill them and in knowing this I know of a reason for spraying them with insecticide. Hume himself thought that even here it is 'strictly speaking' not this action that is rational but the judgement that spraying them with insecticide will kill the greenfly; for only this, and not the action, can be true or false. But anyone who thinks that actions can be rational in this way, and only in this way, makes a minimal concession to the idea of practical reason, constructing this idea essentially from the materials provided by the theoretical conception of reason. Since the result construes practical reason as a matter of know-how, discovering means to ends, I shall call this the technological conception of practical reason.

Popper himself makes this concession in his paper 'Utopia and Violence': 'I believe', he says, 'that it is quite true that we can judge the rationality of an action only in relation to some aims or ends.' But given that arguing is action, and that as ways of doing things violence is to be contrasted with reason as argument in that sense, i.e. as reasoning, this is enough of a concession to raise Feyerabend's insistent questions about the effectiveness of argument, to generate some doubts, only apparently paradoxical, about the reasonableness of reasoning, and to undermine the view, *a priori* or otherwise, that violence is contrary to reason. For if we admit the possibility of practical reason, even in its truncated technological form, and raise the question of the rationality of arguments and reasoning as activities, argument will now have to compete for the accolade of rationality with any other action or activity open to the agent in the circumstances. The question whether it's reasonable to argue with somebody or to reason something out will now depend on what other things one could do in the circumstances, things that in those circumstances one might have more reason to do, and which certainly might be more effective ways of achieving one's aims. For the power of reason, one's own and others', might be limited in such ways as this, that one's capacity to reason may not be adequate to solve one's problem, or that the person one is arguing or reasoning with might be too irrational to be convinced. We are familiar with the idea that in and since the eighteenth century the Enlightenment faith in reason has come under attack from such thinkers as Hume, Marx, and Freud, who are sometimes thought to have claimed that man, far from being a rational animal, is essentially irrational or non-rational. Marx attacked the doctrinaires on the ground that no amount of argument criticizing society, however justified as criticism, and no amount of argument advocating improvements, however desirable the improvements, was enough either to convince people or to effect those improvements. Koestler has said: 'To go on preaching reason to an inherently unreasonable species is, as history shows, a fairly hopeless enterprise.' Yet Marx was not an irrationalist, nor is there here any ground for irrationalism or for despair of reason. For the cunning of reason is inexhaustible and a match for any conceivable circumstances. Its message is that when reason is useless or ineffective, it's unreasonable to use reason and perhaps reasonable to use some more effective means: even violence. The black who is attacked by a white thug and retaliates with violence is not, of course, reasoning with his assailant; but he has good reason to stop the assault, with violence if necessary; and his violence is then itself, though not a piece of reasoning and not a conclusion drawn from premises, an exercise of reason, a literal example of reason in action.

In 'Utopia and Violence' Popper seems prepared to admit this in substance, though he fails to draw the crucial conclusions. Basing his advocacy of reason on a kind of scepticism, he says: 'What I call the attitude of reasonableness may be characterized by a remark like this: "I think I am right, but I may be wrong and you may be right, and in any case let us discuss it, for in this way we are likely to get nearer to a true understanding than if we each merely insist that we are right." ' In the face of violence this modest scepticism is seriously compromised: '... it always takes two to make a discussion reasonable. ... You cannot have a rational discussion with a man who prefers shooting you to being convinced by you. In other words, there are limits to the attitude of reasonableness. It is the same with tolerance. You must not, without qualification, accept the principle of tolerating all those who are intolerant; if you do, you will destroy not only yourself, but also the attitude of tolerance.' Of the person who does not, like himself, hate violence, he says: '. . . you may not be able to argue with the admirer of violence. He has a way of answering an argument with a bullet if he is not kept under control by the threat of counter-violence.' What Popper fails to see, or at least to admit, is that on his own technological conception of practical reason he is committed to the view that for those who do not happen to hate violence, violence is not contrary to reason, and for those who hate it only when they are its victims, violence towards others may be perfectly reasonable. But then, even in the case he does consider, the case of the person who, like himself, hates violence as such, he still fails to admit the crucial conclusions that follow about reason and rationality, namely that as a way of preventing greater violence, counter-violence, which is of course a sort of violence, would not be contrary to reason, and that in the circumstances he describes, what he calls 'the attitude of reasonableness' would be an extremely unreasonable attitude. The qualifications reveal Popper's repeated antithesis between reason and violence as facile and superficial, but it would be cynical to suggest that this is why he fails to make them explicit, even when they are staring him (and us) in the face. Such glaring omissions can be explained, I think, only in terms of the subterranean pressures exerted by an idea of reason that is basically the theoretical conception, but whose confusions have been worse confounded by its being stretched into the idea of practical reason that I have called the technological conception.

But there is an objection that at a practical level is far more serious. The only limit Popper places on discussion in a dispute is when one party resorts, or is prepared to resort, to violence: in that situation, and only in that situation, he seems to think, violence is permissible, i.e. violence is permissible only as counter-violence. Let's consider a case, one in which some people have similarly insisted from the start on 'a dialogue'.

The Ulster government might well have been delighted to continue a dialogue with the Catholics, endlessly if necessary, provided that the Catholics themselves did no more than talk. It needed to exercise no violence against those Catholics other than the violence recognized in any country as that involved in the legitimate sanctions of the law—a kind of violence easily represented, especially in a parliamentary democracy, as counter-violence, justified as society's ultimate weapon against the 'violence and unreason' of criminals and subversives. In general, when there is a dispute in which one party objects to existing arrangements and wishes to change them, but the other party stands to lose by the change, the latter party can resist the change endlessly by agreeing to talk, provided that his opponent agrees to go on talking unless subjected to violence. When the privileged party has political power, the whole range of legitimate political activities between talking and violence may still be ineffective. In these circumstances violence may be the only way of effecting change, and it may be rational even though it's not counter-violence.

Whatever is true of violence, it's in situations of this sort that the continued demand for argument and dialogue is peculiarly reactionary, working in the defence of privilege. It's a demand for reason that plays into the hands of the unreasonable: the same reason that enables liberalism to adopt its characteristic posture of endorsing reasonable aims while condemning the means that may be necessary to achieve them. For any reasonable person, it must be said, there's a point when the futility of argument appalls and when argument itself may involve one in the very corruption one is arguing against. Writing of his participation in lectures, discussions, and forums on Vietnam, Chomsky says (in the Introduction to *American Power and the New Mandarins*): 'Perhaps I should mention that, increasingly, I have had a certain feeling of falseness in these lectures and discussions. . . . Without awareness, I found myself drawn into this morass of insane rationality. . . . By entering into the arena of argument and counter-argument, of technical feasibility and

tactics, of footnotes and citations, by accepting the presumption
of legitimacy of debate on certain issues, one has already lost
one's humanity....' Popper's sceptical modesty, his willing-
ness to suppose that he may be wrong and the other side right,
would of course inhibit any such feelings as these. But though
perhaps a way of avoiding intellectual commitment, this scepticism induces an inactivism that cannot escape moral commitment. In a footnote to his 'Responsibility of Intellectuals'
(reprinted in *American Power*), Chomsky refers to the view put
forward in *The End of Ideology* 'that one who advocates action
... has a responsibility to assess its social cost', and adds in
parenthesis that this is also true of those who advocate *in*action
—'a matter', he says, 'less frequently noted'. Doing nothing is
not doing something, but it is something that can be appraised
from a practical and moral point of view, and for which one
can be held responsible. To do nothing but argue against a
situation when argument is ineffective is to do nothing about
that situation; and if effective ways of changing it are open,
doing nothing is to share the responsibility for maintaining the
situation, and may be contrary to reason.

I concede, finally, something to the view that violence is *a
priori* contrary to reason. But this very concession involves a
denial of the theoretical conception of reason and its associated
technological conception of practical reason. As I've already
suggested these two ideas of reason, though so closely related,
diverge widely on the range of items that each allows to be
reasonable: the theoretical conception excludes all actions and
activities except reasoning, and even, in the purified version, all
actions and activities whatsoever; whereas the technological
conception of practical reason *in*cludes all actions and activities,
not excepting violence, under the weak condition of their being
a means to some end. Any adequate conception of reason (and
in particular of practical reason) will make violence neither so
easy to exclude nor so easy to include.

It's part of the meaning of the word 'violence', then, that an
act of violence against someone involves harming or hurting

that person, or at the least causing him some discomfort or inconvenience. It follows that an act of violence is necessarily contrary to reason in this sense, that the fact that it necessarily involves harm, hurt, discomfort or inconvenience is necessarily a reason against it; and this is so regardless of the agent's aims or ends and in particular of his hatred or otherwise of violence. It may be conscious or half-conscious recognition of this fact that has led to the view that violence is necessarily contrary to reason and therefore always unreasonable. But this does not follow. For someone who does something that is an act of violence will also thereby be doing things of other descriptions; and this necessary reason against violence may therefore, in the circumstances, be overridden or outweighed by contingently related facts that constitute reasons in favour of that act of violence. In other words, when it's claimed that the fact that something is an act of violence is necessarily a reason against doing it the necessity here is in its being *a* reason, not necessarily a conclusive reason, i.e. in its bearing with *some* pressure on what it's a reason against. It is not to be confused with that necessity in which someone who has a conclusive reason against doing something *must* not do that thing. An analogous *a priori* case in favour of the rationality of reasoning with people could also be constructed.

The failure to grasp these matters may itself be due to the influence of the theoretical conception of reason. In the field of reasons for believing things we have the notion of reasons that can conflict, some pointing in favour of some particular belief, some pointing against. But whenever reasons for or against believing some particular thing conflict, the implication is that this conflict is, so to speak, only apparent, since some of the reasons are only apparent, not real, reasons: in other words, such conflicts occur only because our knowledge is deficient in one way or another. The concept of a reason for believing something is such that, with respect to any particular belief, if our understanding were adequate all the facts that constituted considerations relevant to that belief would point in the same direction: they would either all be reasons for, or all be reasons against, believing that thing. Theoretical reason, we might say, is monolithic in this sense. Practical reason is not. Reasons for doing a particular thing can conflict—shall I say?—objectively. Violence is contrary to reason only in this partial and non-monolithic way. It is necessarily regrettable, but it may be a regrettable necessity; and the word 'necessity' signifies the pressure of reason.

Comment

BY G. R. GRICE

I agree in the main with Professor Edgley's remarks about reason. Among other points, I agree with his denial of the classical thesis that only means to given ends are assessable for rationality. Ends, whether aims or desires, are similarly assessable, and not just against other aims or other desires. I take this to be a point of crucial importance. But I wish to take up one remark which suggests that Edgley may be willing to put his important and true claim that there are reasons for *doing* things, as well as reasons for *believing* things, to a weak employment where it may be capable of strong employment, namely that ill-defined area which we call morality.

Edgley says that an act of violence against someone necessarily involves harming or hurting that person, or causing him some discomfort or inconvenience, and that this fact constitutes a reason against doing it; *a* reason, he is careful to point out, not a conclusive reason. Consider two agents, *A* and *B*, and a particular act *x*. Edgley is saying that the fact that *A*'s doing *x* hurts *B* is a reason against *A*'s doing *x*. Are we to take this as self-evident? If not, how is it to be supported?

There is one move which I wish to stigmatize as a weak move. It is to say that '*A*'s doing *x* hurts *B*' is a reason against

A's doing x just because A's hurting B is morally wrong, *prima facie*. (*Prima facie* because we are considering a reason, not a conclusive reason.) Generalized, the move consists in saying that we are to decide whether there is a reason for or against doing an action just by asking whether it is *prima facie* morally right or morally wrong; and we are to decide whether there is a conclusive reason for or against doing it just by asking whether it is actually morally right or morally wrong. I stigmatize this as a weak move because it makes the application of the notions of reason for and against doing things parasitic upon the notions of moral right and moral wrong. If we operate in this way, we shall not be able to decide upon what is morally right or wrong by invoking the notions of reasons for and against doing things. Now it seems to me that the central importance of the discovery that there are reasons for acting, and that any action, aim or desire can be assessed for rationality, is that it opens up a new field of investigation which should enable us to decide what is morally right and what is morally wrong. Or better, that it should enable us to decide what there is good reason for doing, wanting and aiming at and what there is good reason for not doing, wanting and aiming at—and if morality enjoins something different, so much the worse for morality.

I want to illustrate this point with an example. We have been considering the fact that A's doing x hurts B. Let us suppose that A is a sadist, that B is a masochist and that x is an act of whipping. There is a long tradition of substantial moral belief that sadism and masochism are morally wrong, or evils, or what have you, and I dare say this is still the predominant view. Anyone who thinks this and who is prone to the weak move I have described will have no qualms about saying that the fact that A's doing x hurts B is a reason against A's doing x even when A is a sadist and B a masochist. He will have no qualms because he thinks these things are morally wrong and he applies the notion of *reason against* solely on the basis of moral wrong. I think he ought to have a qualm. If an objector says that in these circumstances the fact that x hurts B, far from being a reason *against* A's doing x is a reason *for* A's doing it, it is not evident to me that he is mistaken. And if he is not mistaken, and it is none the less morally wrong for A to do x, it is not evident to me, *qua* rational agent, that I should any longer be interested in this bit of morality.

I hope the discovery that there are such things as reasons for acting is the first step to settling questions such as this. But there are further weak moves which, if not arrested, will largely nullify the importance of the discovery. I now wish to look at another. Edgley holds, as we have seen, that the fact that A's doing x hurts B is a reason against A's doing x. He also holds that the fact that A enjoys doing x is a reason in favour of his doing x. Let us now suppose that x is again an act of whipping, that A is again a sadist who enjoys whipping people but that this time B is no masochist. He does not like being whipped one bit. Edgley and many other philosophers would now say that A has a reason for doing x (he would enjoy it) and a reason against doing x (it hurts B). This is, of course, no contradiction; they are saying only that A has a reason for and against, not that he has a conclusive reason for and against. The question I wish to ask is how it is to be decided whether one of these reasons overrides the other, or is a better reason than the other; and how it is to be decided which overrides the other, or which is the better reason ? There is an answer to this question which is so common that it qualifies as the stock answer. It consists in saying that one of these reasons (it hurts B) is a moral reason, and that the other (A enjoys it) is a nonmoral reason, and that moral reasons override nonmoral reasons. This move is the sister in weakness of the one we discussed earlier. It leaves two crucial questions unanswered. The first is how it is to be determined which reasons are moral and which are not. It is well known that the distinction between moral and nonmoral, supposing there is just one distinction to be drawn, has so far eluded philosophers. But even if this problem were solved, we should have to face the second. How is it to be shown that moral reasons override nonmoral reasons ? What is it about them in virtue of which they

KPR

are overriding? These questions surely demand answers. It is, of course, true that most people most of the time treat certain considerations as overriding. And no doubt most of them, most of the time, would, with a little leading, label these considerations as reasons and as moral reasons at that. But perhaps the time has passed, in the history of philosophy, when we could be content to rely upon such facts.

Let us return to *A*, our sadist, and *B*, our standard model who is certainly no masochist. If *A* gives *B* a whipping, *A* will enjoy himself and *B* will be hurt. We have been looking at the idea that *B*'s hurt, being a moral reason, overrides *A*'s enjoyment, which is a nonmoral reason. Let us now build a little bit more into the case. Suppose *A* is in the grip of nearly irresistible sexual desire. His need to whip *B* is pretty desperate. If he retrains himself he will, of course, be hurt; not physically perhaps, but he will be hurt none the less. Sexual frustration does hurt. Thus someone is hurt whatever is done. There need be, so far as anyone can tell, no difference between the degree of hurt which *B* suffers if he is whipped and the degree of hurt which *A* suffers if he restrains himself. It thus seems that there is equally good reason both for and against *A*'s whipping *B*. The moral consciousness, we should note, would not like this conclusion: its dictate would be that *A* ought not to whip *B*. Can we conclude, so simply, that morality and reason part company?

The obvious rejoinder is that we cannot: that there are other facts about the situation which constitute reasons against the whipping. Now, of course, there may be such additional facts, but so far as I can see, there need not be. And if there need not be, we have only to imagine a situation in which there are none to generate the problem. Let us look at some of these facts which might be thought to constitute reasons. *B* may be humiliated in being whipped. Indeed he may, but he need not be. He need not be that sort of person. Similarly, if it is said that being whipped is an affront to *B*'s dignity, the reply must be that it need not be. He may be too preoccupied with the pain to think of his dignity. Again, being whipped may make *B* angry, and this may be thought to be a reason for *A*'s not doing it. But again, it need not make *B* angry; he may just cry. Moreover, the problems which have already been raised about '*x* hurts *B*' as a reason can be raised again about '*x* humiliates *B*', '*x* is an affront to *B*'s dignity', '*x* makes *B* angry' and so on. I do not think there is any solution to the difficulty in this direction.

Someone wishing to maintain that there is better reason for *A*'s restraining than indulging himself may try to make something of the fact that if *A* is to whip *B* he must have *B* in his power; or of the connected fact that while *A* exercises his choice, *B* does not. Whether anything could be made of such points I do not know. But for present purposes it is neither here nor there. The situation need not be anything like that imagined. *A* and *B* may be supposed to be out in the open with each other and sensibly discussing the rational way for them to act. *A* points out that if he does not whip *B* he suffers. And *B* points out that he suffers if *A* does whip him. They agree that, so far as either can tell, the degrees of suffering are equal, and neither has any other factors to call upon. So far as we have gone, the rational course of action seems to be for *A* to whip *B* on Mondays, Wednesdays and Fridays but not on the intermediate days. They may both accept that this is the rational way to proceed and act accordingly. There need be no question of *B* being in *A*'s power, nor of *A* exercising his choice while *B* does not.

It may now be said that if *A* whips *B* he inflicts unnecessary suffering upon him; that *B*, like everyone else, has a right not to have unnecessary suffering inflicted upon him, and that this constitutes a reason for *A*'s not whipping *B*. In response to this argument I want to make two points, the first small but sufficient, I think, to dispose of it; the second more important. The first point is that if *A*'s whipping *B* inflicts unnecessary suffering upon *B*, *A*'s not whipping *B* inflicts unnecessary suffering upon *A*. I can find no sense in which *B*'s suffering in the one case is 'unnecessary' while *A*'s suffering in the other is not 'unnecessary'. So that if *B* has a right upon this ground not to be whipped, *A* similarly has a right to whip him.

The more important point concerning the idea that in saying that someone has a right not to have something done to him a reason has been cited for not doing that thing to him. It may indeed be the case that if he has a right not to have something done to him, there is a reason for others not doing that thing to him. But it does not follow that, in saying that he has the right, the reason has been *cited*. In other words, it does not follow that the proposition 'So-and-so has a right not to be treated thus and so' is, if true, a reason for not treating him thus and so—although it may well be the case that this proposition implies that there is a reason for not treating him thus and so. The point may be brought out by considering what I take to be a parallel case. If I say to one of my children 'You ought to clean your teeth before you go to bed' I have not cited a reason for his cleaning his teeth. I should cite a reason (or what I take to be a reason) in answering his question 'Why ?'. I should cite a reason in saying, for example, 'If you don't your teeth will decay and you will have a lot of pain, trouble and expense in later life'. I take this point to be evident and we may express it briefly by saying that prudential oughts are not reasons (although they may imply that there are reasons). Granted that, I see no basis for saying that moral oughts are reasons, although it may again be the case that they imply that there are reasons. And I see no basis for saying that rights (moral or others) are reasons, although it may once more be the case that they imply that there are reasons. Whether these implications hold depends, of course, upon whether prudence and morality, on the one hand, and rationality in action, on the other, coincide.

I envisage the objection that 'oughts' and 'rights' are not parallel in this respect as I have assumed them to be. Someone might object that while 'You ought to do *x*' does not cite a reason, '*A* has a right to your doing *x*' does—as indeed does 'You have an obligation to do *x*'. This suggestion is obviously not without sense and has some plausibility. I shall counter it not by argument but by saying that it seems to me a shame that some moral philosophers are content to say that rights constitute reasons for acting. It is to squander the concept of reason without even trying to extract anything valuable from it. The value to be extracted is this: if we can learn to wield this fledgeling concept correctly we should be able to decide what our rights are in the only sense in which rights are of interest to a rational man: that a man has a right to be treated in a certain way if and only if others have good reason for treating him in that way. The fundamental question is: what actions or kinds of action have we good reason for doing, and what actions or kinds of action have we good reason for not doing? To list our putative rights, relying presumably on our moral intuitions, and to wield the concept on the basis of this list, is to kill this crucial question before we have had a chance to ask it, let alone attempt an answer. We want to dig deeper; we do not want to rest content forever in the moral clouds.

I want to see now if we can collect some data which will help us with this fledgeling concept. The first proposition to look at is:

> *A* would enjoy doing *x*

If we consider it as it stands we should have to consider it as *a* reason. Rather than do that I should like to build it up so that we may discuss it as a conclusive reason. Plainly the first step is to modify it to read:

> *A* would enjoy doing *x* and there is no alternative he would enjoy more.

In building it up further I shall speak of the agent's material and spiritual well-being (his well-being, for short) where I have on previous occasions spoken of his interest. 'Well-being' is perhaps no more self-explanatory than I once fondly hoped that 'interest' was, but there is no space here to go into the finer points of explanation. I now add to the original proposition so that it reads:

> *A* would enjoy doing *x* and there is no alternative he would enjoy more; his doing *x* does not adversely affect his overall well-being and none of the alternatives open to him would increase his overall well-being.

I do not wish to say that this is a conclusive reason for *A*'s doing *x*. It may be that moral considerations are relevant and I want to allow for the possibility of its being true and being shown to be true that moral considerations are overriding. Thus the final form of the proposition to be considered is:

> *A* would enjoy doing *x* and there is no alternative he would enjoy more; his doing *x* does not adversely affect his overall well-being and none of the alternatives open to him would increase his overall well-being; no moral considerations are relevant.

I think we now have a conclusive reason for *A*'s doing *x*. Of course, the final conjunct may be otiose. An egoist, for example, would say that all moral considerations are already incorporated in the earlier conjuncts. Or someone may conceivably hold that moral considerations are not overriding and that the final conjunct is therefore not needed. But a philosopher who takes either of these views is only saying that a weaker proposition than that cited is a conclusive reason for *A*'s doing *x*. He is not denying that claim of the stronger proposition we have before us. His views need not, at this point, be heeded.

I want now to return to hurt. Suppose for '*A* would enjoy doing *x*' we substitute '*A*'s doing *x* would hurt *A*' [*sic*]. If we were to attempt to get out of this a conclusive reason against *A*'s doing *x*, we should presumably build it up in the following way:

> *A*'s doing *x* would hurt *A* and there is an alternative *y* which would hurt *A* less; neither *A*'s doing *x* nor his doing *y*, nor any alternative open to him has any effect on his overall well-being; no moral considerations are relevant.

I do not think that we thus attain a conclusive reason against *A*'s doing *x*. Indeed, I do not think we attain any reason at all.

Simply because *A* may enjoy doing *x* even though it hurts him: he may enjoy self-flagellation.

Consider now:

> *A*'s doing *x* would hurt *B* and there is an alternative which would hurt *B* less . . .

the proposition being completed appropriately along the lines already suggested. This is not a conclusive reason for *A*'s not doing *x*, nor indeed any reason. *B* may be a masochist who enjoys having *A* hurt him as much as he can.

A possible objection should be noted. It may be said that in the latter two cases it is not true that no moral considerations are relevant, for hurt is produced and that is a moral consideration. We do not have to take this difficulty seriously. The final conjunct, saying that no moral considerations are relevant, is included only to allow for the *possibility* that such considerations are, and can be shown to be, overriding. I am now arguing that, in the matter of reasons, enjoyment overrides hurt produced and it is not helpful to say that the production of hurt is a moral consideration; no more helpful than saying the production of enjoyment is a prudential consideration.

Suppose now—to revive the final case we had earlier—that *B* is no masochist but that *A* is a sadist. Consider the proposition beginning:

> *A* enjoys doing *x* to *B* but *B* does not enjoy having *A* do *x* to him; there is an alternative which *A* enjoys less and *B* dislikes less . . .

If, by building this proposition up, we try to generate a conclusive reason, or indeed any reason, for *A*'s not doing *x* we shall have to explain why *B*'s not enjoying the activity carries more weight than *A*'s enjoyment of it. This is a problem which we noted earlier, and I want to submit that it is a serious problem for any philosopher who really wants to make the idea of reasons for acting do some work. It is the more serious because in the general case it is perfectly evident that the agent's enjoyment carries more weight than anyone else's. And given this, an explanation is needed of why it is not true, if it is not true, of all cases.

Let us look at the general case. We have already seen that the proposition:

> *A* would enjoy doing *x* and there is no alternative he would enjoy more . . .

is, when built up in the way suggested, a conclusive reason for *A*'s doing *x*. Consider now the proposition, which begins:

> *A* would enjoy doing *x* more than he would enjoy doing *y*; but *B* would enjoy *A*'s doing *y* more than he would enjoy *A*'s doing *x* (e.g. he would more enjoy watching *A* doing *y* than *x*).

It is important to remember the build-up: that neither *A*'s doing *x* nor his doing *y* nor any other alternative has any effect upon the overall well-being of either *A* or *B* or anyone else; and that no moral considerations are relevant, e.g. no promises have been made. I take it to be evident that this proposition constitutes conclusive reason for *A*'s doing *x*, and that it certainly does not constitute conclusive reason for *A*'s doing *y*. For example, if *A* enjoys playing golf more than he enjoys playing tennis while *B* enjoys watching him playing tennis more than he enjoys watching him playing golf, *and if the other qualifications hold*, there is conclusive reason for *A*'s playing golf and certainly not conclusive reason for his playing tennis. If *A* chose to play golf, he could not be charged with *irrationality* on the ground that *B* would enjoy watching him playing tennis more. Moreover I do not think the degree of their respective enjoyment enters into it. Even if it were true that *A* enjoyed playing golf only slightly more than tennis, while *B* enjoyed watching him playing tennis vastly more than playing golf, *A* could still not be charged with irrationality if he chose to play golf.

This seems to show that in the matter of reasons and rationality in action, the agent's enjoyment carries, in the general case, more weight than anyone else's. And if, in the sadist/non-masochist case the weight of reason is, in the end, against the sadist's gratifying himself, it needs to be shown what makes the difference and why it makes the difference. It is pathetic to say at this point that moral considerations are relevant in such a case and that moral considerations are overriding. It may be true, but so far nothing is explained.

I have been criticizing one way, or perhaps a family of ways, in which some philosophers handle the concept of reason for acting. I shall end briefly on a more positive note. Instead of allowing the moral consciousness to dictate to us what are and what are not reasons, I think we should set about formulating what might be called principles of practical reason. There are, I suspect, at least two such principles to be found which I shall call the Egoistic Principle and the Altruistic Principle. I pair them under these names because I think both Egoism and Altruism exaggerate a truth which the other neglects. A preliminary statement of the Egoistic Principle is this:

> If a man gets nothing out of doing an action *x*, there is no reason for his doing it, and he cannot be charged with irrationality for not doing it.

In saying that he gets nothing out of doing the action, I mean such things as this: he does not enjoy it; he does not enjoy the pleasure which his doing it gives to other people; it does not enable him to do something later which he will enjoy; it contributes nothing to a life which would satisfy him; it is in no way a part of that life in which he would find fulfilment, and so on; in short, it contributes nothing to his overall well-being, material or spiritual. This principle seems to me to be evidently true; evidently true *except* in the following circumstance.[1] Suppose he is one of a group of people subject to a system of rules under which he is required to do *x*. Suppose further that the system of rules is such that, from the general obedience to them, he *and everyone else* gains. In this situation he gets

[1] It also needs to be specified that the *status quo* does not already embody irrationality. This is particularly important in political matters, but there is no space to go into the question here.

something out of others acting in certain ways, and they get something out of his acting in certain ways. In this situation, it is no longer *evident* that there is no reason for his doing x even though he gets nothing out of his doing it. I say only that it is no longer evident. But this lack of evidence allows possible truth to the Altruistic Principle:

> It is not the case that all propositions which are reasons for acting are reasons solely in virtue of referring to benefits coming to the agent.

An Egoist takes it as evident that this principle is false, and all I have said is that it is not evident. It is possible that in the matter of rationality in action benefits coming to people other than the agent count *directly*—not, as the Egoist holds, only indirectly; only in so far as, in the end, benefits coming to others benefit the agent.

I do not think it is evident that the Altruistic Principle is true, although I can find no reason for thinking it to be false. If we can be persuaded of its truth, the next step will be to find the form of proposition that does count as a reason for acting in those cases where benefits coming to people other than the agent are relevant. If this can be done, I think we shall have a weapon superior to the moral consciousness with which to meet its deliverances and assess them for rationality.

Comment

BY ANTHONY MANSER

I suspect that Edgley's opening remark, that the belief that violence is contrary to reason 'runs counter to common sense' is in fact untrue. Certainly many people, and not only professional philosophers, find at first sight something odd in the idea that violence could be reasonable; indeed, it almost has the air of a Humean paradox, and Edgley is forced later in the paper to admit that an act's being violent is a reason, though not a conclusive one, against doing it. If pressed, most liberal intellectuals and many other people would agree with this point, and would be inclined to add that prior violence by another was the only thing that made violence legitimate.[1] On the other side, what Edgley calls the 'romantic ideology' of violence also leads to the feeling that there is an antithesis between the two things. To such romantics it may well seem that the liberal stress on reason and talking round a table are precisely a way of avoiding the necessity for action, for getting to grips with an existing problem. Edgley instances the relations between Protestants and Catholics in Northern Ireland. Nearer home, I suspect that this is what many of the student activists believe. I well remember how shocked I was when an American member of the S.D.S. rejected my arguments against his views with 'But you can argue so much better than we can.' The tone of the remark made it clear that it was not intended as a compliment. At the time I did not understand what he meant; this paper may make his remark clearer.

There are, in fact, large numbers of people imbued with what Edgley calls the 'ideology of liberal intellectuals', though no doubt in its strongest form the ideology is found among professional philosophers and other academics. This in itself is not surprising; one would expect to find ideologists located in universities, and, precisely because they are places dedicated to talk and argument, to find the greatest emphasis on these features of reason in them. But although he sees that what is involved in the muddle he wants to discuss is an ideology (or rather two competing ideologies), it seems that he does not take this fact sufficiently seriously, and hence is unable to do justice to the case he wants to make. For the belief that there is

[1] The notion of a 'just war', which does not depend on prior aggression, might seem a counter-example. But I do not think many liberals would accept a declaration of war against another power unless that power had been guilty of violence of some kind, even if only against its own nationals.

an antithesis between reason and violence is both deep seated and connected with many other features of the liberal ideology. Hence it is by no means the result of an over-emphasis on certain theories of logic, as he suggests.

Edgley's conviction that logic is at the root of the trouble leads him to be remarkably unfair to one of those propounding the ideology he attacks. I refer to his remarks on Lord James's 'If you want to change things, as well you may, you will use rational arguments, and never anything else' (cf. p. 121).[2] Lord James was writing in a particular context, and it seems clear that he was not suggesting that no one should ever actually *do* anything, but rather that in the university the right way to change things was by getting agreement that the change was necessary or desirable. Once this had been done, the rational structure of the university was such that the reform would be put into effect by the duly constituted methods. It is worth pursuing this point further, for it will help to bring out both my agreement and disagreement with Edgley's thesis. Lord James is thinking of the kinds of changes which students might wish to make in universities, changes in syllabuses, courses, examinations, etc. And the theory of university government is that these can be altered as the result of discussion in Senate and elsewhere. In one sense this is true; changes in them occur all the time, though they are generally minor ones. The kind of changes that students want are seen as major and revolutionary ones, as altering the whole nature of the university itself. Hence even if students are represented on the appropriate governing bodies, it is unlikely that their suggestions will be accepted, at least as a result of any *arguments* that they can produce.

For those opposing the changes, and this may include most of the academic staff, will be able to produce many reasons which will be acceptable to their fellows in favour of the *status quo* and against the radical changes suggested from below. In their eyes the students' arguments will not succeed in rebutting these. When the debate occurs, to a disinterested observer it may well

2 Unless otherwise stated, page references are to Edgley's paper.

appear not as a confrontation between reason on one side and unreason on the other, but between two different sets of reasons, with neither side recognizing what the other puts forward as reasons. Any dialogue breaks down and the scene is set for the introduction of violence in the form of a sit-in. (I have not yet discussed the definition of violence, about which I have something to say below, but I hope it will be agreed that a sit-in is close to violence.) An analogous situation occurred in the recent dock troubles. Both sides initially appealed to reasons, the government to the rule of law, the dockers to the right to work, loss of dock jobs, etc. Neither side found the other's reasons adequate or compelling and hence there was left only a recourse to a kind of violence. But this recourse to violence occurred after a period of reasoning, albeit ineffectual,[3] and this seems to differentiate it sharply from what might be called 'criminal' violence. For in general a criminal does not try to convince his victim of the justice of his case, and it would be hard to imagine how he could. Certainly a criminal may begin by threatening violence, and this is to give the victim *a* reason for compliance with his demands. But to give someone *a* reason for action is not the same as reasoning with him; it is not what we ordinarily mean by 'reason' in the contrast between reason and violence.[4]

There may be revolutionaries who advocate violence for its own sake, but these seem to be rare; most, whether they be student activists or political revolutionaries in the full sense,

[3] It is not enough to say, as Professor Hare did in the discussion, that when the 'romantics' *lose* the argument they will resort to violence. For in the situations I am describing there is no external way of deciding who lost the argument, unless it is made axiomatic that the majority always wins. I suspect that this is what the liberal ideologists really believe, though it does not seem obvious to me that the Roman Catholics in Northern Ireland had lost their argument with the Protestants before embarking on violence. Hare also said, with this kind of case in mind, that the fact that reason does not always work is no argument against it. But I am not arguing *against* reason, and neither is Edgley. My concern is to investigate the assumptions that underlie the liberal ideologists' characterization of reason.

[4] Roughly, in cases where 'motive' could be substituted for 'reason' without important alteration of meaning we are not in the realm of 'reason' as discussed in this paper.

feel that their resort to violence is necessary because reasoning with their opponents either has got them nowhere, or it is clear that there is no point in trying to reason with the dominant party. Consequently, they feel that stronger methods of 'giving them reasons for accepting the demands' are necessary. If my somewhat sketchy diagnosis is accepted, it remains to explain why both the liberal intellectuals and Edgley himself make the distinction they do between 'reason' and the 'ideology of violence'. Here a remark I made above is relevant, about the belief in 'duly constituted methods' for making changes. In the case of a democratic state this refers to the apparatus of elections and ways of changing governments, in universities to the structure of Senate and Council with the representatives of various groups on them. Behind both these is the notion of a consensus, of a general consent to the institution as a whole and to the method of settling disputes within it. If there exists such a consensus and the appropriate apparatus, then arguing *is* the method to make changes, for acceptance of an argument will naturally result in the change being put into effect by the existing machinery.

It seems to me that this is the central notion that lies behind the quotations that Edgley gives in his opening pages, and that it is this notion that makes the discussion of the relation between reason and violence in general so inconclusive. For it is in those cases where consensus has broken down that the resort to violence, or at least to methods other than those of discussion within the framework of the system, becomes almost inevitable. And if one side fails to realize what has happened, they may see this resort to other methods as gratuitous violence. Edgley indeed sees that discussion may be a means of prolonging oppression (cf. p. 132), but does not realize the full significance of his own example. For it need not be simply a matter of the dominant party losing by the change, but rather that they cannot see the sense of what the opponents are demanding. Such a situation is often evident, as I have indicated, with student radicals in the universities. Neither side can fully understand the point of view of the other. Hence there is no possibility of a 'rational' agreement between them.

Thus, like Edgley, I locate the source of the trouble on the side of 'reason' rather than on that of violence, though more needs to be said about the latter as well. But the account he gives of the origin of the trouble seems to me far from the mark. Though logicians may be responsible for many of the confusions that exist in philosophy, I do not think this is one of them. Certainly logicians spend a great deal of time analysing arguments, though I suspect they are well aware that arguments of the type they study are comparatively rare in human discourse. Indeed, they are not even very common in the prose parts of logic books themselves. It is not logic but something which can be called the 'ideology of reason' which requires examination, though here I can only give a sketch of such an examination. The holders of this ideology believe in the power of reason, in the sense that they think that discussion and dialogue, if carried on 'rationally' will tend to result in agreement. But they further believe, and this is the important point, that if agreement turns out to be impossible, then the 'rationality' of the democratic form of government itself will enable those who differ to accept the majority verdict. Even the most optimistic liberal must envisage that sometimes complete agreement will not be reached, and if he did not believe in a 'rational' way of coping with this disagreement, violence would again become the only method of 'settling' the dispute. Here the assumption is that even if men do not agree on immediate aims, there is at least agreement on more remote ones, including the continuance of the form of society which enables such discussion to take place freely. This is a crucial part of the 'ideology of reason' which Edgley omits.

He rightly takes Popper as a good example of a liberal intellectual holding this ideological view. In the paper he quotes from, Popper also says: 'It is a fact, and not a very strange fact, that it is not so very difficult to reach agreement by discussion on what are the most intolerable evils of our society, and on what are the most urgent social reforms.'[5] But Edgley misrepresents Popper by claiming that he 'tends, in fact, to identify reason with argument' (p. 119), where it is the logicians' type of argument that he means. Certainly Popper does use the two terms interchangeably; just after the passage I have cited he writes: 'This is why we can get somewhere in arguing about them [evils]; why we can profit here from the attitude of reasonableness. We can learn by listening to concrete claims, by patiently trying to assess them as impartially as we can, and by considering ways of meeting them without creating worse evils.'[6] This shows that his conception of 'argument' is wider than that of the logic textbook, for 'assessing impartially' and 'considering ways of meeting' are what would normally be called 'being reasonable' but not 'arguing'. Popper's criticism of utopians makes this even clearer: 'With ideal goods it is different. These we know only from dreams and from the dreams of our poets and prophets. They cannot be discussed, only proclaimed from the housetops. They do not call for the rational attitude of the impartial judge, but for the emotional attitude of the impassioned preacher.'[7]

Thus Popper does not err, as Edgley claims, because he has too narrow a conception of reason. It is not merely because of logical flaws that he rejects the claims of utopians, but because they cannot be discussed within the framework of a consensus. The distinction he is drawing is closely connected with the more central one between science and metaphysics. It is this same constellation of views which leads him to advocate 'piece-meal social engineering' as the only correct method of solving social problems. This follows from his belief that it is easy to reach agreement on what are the major social problems, and is closely connected with a view of the nature of those problems themselves which depends on the liberal 'consensus' theory of society. It is because he assumes that all reasonable men do

[5] *Conjectures and Refutations* (London, 1963), p. 361.
[6] Ibid.
[7] Ibid.

agree on the nature of society that he can think that they will also agree on the major problems and methods for their solution. Only within a general consensus is such agreement possible. The enemies are those who have a large and 'emotive' view and hence demand a radical solution to what they see as the problems. Precisely because they have this kind of view a gradual solution, which can be checked for correct working at every stage, does not appeal to them. In the field of politics they are equivalent to the metaphysicians in the field of philosophy; in both cases there exist no methods of reaching agreement and no comfortable place for accepting a difference of opinion.

Thus what Edgley calls Popper's 'technological' view of practical reason is intimately linked to his whole view of philosophy, including his view of science. For him the progress of science is likewise gradual and step by step, and is founded on a consensus among scientists about what is to count as a legitimate move in the activity. The attack on Popper's view by Kuhn and Feyerabend consists largely in the denial of such a consensus, at least throughout the history of science.[8] For

[8] In his reply at the Conference, Edgley criticized my remarks about Kuhn and Popper by saying that Kuhn needs the notion of consensus for his 'normal science', and that Popper talks of science as 'revolution in permanence'. I accept that both these remarks are true, but I do not think that they are damaging to my thesis. Kuhn's 'normal science' obviously does depend on a consensus, that of the majority of scientists of the period, but his point is that the consensus changes at times of scientific revolution; there is no single 'Logic of Science' which remains the same throughout history. It is the opposite that Popper claims. Precisely because the revolution is a permanent one it must take place within an agreed view of what is to count as a move in science. In his reply to Kuhn ('Normal Science and its Dangers', in *Criticism and the Growth of Knowledge*, eds. Lakatos and Musgrave (Cambridge, 1970), Popper stresses that he is not a relativist, and clearly regards Kuhn as one. What is absolute for Popper is not any particular truth, but the 'logic of scientific discovery' which he regards as marking off science from other human activities. But this logic allows only of gradual changes, in the sense that every new discovery must be commensurable with previous science: 'Thus in science, as distinct from theology, a critical comparison of the competing theories, of the competing frameworks, is always possible' (op. cit., p. 57). I do not here wish to enter into a controversy about the nature of science, but I think that this last quotation indicates a view which Popper carries over into his attitude to social questions, and it is this which I

them, major changes are the result of 'scientific revolutions' which are periods in which one generally accepted view (or consensus) is replaced by another, which no longer fits the paradigms of the earlier consensus. What Kuhn and Feyerabend say about science seems to me also to apply to political revolutions, which, if successful, involve a new consensus. Because Popper thinks of reason as one and the same in all men at all times, because he thinks of it as involving consensus, he can only view revolutions as basically unreasonable. The idea that reason (or what is called 'reason' at any particular time) is itself subject to historical change neither he nor other believers in the liberal ideology can accept. Thus though I agree with Edgley that there is something seriously wrong with the liberal ideology, I locate the trouble in a very different place.

It is noteworthy that Edgley nowhere gives a definition of violence, but seems to assume that we will all agree on what constitute instances of it. This is unfortunate, for part of the clash between the liberal and romantic ideologies depends on a difference of view on the nature of violence. The appropriate section of the O.E.D. definition runs: 'The exercise of physical force so as to inflict injury on or damage to persons or property; action or conduct characterized by this.' This implies, as Edgley points out (p. 122), that the sanctions of the law are not necessarily violent in character. However, it does sound odd to say that imprisoning a man is not doing violence to him, even though we accept that legal sanctions are only counter-violence. On the quoted definition it would seem that legal counter-violence must be rare. Liberals would maintain that this is so in a society founded on consensus. Nevertheless, I am inclined

was concerned with. It is clear that he regards both theories and 'frameworks' as on the same level; Kuhn, in the field of science, is claiming that there is a difference of level. I am pointing out that what Popper considers the political or social 'framework' should rather be thought of as an ideology which can change and be changed. Certainly Popper's view cannot admit political revolution any more than it can what Kuhn calls a scientific revolution. It is also worth noting that Popper concludes his article with an attack on psychology, sociology *and* history.

to agree with Professor Anscombe that in the last resort the law does rest on the possibility of using violence even within the O.E.D. definition: 'In a peaceful and law-abiding country such as England, it may not be immediately obvious that the rulers need to command violence to the point of fighting to the death those that would oppose it; but brief reflection shows that this is so.'[9]

However, there are difficulties with accepting the definition as it stands;[10] mental cruelty can certainly inflict (mental) injury or damage, and this would seem to be doing violence to the victim. Certainly we would ordinarily think of terrorizing someone as doing violence to him, even though no physical damage was done. It is clear that we often think of things as instances of violence which do not fall within the definition quoted above, and some people might be doubtful about the stress on property included.

Nevertheless there is something of a redefinition of the term in the romantic ideology, though I think it is more centrally manifested in the work of Marx. He seems to claim that the situation of the proletariat is the result of violence done to them by the bourgeoisie. The division of labour inflicts injury on the worker, even though not directly, not as the result of intentional action on the part of the employer. In spite of the amelioration of working conditions in the twentieth century, a Marxist can still argue that the alienation which is the lot of the proletariat under capitalism is a form of violence. I am not here concerned with the justice of this claim; it is sufficient that arguments can be produced for it, and that it operates with a conception of violence which is not too far distant from our normal one. This conception can be arrived at by a reasoned series of steps from the everyday notion. However, a Marxist

[9] 'War and Murder' in *Nuclear Weapons, a Catholic Response* (London, 1963), p. 46.

[10] A minor point which deserves mention is the unfortunate difference between 'doing violence to someone' and 'being violent'. A nonviolent man may certainly do violence, e.g. a policeman may stun a suspect in order to take him into custody. We would not therefore call the policeman a 'violent' man.

would further claim that the bourgeois idea of reason is itself part of the apparatus of violence which is used to keep the proletariat in submission. In other words, the Marxists deny that there can be a consensus between the bourgeoisie and the proletariat, and hence that reasons acceptable to one will be acceptable to the other. The two classes may well disagree on 'what are the most intolerable evils of our society, and on what are the most urgent social reforms'. Popper must see the attitude of the proletariat as unreason, and not only because it demands a revolutionary response.

Thus I agree with Edgley that Popper's (and the liberals') conception of reason is too narrow, though not for Edgley's reasons. This narrowness may be visible in the philosophy of logic, but I am sufficiently affected by Marxism to believe that the philosophy of logic of an age is itself only a reflection of other and deeper tendencies within the society. In conclusion, what of the relations between reason and violence? I am still enough under the sway of the liberal ideology to agree with Edgley that there is a *prima facie* case against violence, though no more than that. What I hope I have shown is the lines which an investigation of the ideology of the liberal intellectuals should take.

Comment

BY J. W. N. WATKINS

I am generally averse to trendiness in philosophy. I am particularly averse to trendiness concerning the current trend in some western democracies to resort increasingly to non-argumentative, and more or less violent, political methods.

Edgley's paper gave me the *impression* that he has some sympathy with this—to my mind, ominous—trend, and that he is against old-fashioned (or pre-Chomsky and pre-Feyerabend) critical rationalism. This impression was conveyed chiefly by certain remarks and phrases of his, such as: 'philosophically it's reason that is the chief trouble-maker' (p. 113), 'the alienation of reason' (p. 115), 'the substructure of the ideology of liberal intellectuals ... is a muddle, not to say mystification' (p. 126), 'Popper's repeated antithesis between reason and violence [is] facile and superficial' (p. 131).

But when I searched for his *arguments* what I found—with the one exception of his rejection of anti-psychologism in logic (p. 123), which I pass over in pained silence—consisted of echoes, sometimes somewhat muffled and distorted, from the philosophical tradition he was attacking.

Instead of providing chapter and verse I ask Professor Edgley to take my word for it that the following theses—though some of them are too familiar and obvious to merit the title of *thesis*—have long been accepted within the Popper circle (and, in quite a few cases, outside it too):

(1) Rational discussion and rational action are *problem-oriented*. (Cp. Edgley, p. 127; if the problem has to do with Vietnam, the question of your daughter's measles is not likely to be relevant.)

(2) An action is rational, in a broad but important sense, if it is prescribed by the agent's *de facto* aims and situational beliefs, however immoral or erroneous these may respectively be. (Cp. Edgley, pp. 129–31, and his discussion of the 'technological conception of reason'.)

(3) A do-nothing policy is still a policy, and may be rational or otherwise in the sense of (2) above. (Cp. Edgley, pp. 126 and 133.)

(4) Someone who goes through the motions of arguing but who has resolved in advance (and sticks to his resolve) not to allow any counter-argument to modify his position, is only pretending to argue.

(5) Pretending to argue *may* be rational in the sense of (2) above (cp. Edgley, p. 132), just as trying to argue seriously (with, say, a quick-tempered gunman) may be irrational (cp. Edgley, pp. 127, 129 and 132).

(6) The role of logical inference in argument is not so much to

justify conclusions as to assist the criticism of premisses. (Cp. Edgley, pp. 123–4.)

(7) Inconsistency-proofs apart, there are no *conclusive* arguments in empirical science. (Cp. Edgley, p. 119.)

(8) Science is *not* entirely rational. (Cp. Edgley, pp. 119–20.) For the invention of new ideas is not a rational process. Also, a certain amount of dogmatism and tenacity is actually needed in science.

An idea of Popper's which Edgley might have made use of, but did not, is this:

(9) Rationalism itself cannot be entirely rational. For the adoption of a rationalist attitude cannot itself be an entirely rational process.[1]

These nine theses have no tendency, so far as I can see, either singly or collectively, to favour any shift away from argumentative and peaceable methods of deciding issues in a political democracy towards non-argumentative and violent methods. So I will end by putting two questions to Professor Edgley, one philosophical, the other practical. First: has he any philosophical objections to Popper's critical rationalism (other than the one associated with his wish to see psychology put back into logic) that are *not* already contained in these nine Popperian theses? Second: can he specify any situations where Popper would presumably be against, but he (Edgley) would be for, the use of violence?

---

[1] 'Whether this adoption is tentative or leads to a settled habit, we may describe it as an irrational *faith in reason*. So rationalism is necessarily far from comprehensive or self-contained. This has frequently been overlooked by rationalists who thus exposed themselves to a beating in their own field and by their own favourite weapon whenever an irrationalist took the trouble to turn it against them' (*The Open Society* . . . , 4th ed. 1962, Vol. 2, p. 231).

Bartley tried to eliminate this residual irrationalism with his idea of a *comprehensively* critical rationalism (CCR) (W. W. Bartley III, *The Retreat to Commitment*, ch. V), but I do not think that he succeeded (see my 'CCR: A Refutation', *Philosophy*, Vol. XLVI, p. 175, January 1971).

Comment

BY D. E. MILLIGAN

Edgley's paper suggests that in some discussions of the contrast
between reason and violence there are muddles about the nature
of reason—muddles particularly to be found in the thinking of
some liberal intellectuals who defend reason at the expense of
violence. There may well be some truth in this suggestion.
However, Edgley's paper does also seem to imply that no
worthwhile contrast lies behind the muddles, and that violence
is sometimes, perhaps even often, reasonable or in accord with
reason. What I shall try to do is to outline briefly a legitimate
contrast between reason and violence, to indicate that an
acceptance of this does not imply that violence can never be
reasonable, and to suggest some of the conditions which must
be met before it can be reasonable.

The argument about reason and violence is, I take it, about
ways of settling disputes or disagreements. Ought they to be
settled by reason or by violence? To many the answer is
obvious. They find it difficult to see how anyone could seriously
maintain that a dispute would not be better settled by argument,
discussion and negotiation than by any kind of force. But to
some people violence is justifiable; reason has failed and the
only way to obtain any worthwhile change in society is by
violence. They may regret having to use it, but it is necessary.
However, few of those who advocate reason would suggest that
there are no circumstances in which violence is justifiable. It
might therefore seem as if the disagreement is simply about
what circumstances justify violence. But to discuss this it is
essential to be clear about the alternative to violence, an alternative rightly or wrongly referred to as reason.

In making this contrast between reason and violence we do
not need to limit reason to what Edgley called the technological
conception of reason. To argue that it must be limited in this
way, as Hume did, is, I agree, a mistake. It may be that Popper

was also guilty of that mistake; but my purpose here is neither to defend nor to attack Popper. He and others may have based their contrast between reason and violence on such an idea of reason; but the contrast can be made defensible and closer to what is ordinarily intended if it is based on a rather different conception of reason. I cannot here justify such an alternative view of reason,[1] but can only briefly indicate some aspects of it and apply them to the context of disputes.

As I shall contrast it with violence, reason is a form of activity which is not restricted to arguing deductively or inductively, but consists of a far wider range of activities. To see what this might involve, consider an individual who deliberates about what he should do; he is not necessarily only observing his own desires and working out the means to their satisfaction. To suppose that he does no more is to grossly underestimate the extent and complexity of the thinking, both theoretical and practical, that is involved in action. The estimation of consequences, particularly when they involve the actions of others, cannot be achieved just by predicting on the basis of empirical generalizations. Again, the agent's desires may conflict and suggest incompatible courses of action; this requires the comparison and evaluation of the desires, a comparison which does not just involve the measurement of like against like on the same scale. More difficult are the cases where the satisfaction of desires has to be weighed against the agent's moral or religious beliefs. Other examples of these complexities might equally have been chosen. Thus when an agent thinks about the situation in which he has to act, he will often find that there are good reasons both for and against several different actions. To sort out these reasons, to decide what importance they have, what weight to give them and to come to a conclusion is no simple matter. Such a conclusion does not follow deductively, nor is there a decision procedure for discovering the correct conclusion. But this does not imply that the agent has not been

---

[1] I have discussed it more fully in 'Reasons as Explanations', *Mind* (forthcoming).

reasoning about what to do or that there cannot be objective standards which can be applied to such reasoning. We may say not only that the agent's reasons for what he did were good or bad, but we may also say that the methods by which he reasoned to his decision were good or bad.

The processes by which two parties to a dispute can try to achieve a fair settlement may be similar. They may deliberate with each other, examining the reasons for and against the different courses of action advocated. Just as an individual may have to compromise between his conflicting interests, so the two sides may have to compromise[2] between their respective interests. In discussing their dispute with each other in this kind of way, they are employing reason as a method for trying to settle the dispute. Of course their methods of negotiating may be criticized; just as there are standards of reasoning for the individual, so there are for reasoning between individuals. To approach a dispute in this kind of way is clearly quite different from using violence. A solution may be found by arguing and discussing, or a solution may be forced on the less powerful by the more powerful.

Reason as I have described it is an ideal to which actual practice only approximates to a greater or lesser degree. But, rightly or wrongly, it is this ideal which many people have in mind when they advocate reason rather than violence as a method of solving disputes. The contrast is thus between the view that by negotiation and discussion a fair and just solution is to be found and the view that might is right. Those who defend reason are against war both real and economic and in favour of the United Nations and the International Court of Justice. They are against strikes and in favour of arbitration. They are against conflict and confrontation and in favour of conciliation. They are against the rule of the jungle and in favour of the rule of law.

It is, of course, the case that institutions such as the United

[2] Far more needs to be said about the nature and justification of compromise.

Nations are inadequate, and that they are often used to pursue self-interest and to exercise power, rather than to find a fair and just solution. It is the case that in many disagreements between world powers there is not even any agreement over the principles of justice. It is the case that, by claiming to apply the method of reason and by apparently engaging in many of the activities that method suggests, individuals and institutions may simply be resisting change. It is the case that even if both sides to a dispute claim to be willing to negotiate there is no guarantee of a fair solution being reached and no guarantee that the method of reason will not be taken advantage of and adhered to in name only. But it does not follow from these inadequacies in practice that the ideal of the method of reason should be abandoned. The deficiencies of the United Nations do not justify reverting to policies which rely only on power politics, gunboat diplomacy and war. I would argue, though it is not essential to my case here, that an imperfect system of negotiation is better than none at all, and that the only hope of achieving justice is to support and develop reason as a method of settling disputes whether international or intranational.[3]

So far I have suggested that there is an approach to the solution of disputes which may be referred to as the method of reason and that this may be contrasted with violence. Before going any further a little needs to be said about what constitutes violence. Violence when contrasted with reason is not simply confined to physical injury to persons or damage to property. Almost any kind of student sit-in is called violent; shouting someone down is violent; abuse is violent. Once the notion of violence is extended to cover such things as these, it is difficult to see how in the context of disputes it is possible to draw the

---

[3] There are some who claim that reason is not even in principle a good method of settling disputes; that reason is a tool of the bourgeois used to preserve their position of privilege, and that the working classes only have their strength or power with which to obtain justice for themselves. This is not a foolish argument; but to me the facts pointed to indicate a misuse of reason rather than anything inherently wrong with reason.

line so that it is not coercion which is contrasted with reason. Indeed the interests of clarity would seem to me best served by making the contrast in that way and keeping the term 'violence' for certain extreme forms of coercion. Much of the argument against violence is equally an argument against coercion. Violence may be wrong because of the pain it causes or the damage that is done; but equally other forms of coercion may result in considerable suffering even if blood does not flow and no observable injury is inflicted. But it is not only for reasons such as these that violence is wrong; it is also wrong for a reason that applies to all forms of coercion, that where coercion is the method of settling the dispute it is necessarily the most powerful who wins.

However, the argument of those who defend violence is that coercion, like reason, is justified and is only justified in those cases in which the right solution is obtained by using that method. But who is to say what the right solution is? If reason is used, then there is an attempt by the disputants to come to an agreement about the right thing to do. However, if coercion is allowed, then those who are more powerful have only to decide for themselves what is right and then impose their idea of what is right on those who are less powerful; and this idea is only too likely to be an expression of what they want, rather than what would independently be seen as right. Sometimes right will be on the side of might, but since those who have the power will not in fact be called on to defend their position with reasons or convince others of the justice of their actions, it seems unlikely that might, even if motivated by right, will often have right on its side. Whatever may be the case in particular instances, the method of reason is more likely to achieve fairness for the less powerful than any alternative, and is unlikely to impose unfairness on the more powerful; hence the method of reason is one worth preserving or adopting and anything which serves to undermine it (such as the occasional case in which power decides) is to be avoided.

I do not deny that there may be situations in which coercion may be supported by reasons, and that in some of these the balance of reasons will be in support of coercion rather than reason. Certainly most people would accept this in the case of legal punishment which if not violent is certainly coercive. Thus it might be said that in these particular cases violence or coercion would be reasonable, or even the only reasonable course of action. I have some hesitation in saying this because the overtones of the word 'reasonable' immediately suggest moderation and restraint which seem incompatible with violence, and indeed this may be the cause of Popper and others being reluctant to say that violence is ever reasonable. Waging war on Hitler was a violent action and one that to most people was justifiable; it had an overwhelming balance of reasons in its favour. But to say that it was reasonable sounds odd and not quite in keeping with our ordinary use of that term.

However, ordinary language need not inhibit us greatly here. Though much of our use of the terms 'reasonable' and 'rational' may be ambiguous, vague or imprecise, we can give a clear sense to these terms such that it can be correctly said that particular instances of violence are reasonable, meaning either that there are overriding reasons in favour of violent action in this situation or simply that there are strong, though not overriding, reasons in favour of such action. But to agree that violence is sometimes reasonable is not incompatible with distinguishing between violence and reason as methods of settling disputes, and is even not incompatible with claiming that reason is the right way of settling disputes. To say violence is contrary to reason may mean that violent action is always unreasonable or is *prima facie* unreasonable; it may also mean that the methods of violence and reason are alternative methods of settling disputes, and that in so far as one is using violence one is not using reason. This ambiguity means that it is not contradictory, though it might be misleading, to say that reason is sometimes unreasonable, suggesting that the balance of reasons is sometimes against using the method of reason to settle disputes. Though I think Edgley is aware of this distinction, he does seem to me to leave himself open to misunderstanding here.

Though it does not affect the main part of my argument, I should like to say a little about the circumstances in which violence might be reasonable. It will, in my opinion, only be reasonable in those cases in which the opposite side in the dispute does not observe the method of reason. Thus I would claim that violence or coercion are only reasonable if they are counter-coercion. I do not say it would always be reasonable in such circumstances. The degree to which the method of reason is departed from is rarely sufficiently great to justify violence, particularly before other alternatives have been tried. It may be better to accept injustice and unfairness resulting from the use of power by others than to engage in violence in order to try to bring about justice. Further, the only degree of coercion which is reasonable is the minimum required to redress the injustice; it is incumbent on those who wish to use coercion not simply to produce reasons for using coercion, but to produce reasons for using that degree of coercion which is suggested.

The answer to this which is made by those who think that violence is far more frequently reasonable is that my argument is merely a rationalization of the liberal intellectual's position; he is willing to talk and to join the odd pressure group, but is unwilling to take effective action towards altering society—this unwillingness being the result of his realization that he has so much to lose if society is altered. I recognize the possibility of this; I recognize that it may even be true of all liberal intellectuals. But it does not need to be. Moreover, the wrongness of their motives does not imply the wrongness of their opinions or actions. A more important aspect of the ineffectiveness of the liberal intellectual than his allegedly selfish motives is his failure to recognize the degree or source of unfairness in our society. He does not seem to have noticed the degree to which unchallenged, and often unchallengeable, power rests with certain groups or institutions in our society, a consequence of which is that coercion is being employed in many contexts and in many ways which are never questioned. Such a failure is, no doubt, partly the result of complacency arising from the favourable comparison of our society with others; but is also partly the result of not having had the information, which sociologists and others are now producing, needed to recognize much of the injustice.

If coercion is not to be used or indeed does not have to be used to counteract the coercion exercised in subtle ways by existing institutions, then first such coercion as exists must be discovered; the liberal intellectual must not be content to wait for it to show itself or for those who suffer from it to rebel, but he must rather seek it out. Secondly, he must work to remove such coercion by every means that the method of reason allows. If, and only if, that fails (and indeed not always then) will it be reasonable and possibly obligatory to resort to counter-coercion.

Thus, if violence is to be used it must first be shown that the method of reason will fail to settle the dispute or has failed to change the system so as to get rid of the injustice or of the particular exercise of power. Secondly, it is necessary to show that the unfairness is sufficiently clear and sufficiently great to justify some coercion or violence. Thirdly, it is necessary to show that the degree of coercion to be used is the minimum required to effect the change. Violence is a dangerous weapon; those who use it may easily, if unwittingly, introduce a greater injustice than the one they are trying to remove.

Much that I have said has been the simple expression of values, values which could be defended although not briefly. Much has been a considerable over-simplification, such as the grouping together of all kinds of disputes and disagreements as if they were of the same sort. Much has been taken for granted, such as the possibility of there being a right solution to any dispute. But I hope that none of this vitiates my attempts at clarification of the issues. This clarification seems to me to indicate the likelihood of a greater degree of agreement between the respective backers of reason and violence than might have been expected and to suggest that the disagreement between them is often not about a moral principle but is related rather to what they each take to be the nature of our society and the way in which power is exercised in it. Personally I am against violence, but agree with the analysis of our society and others given by those who are thought to be or who claim to be on the side of violence.

I am not sure how far what I have said is in disagreement with Edgley's paper. It certainly seems to me that he does not say enough about what lies behind the idea of reason when it is opposed to violence, and that he is likely to be read as giving greater support to violence than he perhaps intended. In so far as he claims violence is sometimes the reasonable course of action, in the sense that the weight of reasons favour it, the only people who would disagree are the most extreme pacifists, amongst whom Popper, surely, cannot be counted. Violence would sometimes be reasonable, in Edgley's sense of the term, to Popper and almost all liberal intellectuals. But this would in no way diminish their hatred of violence and their deeply felt commitment to reason as opposed to violence.

Comment

BY R. M. HARE

It is obviously necessary to distinguish between the following two questions:

(a) Ought we to use reasoning rather than some other procedure in deciding what we ought to do?

(b) Ought we to use reasoning or some other procedure in trying to get other people to co-operate with us?

It looks as if some of those whom Professor Edgley quotes (on both sides) are answering question (b). Sense can only be made of his paper if we assume that he is mainly interested in question (*b*); for he seeks to impugn the antithesis between reason and violence, and violence could not be one of the other procedures mentioned in (*a*), though thinking with one's blood could be, or following my leader (both of which are, now as ever, popular procedures). The main connection between the questions is that the decision referred to in (*a*)—the decision as to what we ought to do—may be a decision as to the answer to (*b*). And the right answer to (*b*), as Edgley says, may in *some* cases be that we ought to use some other procedure than reasoning. These will be the cases in which reasoning with people will not achieve co-operation, and in which the end for which the co-operation is sought is so important that the evils that may ensue from abandoning reasoning in favour of some other method are less than that of not achieving the end. *When* this is so, is a question which should itself, if the answer to (*a*) is 'Yes', be decided by reasoning.

Question (*a*) is therefore crucial. I hope that in the middle of Edgley's paper he is not suggesting that when we use reasoning to decide what we ought to do, we are somehow condemning ourselves to inaction (because such reasoning can only be a matter of inferring conclusions from premisses, and merely to do this is not to change the world). This could only be thought by a descriptivist—i.e. by someone who held that when I come to the conclusion that I ought to do something, this conclusion has *of itself* no bearing on my subsequent actions. Most of us, when we are trying, by reasoning or otherwise, to decide what we ought to do, do it because we think that such a decision has necessary implications for another closely-linked decision—the decision what *to* do; i.e. we believe that reason can be practical, or (with Aristotle) that its conclusion can be an action. And this is possibly only if some of the premisses are prescriptive. But of course, as I have argued elsewhere, influenced by Popper, there is much more to practical reasoning than the mechanical drawing of conclusions from given premisses (see my *Freedom and Reason*, ch. 6 *ad init.*).

If the answer to (a) is sometimes 'Yes' (for cases in which it might be 'No', see my paper in *Ar. Soc.* 1972–3), then what we have to do is reason, or try to reach a rational conclusion, about whether to use reasoning or other methods to secure the co-operation of others. Professor Edgley rightly thinks that violence is not the only other method besides reasoning; but reasoning stands in a class by itself, because it is only when the co-operation is secured by reasoning that all parties can be assured (if the reasoning is done correctly) that what they are co-operating in doing is the rational thing to do. This is achieved because all parties have answered 'Yes' to question (a). I take it that this is what the people whom Edgley attacks are trying to convey to their audiences. I hope they succeed, because otherwise we shall go on arriving at bad policies by irrational methods of decision, in our universities as elsewhere. And it will be hard to blame the young for this when they have oldies like Professor Edgley to encourage them, and when Popper, who stands up for reason, gets written off as 'facile and superficial'.

Reply to Comments

BY ROY EDGLEY

I argue among other things that (a) violence is not necessarily contrary to reason, though (b) the fact that something is an act of violence is necessarily some reason against doing it. With respect to these questions, Grice and Manser suggest opposing criticisms: Grice suggests that even my concession in (b) is too much since it's incompatible with a situation in which a masochist enjoys being hurt by an act of violence like whipping, when there's not even a *prima facie* reason against such violence; whereas Manser opens by claiming that my view in (a) 'almost has the air of a Humean paradox', so that I am 'forced later . . . to admit that an act's being violent is a reason . . . against doing it'. Let me say at once that to describe me as being 'forced . . . to admit' (*b*) implies or presupposes either or both of two false-hoods, namely that I was reluctant to assert (*b*) and that (*b*) is inconsistent with (*a*).

G. R. GRICE

I agree with much of what Grice says about morality and reasons for doing things, but none of it, I think, is incompatible with my views on reason and violence. As I've already sugges-ted, the point at which Grice's reply does seem to conflict with those views is in his early paragraphs on sadism and maso-chism. I had said: '. . . the fact that it [an act of violence] necessarily involves . . . hurt . . . is necessarily a reason against it . . .' (p. 134). Grice in effect asks whether this is true even when the act of violence is a whipping given to a masochist, who enjoys being hurt. My difficulty with this is that I find maso-chism conceptually less straightforward than does Grice. Somebody might enjoy being whipped; somebody might get moral satisfaction out of being hurt; somebody might need to be hurt in order to get pleasure, e.g. out of sex.[1] All of these could be described as 'masochists', but in no case would it follow that what the masochist enjoys is being hurt. On my view that description of masochism would be self-contradictory, or as near to it as concepts with such broad borderlines allow. Grice would agree, I take it, that enjoyment has a contrary, e.g. disliking (he uses the word 'dislikes' once, and then (pp. 143–4) apparently as the contradictory of 'enjoys'). It seems to me that this contrary of enjoyment is involved in the concept of being hurt, in the sense that *A* must dislike being hurt; and that's why the fact that doing something would hurt somebody is necessarily a reason against doing it. If I may adapt a quota-tion from Grice (p. 143): in the matter of reasons, enjoyment is no more fundamental than disliking.

Grice doesn't, I think, clearly enough distinguish that matter

[1] A possibility mentioned to me by Robert Kirkham.

from problems involving the distinction between the agent and others. Sadism is conceptually less problematic than masochism because what the sadist enjoys is hurting *somebody else*. Most of the problems Grice considers in this area are problems of acute inter-personal conflict, acute because the conflict is not of the ordinary kind usually considered under the heading of 'conflict of interests': in these cases the very object of one person's enjoyment (or dislike) is another's hurt (or enjoyment). But this is a good enough reason for regarding such attitudes as pathological. When Grice says of his sadist *A* who 'is in the grip of a nearly irresistible sexual desire' to whip *B*, though *B* would strongly dislike being whipped, that 'So far as we have gone, the rational course of action seems to be for *A* to whip *B* on Mondays, Wednesdays, and Fridays but not on the inter-mediate days' (p. 139), he's neglecting a less jokey but still more rational possibility: curing *A* of his perversion. The rationality of this course of action still depends on the basic connection between practical reason on the one hand and enjoyment and dislike on the other. Grice's failure to see this is no doubt due to his insistence on the prime importance of the *agent*'s enjoyment. On this topic there's certainly, as he says, 'a serious problem for any philosopher who really wants to make the idea of reasons for acting do some work'. But the problem is one in the pathology of philosophical ideas: why some philosophers have conceded so much to egoism. The ideology of capitalism is an obvious candidate, but that's another story.

ANTHONY MANSER

Manser in his reply spends much of his time arguing for a view I accept, though he takes me to be denying it. His objection, made in many places, can be regarded as summarized in the following criticism: '. . . the account he gives of the origin of the trouble seems to me far from the mark. Though logicians may be responsible for many of the confusions that exist in philosophy, I do not think this is one of them' (p. 151). In his final paragraph he says: 'I agree with Edgley that Popper's (and the liberals') conception of reason is too narrow, though not for Edgley's reasons ... the philosophy of logic of an age is itself only a reflection of other and deeper tendencies within the society' (p. 156). Why does he think that what I've said about the relation between modern philosophy of logic and the liberal ideology of reason is incompatible with this last quoted remark, which I fully accept? Manser himself maps part of the liberal ideology of reason in terms of the notion of consensus without regarding this as conflicting with the idea that this ideology reflects 'deeper tendencies within society'. I take it that philosophy succeeds in *producing* ideology in the sense that it articulates and systematizes ideas already 'in the air', ideas changed and developed by being made clearer, more plausible, and more defensible by this philosophical activity, but in their inexplicit form attributable chiefly to the changing forms, economic, social, and political, of workaday life in general, which thus prepares the way for their intellectual reception.[2] In other words, ideology results from the interaction of philosophical and other intellectual clarification with social phenomena and the ideas that spontaneously reflect them: a cloud of industrial smog condensed into a drop of refined social oil. The effect of philosophy is thus in this way to justify half-formed and half-forming common ideas, and so to support and sustain their acceptance at an intellectual level. By reflecting and sustaining it, philosophy in both ways *reproduces* the changing social order. In a society in which specialization of labour distinguishes a class of intellectuals, we can, therefore, for the sake of analysis, conveniently (though at the risk of misleading) identify an ideology of intellectuals and seek to understand that; and this will allow us to concentrate on the internal structure of the ideology, and in particular on the logical or quasi-logical articulation of its component ideas, seeking to understand the ideology from the inside, while ignoring for the moment the

[2] My views on ideology owe much to John Mepham's, 'The Theory of Ideology in Capital' (*Radical Philosophy* 2).

social conditions that those ideas, in their comparatively in-
articulate and unsystematic form, spontaneously reflect in the
non-intellectual consciousness. This is what I tried to do in my
paper. Its sub-title refers explicitly to 'the ideology of liberal
intellectuals'; I took care to say of the antithesis between reason
and violence that 'it's a common misconception of reason . . .
that generates, *or at least supports*, the antithesis' (p. 113); and
I claimed that in modern philosophy of logic liberalism's
Hamlet syndrome finds not its origin but 'a philosophical
rationale' (p. 125).

I've already pointed out that Manser himself, in his argument
about the role of the notion of consensus in the liberal ideology
of reason, offers an internal account of that ideology, of the
same general type as my own. But he seems to be in some doubt
as to whether the two accounts are in competition, and therefore in doubt about whether my account in terms of the
philosophy of logic is wrong or only a part of the truth. Manser
is certainly right to emphasize the importance of the notion of
consensus in liberal ideology. But this would be incompatible
with my views only if I had claimed to be giving a picture of
the whole of the liberal ideology of reason. I have not claimed
this. What I've done, as a careful reading will show, is to indicate frequently that my paper concentrates on what is just a
part of a much bigger and more complicated story (e.g. my
sub-title refers to 'A *Fragment* of the Ideology of Liberal Intellectuals'). I am not denying that 'the belief that there is an
antithesis between reason and violence is both deep seated and
connected with many other features of the liberal ideology'
(pp. 147–8).

There are, however, signs of a substantive disagreement
between Manser and myself. Let me introduce the matter via
his defence of Lord James. It may be true that when Lord
James wrote, 'If you want to change things . . . you will use
rational arguments and never anything else', he failed to
make explicit two other claims that imply the claim he does
make: namely the one Manser attributes to him, that 'the right

way to change things was by getting agreement that the change was necessary or desirable' (p. 148), and the claim that the right way to get agreement is by rational argument. As I suggested (p. 134), I think an *a priori* case could be made out for something like this latter claim, at least as a *prima facie* principle. But it's a platitude, as Manser points out, that rational argument, or argument that its proponents take to be rational, may be ineffective in achieving agreement, and the crucial question is what is to be done then. Manser says that it's part of the liberal ideology of reason at this point to suppose (*a*) that the *rational* way of coping with this disagreement is to agree to accept the majority verdict and (*b*) that men *will* agree to this because they agree on the remote aim of maintaining a society in which free discussion is possible. Manser himself seems to assert that (*b*) is false; and it seems clear as a matter of fact that it is false. But what he apparently offers as the ground of its falsity seems to imply the falseness of (*a*) also. His argument, supported with references to Kuhn and Feyerabend, is that what is really wrong with the liberal ideology of reason, exemplified in Popper, is that it 'thinks of reason as one and the same in all men at all times', whereas the truth is that 'reason . . . is itself subject to historical change . . .' (p. 154).

Now I suspect that not many people, liberal or not, accept (*b*), though I agree that (*a*) has a strong claim to be regarded as essential to liberal ideology. Manser quotes Anscombe's claim that behind the law of a liberal country stands the possibility of state violence, and liberals could presumably argue the need for the state to be able to command violence precisely on the ground that (*a*) is true and (*b*) sometimes not. Thus when Manser says that 'there is something seriously wrong with the liberal ideology', he will have failed to show this unless he shows that (*a*) is at fault. I think that his argument fails to show this.

It may be the case that different groups of people, at the same or at different times, have different ideas of reason. This is compatible with (*a*): for some of those ideas of reason may be mistaken, muddled, misconceptions, and (*a*) may not. This is compatible also with the possibility that the people with those muddled ideas may be unable to see that they are muddled and give them up in favour of superior ones. But there is a stronger way of interpreting Manser's thesis, a way that does imply the rejection of (*a*): this is to say not merely that different people may have different conceptions of reason that they are unable to reconcile, but that none can be more acceptable than any other. This is the relativist and idealist conception of rationality that some interpretations attribute to Kuhn: it's not merely that what is *thought* to be rational varies from group to group and time to time, but either that what *is* rational varies or that when such differences occur neither side's view is more or less rational than the other's. Some of the things Manser says, especially his footnote 3, suggest that this is his view. But it seems to me paradoxical, and not the only alternative to the liberal doctrine, since it's certainly non-Marxist. Briefly, what makes it paradoxical is that under this interpretation the concept of reason becomes essentially a third-person (or spectator's) concept, useful for seeming to express a detached Olympian attitude towards disputing parties, but delusively so to the extent that such a case is *argued for*, which employs a concept of reason that is first-person, essentially committed and participant.

In any case, Manser seems prepared to accept the basic step that I chiefly question in the liberal ideology: the identification of reason with reasoning involved in the antithesis between reason and violence. He says (p. 149): 'But to give someone a reason for action is not the same as reasoning with him; it is not what we ordinarily mean by "reason" in the contrast between reason and violence'. A footnote adds: 'Roughly, in cases where "motive" could be substituted for "reason" without important alteration of meaning we are not in the realm of "reason" as discussed in this paper.' There is a double confusion here. Manser supposes that in discussing the contrast between reason and violence we must agree that 'reason' here means 'reasoning'; but he also implies either that by reasoning with someone we can't give him a reason for action in the sense of *stating* a reason for him to do something, or that in stating a reason for him to do something we're not giving him a motive for doing it. If I give a worker a reason for striking by saying to him 'A strike would force the management to yield on the pay-claim' am I not also giving him a motive for striking? How then can Manser think that even if we restrict the discussion to reasoning we shall not be discussing motives for doing things? I can only hazard the guess, supported by that tell-tale footnote, that Manser shares with liberal intellectuals that very misconception of reason I stigmatized as the theoretical conception, though in the sophisticated form of supposing that the word 'reason' is ambiguous between 'a reason for believing that so-and-so' and 'a reason for doing so-and-so'.

If so, it would presumably explain why he fails to see either that logic and the philosophy of logic are involved or that his defence of Popper against my criticism is beside the point. To start with the former, Manser's view that 'it is not logic but something which can be called the "ideology of reason" which requires examination' (p. 151) is baffling in the extreme. We are concerned with the ideology of reason. We are concerned with this ideology as a part of liberalism, whose historical roots are deep in the European and American intellectual tradition of the past three centuries. We are concerned (at least *I* was concerned, as my sub-title indicates) with this ideology as it manifests itself in the thought of contemporary intellectuals. Reason and logic are intimately related. The specialist discipline of logic, after centuries of slumber, has in the last hundred years awoken in Europe and America, has undergone a revolution and decades of intense activity, and now occupies a place of respect and influence in the intellectual scheme of things. Is it surprising that this subject with this history should have profoundly impressed twentieth-century philosophers and other intellectuals, and should have helped to shape their conception of reason? That conception bears clear marks of thinking in and about logic, especially in respect of its anti-psychologism, the fact-value distinction, and the linguistic conception of logic. It's precisely in these respects that in a society heavily dependent on tame experts, and in particular apolitical scientists and technologists, this conception of reason is ideologically valuable. It's precisely in these respects that this conception of reason answers to liberalism's inactivism. Popper has been a consistent advocate of at least the first two doctrines.

Manser seems to think that when I talk of 'the logician's conception of argument' I include features that distinguish arguments of the type they study from arguments of other types (p. 151). But my characterization of the logician's conception of argument (p. 123) is in itself wide enough to cover any type of argument 'in human discourse': all it needs is some conclusion being argued for, and some premiss or premisses given as reasons that are taken to argue for that conclusion. The contrast I am concerned with is not between types of argument in this sense, but between arguments of any type in that sense, i.e. sets of assertions or propositions, and argument as the *activity* of arguing, and with it any other activity or action. I call the former 'the logician's conception' because logicians have typically studied arguments in that sense and the associated conception of reason: their concern has been with the rationality of arguments in that sense, rationality or validity being thus thought of as a function of the 'logical relations' holding between the component propositions of the argument, these logical relations in their turn being construed as relations of truth and falsity resulting from the syntax or semantics of those propositions. It's this conception of argument and its associated conception of rationality that lend ideological support to the view that the only things that can be rational are words and thought, not deeds or emotions. Manser's claim (p. 152) that Popper's 'conception of "argument" is wider than that of the logic textbook' is therefore beside the point. Popper's notion of 'reasonableness' is still essentially linked, like the liberal preference, to words, thought, and argument, in contrast to deeds and emotions. Indeed, in the passage Manser quotes in this same paragraph, Popper explicitly contrasts 'the rational attitude of the impartial judge' with 'the emotional attitude of the impassioned preacher'—as if, for instance, it couldn't be a rational attitude to react in an emotional and impassioned way, with horror, indignation, and anger, to the American terrorist bombing of North Vietnam. What could be more rational than loathing what is loathsome, even if that does happen to be the President of the U.S.A. and his policies?

J. W. N. WATKINS

Watkins insists on trying to put me into a pigeon-hole and then complains that he can't find any arguments in my paper. Of course arguments will sound like 'echoes . . . muffled and distorted' (p. 157) to anyone capable of recognizing something as an argument only if it conforms to a pattern characteristic of an established 'trend' or 'tradition', and in particular the 'tradition' of critical rationalism or some familiar opposing 'trend'. On that issue, my p. 119 should make it clear that in my opinion both sides misconceive reason, and in the same way. But I don't expect comprehension from critical rationalists. The 'pained silence' in which Watkins 'passes over' my remarks about anti-psychologism seems fairly typical of what their anti-dogmatism comes to in practice.

Watkins presents nine theses and claims that they don't tend to favour 'non-argumentative and violent methods' rather than 'argumentative and peaceable methods' of deciding issues (p. 158). The presupposition that non-argumentative methods are violent I criticized on p. 122, so this must be another part of my paper that Watkins has decided to 'pass over in pained silence'. I wonder whether silence, pained or painless, is an argumentative or violent method? An answer is needed, because it seems to play a vital part in the technique of critical rationalism.

Presuppositions aside, Watkins' claim about his nine theses seems to me either to be false, or to be trivially true because the theses have no bearing on the question of what methods should be used. My argument was that logically speaking only a hair's breadth divides the theoretical conception of reason from the technological conception of practical reason, though the former denies that actions and activities, with the possible exception of reasoning itself, can be rational, whereas the latter imposes only weak conditions on the rationality of actions, including violence; and that these conceptions, or rather misconceptions, underlie and help to explain much liberal thinking about reason and violence, such as Popper's. On pp. 128–31 I point out how the opposing pressures of these two doctrines account for the ambivalence and confusion in Popper. Watkins' theses exhibit signs of the same ambivalence, though a version of the technological conception (in thesis 2) now dominates. Thesis 4, for example, looks like the beginning of an argument for Popper's 'attitude of reasonableness', and as such it invites an adaptation in reply: someone who goes through the motions of arguing, e.g. in favour of taking industrial action, such as striking and encouraging others to strike, but who resolves not to take any such action because there might be counter-arguments that would modify his position, is only pretending to argue. However, as Watkins points out in thesis 5, given thesis 2, there is no general argument from thesis 4 to Popper's claim that arguing and reasoning are preferable to violence.

Isn't it the case, then, contrary to Watkins' assertion, that thesis 2 does favour a 'shift . . . towards non-argumentative and violent methods'? It would, for instance, make Hitler's persecution of the Jews rational. Wouldn't that 'favour' such violence, and any like it, in opposition to those who object to it as irrational? Perhaps not, for any purposive action whatsoever would presumably be rational according to thesis 2, not excepting the actions of criticizing or speaking in favour of some other action. That sounds like rationalism of an idiotically *un*critical kind, ideal for the defence of the status quo. This 'broad and important' sense of 'rational action' is, in fact, a simple-minded sense articulated by philosophers, and important only in spreading confusion in the defence, among other things, of their theories.

My answers to Watkins' two questions (p. 158) are therefore as follows. First, Popper's critical rationalism is relevant only so far as that doctrine is applied in his views on reason and violence, and my objections to those views are contained in my paper and these replies; as to the suggestion that Watkins' 'nine Popperian theses' do contain 'philosophical objections to Popper's critical rationalism', I've indicated in this note their relevance (or lack of it) to the problem of reason and violence. Second, since, as I've pointed out (see especially pp. 128–31), the opposing pressures of the theoretical conception of reason and the technological conception of practical reason make Popper's views on that problem hopelessly muddled and ambivalent, distinguishing the situations in which Popper would be against from those in which he would be for the use of violence is largely a matter of guesswork. However, putting aside what his general theories imply on this matter, if anything, what he explicitly seems to commit himself to, as I say on p. 131, is that violence is legitimate only as counter-violence. I there argue against that view, so that one reply to Watkins' question is already explicit in my paper, for anyone who can read. Between the confusion of Popper's general arguments and his explicit commitment to violence only as counter-violence it's perhaps possible to discern a political way of reconciling the opposing tendencies of the theoretical conception and the technological conception: the former might be allowed to support the view that for subjects of the state argument and discussion are the only legitimate political methods of settling issues and effecting change, while for the state itself violence, and any other means necessary to achieve its aims, are permissible in accordance with the technological conception of practical reason. Whether or not this idea is present in Popper, its ideological potential for a liberal democratic technocracy is obvious. Though referring to a different kind of political set-up, Kant's summary of Frederick the Great's policy is worth remembering as a description of liberalism's reconciliation of rationality with law and order: '*Argue* as much as you like and about whatever you like, but *obey*!'

D. E. MILLIGAN

Milligan's careful reply takes caution to excess when he says (p. 164) '... I think Edgley is aware of this distinction'. The distinction he refers to, between what's reasonable and what's reasoning, I first promise in the title of my second section, I make it explicit on pp. 123–5, and in the course of the rest of that section and the first two paragraphs of the next I use it to draw several aphoristic conclusions and contrasts. Perhaps this also shows that Milligan is wrong when he says (p. 159) '... Edgley's paper does ... seem to imply that no worthwhile contrast lies behind the muddles'. In any case, I point out on pp. 133–4 that there is something in the view that violence is *a priori* contrary to reason and reasoning in conformity with it.

So far, then, Milligan and I seem to agree. But I reject the additional argument he gives against violence (p. 163), I think that much of the early part of his paper sits uneasily with the conclusion he comes to on p. 164, and in the later part of his paper, which at least heavily qualifies that earlier part, he still fails to rid himself of what I can only call 'liberal prejudice'. In all cases, Milligan seems insufficiently aware of the power of ideology. He suggests (pp. 162–3) that violence is a form of coercion and that it's coercion that should be contrasted with reason; and it's with this contrast that he leads into his additional argument against violence—'it is also wrong for a reason that applies to all forms of coercion, that where coercion is the method of settling the dispute it is necessarily the most powerful who wins' (p. 163). But this last clause sounds like a tautology, and one equally applicable to the method of settling disputes by reasoning. Thinking, reasoning, arguing, and discussing are certainly exercises of our powers, and in doing these things we may exert power and coercion on ourselves and others, as social forces exert their power on our thinking and arguing. Thus the alternatives offered on p. 161, e.g. 'A solution may be found by arguing and discussing, or a solution may be forced on the less powerful by the more powerful', are not exclusive: a solution found by arguing and discussing may be forced on the less powerful by the more powerful. Milligan takes some account of these things, pp. 161–2, but says in a footnote that they 'indicate a misuse of reason rather than anything inherently wrong with reason'. Of course this last point is right in those uses of the concept in which it carries a favourable evaluative force (see my p. 124). But Milligan is supposed to be talking about the activity of reasoning, and as I argue on p. 126 and p. 127 there is no straightforward transfer of that evaluative force to this use of the concept.

In any case, as he seems to see on p. 163, from the fact that it's the most powerful who wins it doesn't follow that exercising power is wrong. Such a view is in danger of implying that a method is right only if it's ineffective. So whether it's Milligan's contrast or one attributed by him to others, the contrast stated on p. 161 'between the view that by negotiation and discussion a fair and just solution is to be found and the view that might is right' is simply not the contrast before us. Denying that by negotiation and discussion a fair and just solution is to be found doesn't commit anyone to the idea that might is right. And as for 'they are against the rule of the jungle and in favour of the rule of law', the rule of law may be a sophisticated form of the rule of the jungle, and certainly a way of exercising might in the guise of right. Of course reason is necessarily right and is to be contrasted with coercion, which is not necessarily right. But it doesn't follow that coercion is wrong, nor does it follow either that reason*ing* is right or that reasoning can't be coercive. Milligan admits that 'sometimes right will be on the side of might' but argues that this won't usually be the case because 'those who have the power will not in fact be called on to defend their position with reasons or convince others of the justice of their actions', so that 'whatever may be the case in particular instances, the method of reason is more likely to achieve fairness for the less powerful than any alternative' (p. 163). How many 'particular instances' do we need to undermine this view? History doesn't seem to me to show that what fairness, equality, and justice there is could have been achieved without the violent struggle of rebellion and revolution, and other such exercises of power in their cause. The contemporary situation hardly suggests otherwise: South Africa, Rhodesia, Greece, Portugal, Spain, are simply the obvious examples. In examples that are less obvious, 'those who have the power' precisely *do* 'defend their position with reasons or convince others of the justice of their actions'—not, perhaps, with crudely explicit propaganda, but implicitly by means of an ideology that in a variety of hidden ways shapes thought and discussion into relatively innocuous forms, so that common reasoning itself, exerting its power on the side of the status quo, becomes one of the modes through which political power expresses and consolidates itself.

Milligan agrees that liberals often fail to see that 'coercion is being employed in many contexts and in many ways which are never questioned' (pp. 165–6). But this doesn't shake his faith in the method of reason as even here 'more likely to achieve fairness for the less powerful than any alternative'. And even if reasoning fails, he claims, it must be tried first, for 'it must first be shown that the method of reason will fail to settle the dispute' (p. 166). But there is here an unanswered question and a connected assumption. How can trying the method of reason show that it will fail? In itself, trying it and failing shows only that it has so far failed, and then the liberal will exhort us to try, try, and try again. But how much trying, and for how long, is necessary to show that it will fail, and will continue to fail, in the future? If past efforts and failures are to show, i.e. constitute grounds for thinking, that future efforts will also fail, we need an argument and theory. But if we have such a theory, actual trying on any particular occasion may be unnecessary: it may be possible to show without trying that trying will fail. We don't, after all, need to show by trying that if we jump out of an upstairs window and try to fly by beating our arms like wings, we shall fail. Is it any more than slightly less evident that the South African blacks will fail to get justice by reasoning alone? Was it any more than slightly less evident at the time of the Tolpuddle martyrs, and since, that workers wouldn't succeed in improving their pay and conditions by 'the method of reason'?

Has Milligan forgotten such cases when he says 'Violence is a dangerous weapon; those who use it may easily, if unwittingly, introduce a greater injustice than the one they are trying to remove' (p. 166)? For that statement has a counterpart exemplified by these cases: non-violence is a dangerous weapon; those who use it may easily, if unwittingly, maintain a greater injustice than any they might introduce by using other methods. The fact is that any method is dangerous, but some are less *obviously* so than others. Views like the one I've quoted from Milligan help to obscure the fact because of the assumption that since our conduct can be identified in terms of the effects or consequences attributable to it we are responsible only for 'introducing' features to, or 'removing' features from, our situation, i.e. only for changes we bring about. Underlying this assumption, no doubt, is a well-known doctrine of causality according to which both cause and effect must be events, changes, or happenings. It then seems to follow that inaction, or doing nothing, is the safest or least dangerous policy, since no changes at all can be attributed to it, and objectionable features of the situation can be blamed on something or somebody else. Still better, for liberalism, is the time-honoured liberal policy of acting ineffectively, for then one has both avoided introducing a 'greater injustice' and at least tried to change a situation for whose objectionable features one is not responsible. Given normal circumstances, the method of reason is ideal for this purpose. But its ideological nature is obvious. Lacks, omissions, and negations can have effects or consequences, and neither need those consequences be changes: seeds may fail to germinate because of lack of sun. Similarly by failing to change an oppressive situation that could be changed, ineffective methods help to maintain it. Since at the same time they promote the illusion that 'something is being done' about that situation, they may be doubly 'dangerous'.

In his last paragraph Milligan proposes reconciliation between us all, Popper and other liberals included, under the umbrella of the doctrine 'Violence would sometimes be reasonable' (p. 167). As I've already pointed out, Popper's general views imply two extreme and inconsistent positions about reason and violence, one that violence is never reasonable, the other that violence is (nearly) always reasonable; and between these he commits himself to the idea that violence is legitimate only as counter-violence. As far as I understand him, Milligan agrees with me in rejecting all three of these positions: he claims that violence may be reasonable not only as counter-violence but more generally as counter-coercion. But though this condition on the legitimacy of violence is weaker than Popper's, I've argued that the additional conditions he imposes are still too strong, and still concede too much to the liberal ideology. Perhaps we should agree that our 'method of reason', as in so many other cases, has turned out to be a method of reaching *dis*agreement.

R. M. HARE

Hare hopes that in this controversy I shall fail and my opponents succeed, 'because otherwise we shall go on arriving at bad policies by irrational methods of decision, in our universities as elsewhere'. Representing Popper as one who 'stands up for reason' he insinuates by contrast that I am an irrationalist. I hope that his readers, unlike the author, won't need me to draw attention to the fact that his arguments provide not the slightest support for these conservative prejudices. It is, indeed, a typical performance: Hare's writings are characterized by hard professional arguments that entirely fail to justify the deeply conservative temperament revealed in their setting of conventional

examples and complacent assumptions about the social framework.

Of course Popper 'stands up for reason'. So do I and count-
less others who nevertheless disagree about what reason is and
can do. I agree, as I indicate on my p. 124 and p. 134, that
'reasoning stands in a class by itself'. What, then, according to
Hare, is supposed to be the disagreement in which I can be
seen to be attacking reason while he and Popper unitedly
'stand up' for it?

Let me approach the matter by way of a couple of prelimin-
aries that help to bring out the gulf between Hare's position and
Popper's. First, Hare supposes that 'those whom Professor
Edgley quotes (on both sides) are answering question (*b*)'. On
my p. 121 I point out that Lord James discusses reason as 'a
way of changing things', whereas Popper considers reason and
violence as 'ways of settling disagreements or disputes between
people'. It seems evident, especially in view of the questions I
raise on p. 122, that both are concerned with contexts that are
wider than the one selected by Hare in his question (*b*), which
considers reasoning as a way of 'trying to get other people to
co-operate with us'. Narrowing the question to ways of trying
to get co-operation clearly loads the dice in favour of reasoning;
though even so, Hare admits both that there will be 'cases in
which reasoning with people will not achieve co-operation', so
that other procedures may be preferable, and that 'violence is
not the only other method besides reasoning'. We are already
some distance from Popper's refusal to deny that even in the
more general context of ways of settling disputes, and even when
other methods are 'necessary', violence is the only alternative
and reasoning is the only reasonable response.

Second, Hare says that the question when to abandon reasoning 'is a question which should itself, if the answer to (*a*) is
"Yes", be decided by reasoning'. But the condition about the
answer to (*a*), he holds, is not always fulfilled. I agree with that,
though not on the grounds he advances in his presidential
address to the Aristotelian Society. The most general ground

is an application of the distinction central to my paper, between reason and reasoning: some of the things a person does may be rational, and done for good reasons, without his having gone through a process of reasoning to decide what to do. Hare's idea that this distinction needs support from the special rule-utilitarian, puritanical and elitist arguments of his presidential address is the result of his long-standing tendency, which despite his disclaimers about 'the *mechanical* drawing of conclusions from *given* premises' is exhibited clearly here in his second paragraph, to identify practical reason with practical inference, and consequently to misunderstand the basic concept of a reason for doing something. I have reasoned with him on these matters elsewhere,[2] but apparently without achieving his 'co-operation'. However, whatever the ground of the admission that the answer to (*a*) is not always 'Yes', Hare is here again seriously qualifying Popper's faith in what Feyerabend calls 'the omnipresence of argument'.

Notwithstanding these limitations on its scope, reasoning, according to Hare, 'stands in a class by itself because it is only when the co-operation is secured by reasoning that all parties can be assured (if the reasoning is done correctly) that what they are co-operating in doing is the rational thing to do. This is achieved because all parties have answered "Yes" to question (*a*).' Hare's bland assumption, in the following sentence, that 'this is what the people whom Edgley attacks are trying to convey', and presumably therefore that this is what I am attacking, is nowhere argued for. Having disagreed with Popper in the respects already described, Hare has now achieved agreement, if at all, at the cost either of trivializing the argument by formulating a tautology as the substance of Popper's message, or of adopting a position that holds only for a range of basic cases and not otherwise. Of course, *if a person reasons correctly* about what to do, he can be assured that what he thereby decides to do is the rational thing to do; and *if two people reason correctly*

---

[2] *Reason in Theory and Practice* (especially 1 and 4.8) and 'Hume's Law' (*Aris. Soc. Supp. Vol.* XLIV, 1970).

together about what one or other or both should do, they will
necessarily agree and 'co-operate' and can be assured that what
they agree should be done is the rational thing to do. I don't
attack that view, nor does Popper defend it. But does it follow
that it's *only* if co-operation is secured by reasoning that all
parties can be assured that what they are co-operating in doing
is the rational thing to do ? Yes, given that the reasoning is done
correctly, a condition that restricts the claim to those basic
cases in which each side needs to consider only the *rationality* or
otherwise of the other's view, and not the *fact* that the other side
has that view and might act on it. But these latter cases, though
parasitic on the basic ones, are perfectly common; indeed, since
if the reasoning of both sides has been done correctly there will
be agreement and no dispute, these cases are typical for disputes.
In that event, the situation I described on my p. 122 will hold,
in which reasons can be given to people in other ways than by
argument and reasoning. Thus if workers demand a higher
wage and their employers refuse, the workers might secure
co-operation not by reasoning but by striking, thus giving their
employers a reason for agreeing to their demand and so convincing them that in the circumstances the rational thing to do
is what the workers believe is the rational thing for them to do,
namely agree to a wage increase. Even if all parties have answered
'Yes' to question (*a*), therefore, Hare's principle will not be
generally true.

It seems clear that what Hare is really objecting to in his
penultimate sentence is not 'arriving at bad policies by irrational
methods of decision' but 'pursuing anti-conservative policies
by methods other than simply reasoning'. And talking of who,
if anybody, is to blame for what 'the young' think and do, we
should bear in mind this possibility: that the tendency among
twentieth-century English philosophers to identify reason with
reasoning, and to suppose that reasoning must confirm established prejudices, is partly to blame for the attitude of those who
reject reason itself.

V / Kant's Concept of Practical Reason

W. H. Walsh

Hume said that reason is and ought only to be the slave of the passions. The question I want to ask is whether Kant supplied convincing grounds for rejecting this claim. My approach will, I fear, have to be largely exegetical, though I hope that some points of mild philosophical interest will emerge at the end.

According to Kant, reason is either theoretical or practical. Theoretical reason, taken in the widest sense of that term, has as its business what Hume called the discovery of truth or falsehood, either at the primary level, where it is a matter of establishing facts, or at the secondary level, where it is a matter of connecting and explaining them. The first of these activities involves the formation and application of concepts, the second the formation and application of theories, among other things. Now forming and applying concepts and theories in each case demands skill, and to that extent the exercise of theoretical reason itself requires there to be such a thing as practical intelligence. But so far as I know Kant was not explicitly aware of this point. He does, of course, consistently present the understanding (and by implication theoretical reason when taken as a separate intellectual faculty) as essentially active: in contrast to the senses, which are passive, the intellect is to be defined in terms of 'spontaneity'.[1] Spontaneity manifests itself in two

[1] *Critique of Pure Reason*, B 75/A 51, A 126, B 129–30.

ways in human thought, first at the logical level in the production of concepts and their use in judgement, second in a more substantial sense in the production and application of *a priori* concepts. But though Kant goes to enormous pains to try to explain what such concepts are and why they are necessary if we are to have knowledge, he sees no special difficulties in our intelligent use of them. Or to be more accurate, the difficulties he sees in their application have to do with the alleged heterogeneity of *a priori* concepts and sense-particulars generally, not with what makes us able to use them successfully on particular occasions. Kant recognizes in one passage[2] that judgement is a matter of know how: it is, he says:

a peculiar talent which can be practised only, and cannot be taught. It is the specific quality of so-called mother-wit; and its lack no school can make good. For although an abundance of rules borrowed from the insight of others may indeed be proffered to, and as it were grafted upon, a limited understanding, the power of rightly employing them must belong to the learner himself.

But he makes nothing of this apparent insight: in the third *Critique* 'determinant' judgement is treated as quite uncontroversial. Nor does he press at all far his somewhat uncertain appreciation that judgement of what is the case must be free in precisely the same way as practical decision. In fact, of course, the whole business of discovering truth and falsehood, exploring and comprehending the world, involves a variety of intellectual skills; it is emphatically not simply a matter of the passive acquisition of truths. Kant knew that much, but not all that was demanded by the alternative view.

In general, Kant said nothing about theoretical reason which conflicts with Hume's dictum on reason and the passions. He advanced doctrines with which Hume would certainly have disagreed, about causality for instance, and he embraced an overall position which is fundamentally different from Hume's (for him reason is obviously not just a 'wonderful and unintel-

[2] Op. cit., B 171/A 132 ff.

ligible instinct in our souls'). But he did not argue that the discovery of truth or falsehood is itself an intelligent activity, and that reason must accordingly be practical. If he refuted Hume on this head at all, it was on another ground and by other arguments.

I turn now to 'practical reason', which comes for Kant in two forms: what may be called everyday or empirical practical reason and what Kant calls 'pure' practical reason. The first of these is, broadly, reason in the service of desire, and to point to it is certainly not to refute Hume. Admittedly, Kant's picture of the general practical situation differs in some respects from Hume's, in so far as Kant made more of the differences between human and animal behaviour and laid more stress on the antithesis between acting from impulse and acting to promote one's long-term interests. Rational beings, as Kant puts the point in a well-known passage in the *Groundwork*,[3] differ from things that are merely natural in that while the latter work in accordance with laws, 'a rational being has the power to act in accordance with his idea of laws, that is in accordance with principles'. One suspects a certain sleight of hand in this passage (on the face of it Kant moves all too easily from laws which describe how things are, to laws which prescribe how things ought to be), but it can perhaps be given an innocuous interpretation on the following lines. Rational beings understand their situation as stones and even animals do not, and this necessarily affects the character of their actions. Because they have the power of conceptual thought they can grasp what is going on and envisage what is to come; accordingly they can formulate and pursue long-term aims as well as immediate satisfactions and can discover effective or more effective ways of attaining their ends. In particular, the human ability to handle general ideas has an important bearing on men's practical activities: it gives them a control over what they do to which there is no parallel among inanimate objects and it introduces into their

[3] *Groundwork of the Metaphysic of Morals*, Academy edition, IV, 412; Kant's 2nd edition, p. 36.

lives an element of choice, between immediate and more remote satisfactions, which is not quite like anything found in the natural world (an animal may refrain from gratifying an immediate impulse out of instinct, or because of the presence of a stronger desire, but scarcely as a result of deliberate policy). Kant is not wide of the mark when he connects these facts with the human possession of a will. But despite his celebrated remark (in the same passage) that 'the will is nothing but practical reason', it is clear that he would not himself regard the considerations so far adduced as decisive against Hume. To show that reason can be something else than the servant of the passions, we can imagine him saying, you have to establish the existence not just of practical reason, but of *pure* practical reason. You have to show, in other words, that reason on its own has the power to *originate* action, not simply to *influence* or *facilitate* it. Reason can be practical in a general sense, as Aristotle thought it was, without being itself an independent spring of action.

It is important in this connection to insist that, in his account of the motivation of non-moral conduct, Kant adopts a position which is almost crudely hedonistic. For him, as for Bentham, Nature has placed mankind under the governance of pleasure and pain, and as empirical beings, parts of the natural order, men inevitably pursue the one and avoid the other. At this level desire alone initiates action. Nor will Kant agree that a distinction between coarse and refined desires and pleasures has any bearing on the issue. We can certainly make that distinction, he tells us in the *Critique of Practical Reason*:[4] more refined joys and delights are 'more in our power than others' and 'do not wear out'; they 'delight and at the same time cultivate'. But:

this is no reason to pass off such pleasures as a mode of determining the will different from that of the senses. For the possibility of these

---

[4] *Critique of Practical Reason*, Academy edition, V, 24; Beck translation, pp. 22–3 (Liberal Arts Library).

pleasures, too, presupposes, as the first condition of our delight, the existence in us of a corresponding feeling.

A man who finds satisfaction in the exercise of power, the consciousness of his spiritual strength in overcoming obstacles or the cultivation of his talents, to use Kant's own examples, does so because he is fundamentally a sensuous being; he is looking for pleasure in different quarters from the simple voluptuary, but looking for it just the same.

It emerges from this that what I have called everyday or empirical practical reason is not a separate faculty, but simply the theoretical intellect co-operating with and, as was said before, serving desire. Its recognition by Kant confirms Hume rather than contradicts him. Hume thought that reason had two functions in regard to conduct: to establish for the agent the true facts of his situation, so that the appropriate desire could be manifested, and to discover the proper, or the best, means to an end which is desired. In both, of course, it is a matter of arriving at true propositions, rather than of willing or initiating action. So far as I know, Kant does not discuss the first of Hume's functions, but he makes it crystal-clear that he agrees with him whole-heartedly about the second. This comes out in a striking way in a discussion at the beginning of the *Critique of Judgement* in the course of which Kant protests against the contemporary tendency to put such things as 'domestic, agricultural or political economy, the art of social intercourse, the principles of dietetics, or even general instruction as to the attainment of happiness' under the heading of practical philosophy. These activities are taken as practical because they bear on the production of objects, as opposed to the knowledge of them. But the injunctions in which they issue rest on theoretical understanding; basically they depend on ability to trace causal connections. And that being so they should properly be reckoned 'only as corollaries of theoretical philosophy', and not as having anything to do with practice in the proper sense of the word. Rules of skill and counsels of prudence, to use the terminology of the *Groundwork*, have the form of imperatives, but are parasitic on statements of what is the case. They are accordingly only 'technically-practical' and are irrelevant to what Kant in his *Lectures on Ethics* called 'the philosophy which provides rules for the proper use of our freedom'.[5]

This discussion, it may be remarked in passing, provides further evidence that Kant had no clear knowledge of the distinction between 'knowing how' and 'knowing that'. The arts or sciences mentioned in the previous paragraph all involve practical skills as well as knowledge of what is the case, but Kant says nothing about this aspect of the situation. Instead, he proceeds as if all that was in question was the mechanical application of rules which rest on theoretical knowledge and have only a formal existence apart from the latter. Our mastery of such rules is not a matter of simple contemplation, but is presumably 'technically-practical'. Nevertheless it depends on knowledge of truths and receives no independent attention from Kant. To put the point crudely, it is as if he supposed that the skill of a surgeon lay not in his hands but entirely in the textbooks written by medical professors.

Despite this, there is a sense in which Kant did distinguish sharply between theory and practice. Intelligence manifests itself in action as well as in the acquisition of truths. But the action in question is action of a special sort, action governed not by the 'technically-practical rules' just mentioned, but by rules of a different kind which Kant calls 'morally-practical'. It is on the existence of this kind of action that Kant grounds his belief that pure reason can be practical. We must now attempt to reconstruct his argument for this point.

It will be convenient to begin by considering a striking passage on the subject which occurs in the discussion of the freedom/natural necessity antinomy in the *Critique of Pure Reason* (Kant's views on ethics were not fully worked out in the

[5] *Lectures on Ethics*, translated by L. Infield, p. 2. The quotations given above come from Section 1 of the Introduction to the *Critique of Judgement*. Compare the longer version in the first introduction to that work (Haden translation, pp. 3–8), along with *Critique of Practical Reason*, V, 26 (Beck, p. 25) and *Groundwork*, IV, 417 (45).

first *Critique*, but were reasonably complete in this particular respect). 'That our reason has causality', Kant writes:[6]

or at least that we represent it to ourselves as having causality, is evident from the *imperatives* which in all matters of conduct we impose as rules on our active powers. *'Ought'* expresses a kind of necessity and of connection with grounds which is found nowhere else in the whole of nature. The understanding can know in nature only what is, what has been, or what will be. We cannot say that anything in nature *ought to be* other than what in these time-relations it actually is. When we have the course of nature alone in view, 'ought' has no meaning whatsoever.

The term 'ought', of course, has non-moral as well as moral uses, and it is possible that Kant is arguing here from its occurrence in either form. But what he says about its expressing a kind of necessity and having a special connection with grounds makes better sense if we concentrate on its specifically moral use. When Kant spoke of the unique kind of necessity which attached to what I am taking to be the moral 'ought' he may have had two things in mind: the unconditional character of moral obligation, and what might be called its ineluctability or omnipresence. The first of these is familiar enough in the celebrated distinction of categorical and hypothetical imperatives: the latter have force only if the person to whom they are addressed happens to want a particular end, the former demand obedience for their own sake and regardless of wants or aspirations. And this connects closely with the other point about the ineluctable character of the moral 'ought', which is brought out in Kant's example[7] of the man whose sovereign threatens him with sudden death unless he is willing to bear false witness against an honourable man whom the ruler wishes to destroy. Would the first man in these circumstances be able to overcome his love of life and resist the threat? Kant says that whether he would or not is always problematic, but that he would admit without hesitation that it would always be

[6] *Critique of Pure Reason*, B 575/A 547.
[7] *Critique of Practical Reason*, V, 30 (Beck, p. 30).

possible for him to do so. The story is immediately about freedom, but I take its relevance for our present purposes to lie in the implied claim that what we ought to do can always weigh with us; it is a force whose presence is constantly felt, if not constantly attended to. In this respect it contrasts sharply with sensuous springs of action, which may or may not be present in a particular individual at any particular time. This, indeed, is Kant's main ground for rejecting moral sense theories of ethics: if morality rested on feeling, whether or not anyone felt the force of moral considerations would be entirely a matter of accident. I might lack a moral sense as I lack a discriminating palate or an ear for music, and so be conveniently deaf to the call of duty.

Kant of course agrees—indeed, emphasizes—that there is one end in which all imperfectly rational beings may be presumed to have a natural interest: the end of their own happiness. But he does not draw the conclusion that counsels of prudence have the same force as moral commands. Why not? His official reason is the rather weak one that, because the concept happiness is itself indeterminate,

we cannot act on determinate principles in order to be happy, but only on empirical counsels, for example, of diet, frugality, politeness, reserve, and so on—things which experience shows contribute most to well-being on the average.[8]

Imperatives of prudence, though they are 'assertoric', cannot exhibit actions as practically necessary because they are not themselves universally valid, but hold only for the most part. They offer prescriptions which work in most cases, but not necessarily in all. Kant speaks sometimes as if this were not a mere contingent fact, but a necessity following from the nature of the concept of happiness, which as an Ideal of imagination cannot be made determinate.[9] But he appears to have thought the cases of morality and prudence to be distinct quite apart

[8] *Groundwork*, IV, 418 (47); cf. *Critique of Practical Reason*, V, 36 (Beck, p. 37).
[9] Ibid.

from this point. The difference comes out in the claim that morality makes demands on us which prudence never does. Despite the fact that we all have a natural interest in our own welfare, the fact is that this interest can be overridden on particular occasions. It is not the case that I *have* to pursue my own happiness come what may; if morality demands that I forgo the pursuit I am perfectly capable of doing so. And that means that counsels of prudence, quite apart from their lack of universality, are ultimately without authority. Although not concerned, as are rules of skill, with the attainment of arbitrary ends, they nevertheless have something optional about them. By contrast, moral commands are not mere pieces of advice. Certainly they too can be overridden, in the sense that they can be ignored: we can, if we choose, consult our own interest or gratify some personal whim rather than do what morality requires. But though we can and often do take no notice of the voice of duty, Kant's point is that we cannot shut it out: it will, in a way, continue to make itself heard even in cases where its injunctions have been rejected, showing its presence in remorse and shame on the part of the agent concerned. The demand that we obey moral requirements thus carries with it a necessity unlike anything to be found in the rest of nature, a necessity which is at once unconditional and ineluctable.

On what might be described as phenomenological grounds Kant appears to have a strong case (a) for his contention that men can be moved to act by moral considerations as well as in response to desire, and (b) for his claim that such considerations possess a unique kind of authority and for that reason demand to be heard as nothing else does. No doubt the situation is not equally clear-cut in all human agents; it could be that Kant made things easier for himself than he should by assuming that men generally must share his own attitude to the moral life and treat the moral law as an object of awed respect. Attention to the history of morals, or even the history of ethics, would suggest that the assumption is at least open to question. But Kant's overall position has enough immediate appeal to carry some conviction even in conditions very different from his own: men today are less inclined than he was to apostrophize duty, but that does not mean that they ignore it altogether. However, the problem that should concern us now is not so much that of whether morality has the force he claims for it, but rather this: granted that moral considerations do have force, does that show that pure reason can be practical?

Why was it that Kant supposed that moral behaviour must be rational behaviour? Why did he say that moral concepts 'have their seat and origin in reason completely *a priori*',[10] so much so that morality has nothing properly to do with *human* (as opposed to *rational*) nature as such? His thought on these subjects is to say the least obscure, and I may as well confess at once that I do not know how to make it convincing. But I can mention a number of points which weighed with Kant when thinking about the subject.

1. The passage from the third Antinomy quoted on p. 195 above is followed a few lines later by these words:[11]

This 'ought' expresses a possible action the ground of which cannot be anything but a mere concept; whereas in the case of a merely natural action the ground must always be an appearance.

A 'merely natural action' in this connection is, of course, a happening in the physical world, the ground or rather cause of which is, according to Kant, always some preceding phenomenon. By contrast, any action proper, whether done in response to the moral 'ought' or of a non-moral nature, is in a sense determined by an idea or concept; it represents an attempt to translate some idea into reality. Actions are grounded as natural happenings are not, and find their grounds in thoughts. Now Kant might conceivably have been influenced, in connecting morality and rationality, by the reflection that moral actions have grounds and to that extent are rationally determined; it will be remembered that in the main passage quoted he spoke of 'ought' as expressing not only a special kind of necessity but also

[10] *Groundwork*, IV, 411 (34).
[11] *Critique of Pure Reason*, B 575–6/A 547–8.

a special connection with grounds. It is clear enough, however, that emphasis must be put here on the word 'special' in both cases. As we have seen, Kant does try to explain the sense in which the necessity which attaches to the moral 'ought' is unique. But in this passage at any rate he does nothing to justify the corresponding claim about grounds. He is content to point out that action of any sort can be said to be grounded as opposed to caused, a fact which shows in his own terminology that reason is practical, but not that pure reason is practical. For the latter to hold it must be established not just that thoughts or ideas must be invoked in the explanation of an action, but that there are actions whose origin is to be found wholly and solely in thoughts.

2. The necessity which attaches to the moral 'ought' has, as we have seen, every appearance of being unconditional: moral injunctions demand to be obeyed, regardless of particular inclinations or desires. It is not a case of our being obliged to do something *if* we want something else, but of our facing a categorical command to do something for its own sake. Kant's belief that moral action is rational action was undoubtedly strengthened by reflection on these facts. For he had argued in his theoretical philosophy that reason, as opposed to understanding, is the faculty which forms the idea of the unconditioned. The intellect in its everyday empirical employment is engaged in endless movement from that which is conditioned to its condition, and thence to what conditions that; whatever condition it arrives at must always proceed to something further, but reason conceives of something which will complete the series and not refer beyond itself since it is self-explanatory and hence unconditioned. And though Kant is at pains to show that such an idea cannot have constitute force in human thinking, i.e. cannot have direct application to an object whether in experience or beyond it, he nevertheless claims that it has a legitimate regulative use. Scientific investigation must be carried on under the guidance of this idea; we must conduct our inquiries as if we hoped to find the ultimate condition of

whatever we examine, even though we know that the hope can never be satisfied. This 'idea of reason' is persistently misused by metaphysicians, but even so has a proper and indeed highly important empirical employment, when it is brought to bear not directly on the data of experience, but at the second level on our attempt to comprehend those data.

But even if all this is correct, does anything follow about the rationality of moral ideas ? The parallels between the two cases are far from exact. Theoretical reason goes off the rails if it attempts to use the idea of the unconditioned on its own account; it finds a proper use for that idea only by letting it guide the operations of the understanding. But moral reason, in Kant's submission, does its job only if it detaches itself from the senses altogether; it is not its business to co-ordinate and systematize efforts to get what we want, or indeed to get what anyone wants. Nor is the situation much better if we consider the type of necessity involved in the two cases. The scientific understanding proceeds on a principle that is analytic, namely that there is a condition for everything conditioned; theoretical reason, by contrast, assumes the truth of the synthetic principle that, if anything is conditioned, there must be something un- conditioned. In the sphere of conduct things are at first sight much the same: everyday practical reason issues hypothetical imperatives on the strength of the analytic principle that he who wills the end, wills also the indispensable means thereto, whereas the categorical imperatives of morality clearly rest on a principle of quite a distinct nature. Kant is apt to describe this principle as 'synthetic *a priori*', but one wonders what good the hackneyed label does him in this context. Quite apart from this, however, there is the difficulty that the alleged synthetic *a priori* principle of morals and the corresponding principle of theoreti- cal reason are supposed by Kant to function very differently. To reach the unconditioned is set as a task to theoretical reason, a task which we know from the first can never be fully accom- plished. Morality by contrast issues its commands as uncondi- tionally binding; talk of 'asymptotic' approximation in this context is absurd. To say that it is one and the same faculty which is engaged in these very different activities seems on the face of things quite gratuitous.

In general, Kant's case for connecting morality with reason by means of the notion of unconditionality carries little independent conviction. It looks moderately respectable when stated in Kant's own terms, since he assumes that reason, and only reason, is the faculty of the unconditioned. But perhaps here we are bamboozled by the mysterious phrase 'the unconditioned'. It should be noticed in this connection that in the *Critique of Pure Reason* Kant is interested in the unconditioned as a possible entity or existent; the necessity which concerns him here is the necessity of a necessary being. But in his moral philosophy any such notion is set aside as strictly subsidiary, and the only necessity in question is that supposed to attach to a moral command. Of course one could not grasp and characterize that necessity without bringing the intellect into play, perhaps even without bringing theoretical reason into play. But that by itself will certainly not show that moral commands are issued by pure practical reason.

3. Kant was obviously influenced in his thinking about morals by some old speculations of his about the world of matter and the world of spirits. To explain this will require a short historical excursus. In the year 1766 Kant published an essay entitled *Dreams of a Spirit-Seer, elucidated through Dreams of Metaphysics*. A main object of this curious piece was to allow Kant to comment on claims made by or on behalf of his contemporary Immanuel Swedenborg to possession of the power to communicate with spirits, irrespective of whether or not they were embodied and, if the latter, of their positions in the spatial and temporal orders. Kant's correspondence shows that he took a lively interest in Swedenborg; he is even said to have written to him direct, without getting any answer.[12] But

---

[12] For the whole subject see C. D. Broad's essay 'Immanuel Kant and Psychical Research', reprinted in *Religion, Philosophy and Psychical Research: Selected Essays*, pp. 116–55.

in the *Dreams* he deals with Swedenborg only in the concluding 'historical' section; the longer 'dogmatic' part of the work is given up to more philosophical topics. Here Kant investigates first what is involved in the concept of a spirit, as opposed to a material thing, and then what would be involved in the notion of a world or community of spirits. His conclusion on the first question is that the only notion we can form of a spirit is of a being which occupies or operates in a space without filling it; spirit is, in effect, non-matter. As for the idea of a community of spirits, we can say that if there were a world of immaterial beings it would operate according to laws of its own and that the relations between its various members would normally be direct, as opposed to through the medium of any bodies with which they happened to be associated. Spirits could thus communicate without being restricted, as men are, by the conditions of space and time: with them telepathy and precognition would be entirely normal.

Kant writes about these topics in a bantering tone which suggests that he regarded the whole subject as a matter of idle speculation, and the predominant impression he conveys is of thinking that we know little or nothing about spirits. But he nevertheless 'admits' that he is 'very inclined to assert the existence of immaterial natures in the world and to place my soul itself in the class of these beings', on the ground that souls, and indeed living things generally, have the power of self-movement, as opposed to material things which are pushed and pulled about by forces outside them.[13] The union of soul and body remains utterly mysterious, but that they are distinct seems clear enough. As for the idea of a realm or community of spirits, it appears at first sight to be quite gratuitous, especially when elaborated in a way which fits in with claims of the Swedenborgian type. Yet Kant goes out of his way to produce what he clearly thinks of as empirical evidence in its favour.

The evidence in question is drawn from morality. The fact is, Kant argues, that human beings find themselves checked in

[13] Academy edition, II, 327 (Goerwitz translation, p. 52).

their judgements and decisions by the feeling that they must have regard to the opinions and welfare of others. It is as if there were active in us a foreign will as well as our own, which moves us on occasion to set aside personal satisfactions and pursue a more general good. Both 'the strong law of duty' (*Schuldigkeit*) and 'the weaker law of benevolence' involve us in much self-sacrifice; both can be and are overridden by selfish inclinations, yet both make their presence felt in our lives. Thus, to quote Kant's own words,[14] 'we recognize that, in our most secret motives, we are dependent on *the rule of the universal will*, and thence arises in the community of all thinking beings a *moral unity* and systematic constitution according to purely spiritual laws'. To speak of the necessitation we feel to bring our will into agreement with the universal will as 'moral feeling' is to draw attention to an unexplained fact, just as Newton drew attention to an unexplained fact when he spoke of gravitation. But Newton took gravitation to be 'the true effect of a general interaction of matter', and similarly here it may be suggested that moral feeling is:

the consequence of an actually active force through which spiritual natures influence one another. The sense of morality would be *this experienced dependence* of the private will on the universal will; it would be a consequence of the natural and universal interaction through which the immaterial world attains its moral unity, in so far as it forms itself into a system of spiritual perfection according to laws of this its own cohesion.[15]

The fact of moral feeling is the effect in the material world of man's membership of the immaterial world. It testifies to the working of forces quite different from any which are found in the sphere of nature.

The interesting thing about this is that precisely the same doctrine is found in the *Groundwork*, where moral feeling is described[16] as 'the subjective effect exercised on our will by the law and having its objective ground in reason alone'. We have

[14] II, 335 (Goerwitz, p. 64).
[15] II, 335 (Goerwitz, pp. 64–5).
[16] IV, 460 (122).

to do here with a phenomenon which, as it were, points beyond itself to something non-phenomenal. Kant's fundamental metaphysical doctrine had certainly changed in important ways since 1766: instead of speaking of the material and immaterial orders Kant now uses the contrast of phenomenal and noumenal and instead of treating these as naming distinct existents he tries to get by with the idea that they characterize alternative points of view. But already at one point in the *Dreams*[17] he uses the Latin phrase *mundus intelligibilis* in speaking of his world of spirits; the change in his general terminology, no doubt occasioned by his reading of Mendelssohn's *Phaedo*, is not significant in this connection. The noumenal order was also made up of immaterial beings, operating according to laws of their own. And though the introduction of the doctrine of the two standpoints was an innovation of great importance for Kant's philosophy generally, its bearing on the problems which now concern us is minimal. Kant still says that, when they act morally, men transfer themselves in thought to another realm, the non-natural or noumenal order, and still thinks of morality as giving us whatever understanding of that realm we possess. That it is now a matter of conceptions rather than facts scarcely affects the main question.

If all this is correct Kant's tendency to connect morality with rationality and to think of moral behaviour as behaviour determined by rational as opposed to merely natural principles is entirely intelligible from the historical point of view. For twenty years or so before he wrote his first major work on ethics he had not only accepted a sharp distinction between moral and non-moral motives, but also interpreted morality as having essentially to do with a non-natural order to which men could be taken to belong in their capacity as spiritual or rational beings. The inference that moral actions were the product of pure practical reason was natural enough in these circumstances. But to say it was natural or historically intelligible is not to justify it from the philosophical point of view. So far as I can see there

[17] II, 329 (Goerwitz, p. 56).

is nothing in the doctrines examined to show that actions motivated by moral considerations have any special connection with reason.

4. However, this is not the end of the matter. Kant in his mature philosophy was entirely clear that we cannot have any direct knowledge of things supersensible but nevertheless held that what he called the 'inexplicable fact' of the moral law not only 'points to' a purely intelligible world but 'defines it positively and enables us to know something of it, namely a law.'[18] It turns out that we can know something of a formal nature about the supersensible, that this fact supplies us with a criterion by which to separate off the morally permissible from the morally forbidden and that this in turn is thought to have a bearing on the question whether acting morally is acting rationally. I must now try to sort out some of the complicated issues involved in this line of argument.

The first step is relatively simple. If there were a world of noumena or pure spirits it would share at least one characteristic with the world of phenomena or merely natural beings, namely that of being ordered. To say that a world is ordered is to say that it is governed throughout by law. Already in the *Dreams* Kant had made clear that the principles which would regulate his hypothetical spirit world must be entirely different from those which govern things material; if this were not so, in the terminology he came to adopt later, heteronomy would prevail everywhere, and morality be accordingly impossible. But though the law of nature and the law of the supersensible must thus be distinct in content, they will nevertheless agree in form: both will and must apply universally in situations answering the same description. They will, or would, be laws in the same sense of the term.

The next move in the argument depends on the assumption that 'the fundamental law of supersensuous nature and of a pure world of the understanding'[19] is revealed to us in the shape

[18] *Critique of Practical Reason*, V, 43 (Beck, p. 44).
[19] Ibid.

of the moral law. Even if it is we are left with the problem of determining its content. Kant's solution to this problem is to treat the law of nature as the *type* of the moral law.[20] We have no insight into the moral order, but we know that any principle which qualifies as a moral principle must hold with the universality which characterizes laws of nature. Accordingly we can decide whether a proposed action is morally permissible by taking the maxim or general description which underlies it and asking if it could hold as a law in a system of nature. Where this condition is not met, the maxim in question must be rejected as immoral.

It is not my intention now to discuss this celebrated doctrine for its own sake; I want rather to try to determine precisely what Kant is claiming and then to assess its bearing on our general subject. Obviously more is being said than that reference to the formal properties of law as such will supply a test by which to sort out the permissible from the forbidden; a test of that kind could be accepted by someone who had little or no sympathy with ethical rationalism. What Kant appears to take for granted in addition is that the bare thought that a proposed action is formally in accordance with law can serve to bring about the action or, in Kant's terminology, serve to determine the will. In the *Critique of Practical Reason*[21] Kant argues explicitly that nothing short of this could properly weigh with a free will. The material of a practical law, i.e. the content of a maxim, can only be given empirically, but a free will must be independent of empirical considerations, on pain of forfeiting its freedom. It must therefore 'find its ground of determination in the law', but:

independently of the material of the law. But besides the latter there is nothing in a law except the legislative form. Therefore, the legislative form, in so far as it is contained in the maxim, is the only thing which can constitute a determining ground of the free will.

[20] V, 67 ff. (Beck, pp. 70 ff.).
[21] V, 29 (Beck, pp. 28-9).

It this is correct, it looks as if 'pure practical reason' will be pure thought determining the will, a situation which holds only in highly special circumstances. In general, Kant agrees with Hume and Aristotle that thought by itself is impotent; in non-moral conditions thought can be effective only if associated with a corresponding desire. But things are different where questions of morality arise; then, and then only, the mere intellectual appreciation that a proposed act would have a certain character-istic can suffice to recommend that act, and the mere intellectual appreciation that it would lack that characteristic can in itself inhibit action. So it is reason, in the shape of mere thought, that originates moral action or prevents immoral action from coming about.

But is it reason alone ? Would the bare thought that something we want to do is contrary to law have any weight with us if it were not for the existence of moral feeling ? Kant has already admitted that we do have a special feeling about morality, and that this must be treated as a phenomenon in the natural world. Humeans might well say that moral considerations are effective only because we have this feeling, and that this means that reason is in precisely the same position here as it is in non-moral cases. Thought has an effect on action, but not directly; it is desire or feeling alone which is the immediate cause of everything we do.

We know already that Kant regards this position as in-compatible with recognition of the ineluctable character of moral obligation, though to say only that will surely not establish its contradictory. He needs to make clear at least how one can admit the fact of moral feeling without going along with Hume's view. His attempt to meet this need is made in the third chapter of the Analytic of the *Critique of Practical Reason*, entitled 'The Incentives of Pure Practical Reason'. There the argument is developed that moral feeling is 'practically', not 'pathologically' effected; the cause which determines it 'lies in the pure practical reason'.[22] It is not the case that we act morally because morality attracts us; the situation is rather that

[22] V, 75 (Beck, p. 78).

intellectual grasp of the moral law produces a special feeling in us. We reverence the moral law and this reverence weakens our self-conceit, but, as the point was put in the *Groundwork*:[23]

although reverence is a feeling, it is not a feeling received through outside influence, but one self-produced by a rational concept, and therefore specifically distinct from feelings of the first kind, all of which can be reduced to inclination or fear. What I recognize as law for me, I recognize with reverence, which means merely consciousness of the subordination of my will to a law without the mediation of external influences on my senses. Immediate determination of the will by the law and consciousness of this determination is called 'reverence', so that reverence is regarded as the effect of the law on the subject and not as the cause of the law.

How a 'rational concept' can exert this 'intellectual causality' is beyond all human understanding; it is opaque in the way in which freedom itself is opaque. Nevertheless, Kant is quite sure that the law, or rather the intellectual grasp of the law, is the ultimate moving principle in a case like this. We are not led to take an interest in morality because we view it with special respect, which would be a purely contingent matter. The truth is rather that moral considerations determine the will directly, thanks to the authority with which pure practical reason, in striking down our self-love, invests the moral law.[24]

I do not see how anyone today could accept this story precisely as it stands, if only because it is impossible to specify what would count for or against it. The causal transaction to which it purports to refer is one which belongs neither to the phenomenal nor to the noumenal world, but to the supposed interaction of the two; *ex hypothesi* it cannot be an object of knowledge or experience. One could perhaps get by with the suggestion that it is an object of belief in Kant's peculiar sense of that term; but only at the expense of leaving doubters entirely unsatisfied. The truth seems, however, to be that no reasonable case can be presented here in Kant's support.

[23] IV, 401, note (16).
[24] *Critique of Practical Reason*, V, 75–6 (Beck, p. 78).

The position may, indeed, be worse than has so far been suggested. Moral feeling is a fact in the phenomenal order, something that occurs as part of our normal experience. As such, so far from being unique in having an 'intellectual' cause, it *must* be determined by something phenomenal. Moreover, it must be seen as exerting causality in precisely the same way as anything else of its kind in the phenomenal world. For Kant that means that it will attract in so far as it is judged to be pleasant and repel in so far as it is judged to be the reverse. In other words, Kant's admission that feeling has an indispensable part to play in the process by which moral considerations produce or prevent actions is fatal to the central doctrine which he seeks to establish. On his own terms pure reason, that is reason acting entirely by itself, cannot be shown to be practical.

Reflection on the material presented in the foregoing pages suggests to me the following conclusions.

First, Kant has nothing of real interest to say about practical reason generally. Practical reason in the everyday or empirical sense is simply theoretical knowledge employed for practical purposes. That action might involve a special kind of knowledge of its own does not seem to have crossed his mind. In this respect Kant makes no advance on Hume; both are a long way behind Aristotle.

Second, although he was correct in seeing that the fact of moral action constituted a challenge to the account of conduct given by writers like Hume, Kant's own analysis of moral knowledge is deeply unsatisfying. His general picture of the moral situation is clearly shaped in many important ways by his acceptance of a two-world metaphysic; except with this assumption the all-important connection between morality and rationality cannot be made intelligible. But this dualism, though it enabled Kant to solve certain problems, left him with others which proved quite insoluble. In particular, it left him with the mysterious phenomenon of moral compunction or moral feeling, the rock on which his whole attempt to establish the reality of pure practical reason founders.

It is astonishing that, despite everything he says about sound moral judgement being within the compass of the plain men, Kant has so little of value to put forward about its operation. He writes as if being moral were a matter of simply laying oneself open to influences from the intelligible world, together with use of the universalization test. There is not a word about how reason shows itself to be practical in particular situations, by exhibiting a knowledge of what to do or avoid. Nothing is said of the fact that one can improve one's moral judgement by modelling oneself on another; indeed, the implication is that to do so is positively immoral.

Kant makes a great thing about morality being the supreme manifestation of reason, without making clear in just what way the agent exhibits irrationality when he behaves immorally. He gives a clear and correct account of the rationality of prudence, but is altogether less convincing when he comes to the rationality of morals. In general, he seems disposed to think that being moral (or at least being alive to moral claims) is part of what is meant by being rational; the metaphysics, or mythology, of the phenomenal and noumenal worlds was particularly influential at this point. For further light on his views on this subject we have to look at the passages in his writings which concern the application of the universalization test. On the face of things these passages seem to present the irrationality of immoral action as involving a species of logical impossibility or logical inconsistency and in so doing appear to bring the rationality of morals close to the rationality of prudence. But the attempt to show that the immoral man is irrational in this sense fails in any case, as I have tried to show elsewhere.

In what way should Kant have proceeded to produce a genuine doctrine of practical reason? I suggest he needed to recognize first that practical rationality is not confined to the sphere of morals. Morality is of interest to the philosopher who reflects on Hume's dictum about reason and the passions because it presents a case in which Hume's position seems singularly implausible. But it is not the only case of this kind. The truth is rather that the possibility of rational action of any sort refutes Hume, by exposing the unsatisfactory nature of the psychology on which he relies. The idea that men and animals alike are impelled by 'desire', which can be assisted or impeded by reason but is not itself rationally produced seems quite unacceptable. As was claimed at an early stage in this paper, the fact that they can reason and grasp things conceptually has profound effects on the whole practical life of human beings; it makes talk about the separate contributions to conduct of reason and the passions impossibly crude. Aristotle again was wiser than Hume in this matter, in his recognition that *boulesis* or rational wish is something very different from animal *epithumia*. Kant, as I tried to suggest, had some grasp of these differences but was not sufficiently alive to their importance to jettison the overall moral psychology he shared with the empiricists. He gets the point right in so far as he insists on the authority of the moral law, as opposed to its mere weight. But he loses whatever advantage he gains there by bringing in his impossible doctrine of moral feeling.

The other respect in which Kant's account of moral thinking needs supplementation is by the development of a theory of moral know-how. It seems to me plain that being virtuous involves skill as well as will; the virtuous man needs to know what to do in particular situations, as well as to have the resolution and determination to do it. Kant has plenty to say about the element of will which is necessary to virtue, but is silent on the element of skill, perhaps because he wanted to make out that morality was wholly in men's power. He is of course right in arguing that being moral is not a mere accomplishment, like being able to play the piano well, but something that requires character. But that fact could be recognized without leaving skill out of the story altogether. If it has no place in the moral life, what is meant by describing one person as more morally sensitive than another, or by saying that one can make moral decisions with intelligence or the lack of it? How can one hope to improve on one's past moral performance, on this account of the matter? The morally wise man is not necessarily the man with the strongest will or the widest knowledge of truths; he needs both, but he needs knowledge of another kind as well.

Comment: 'Moral Objectives'

BY ANSELM WINFRIED MÜLLER

Although a commentator on Professor Walsh's paper could be expected to read a critique of a critique of a Critique I prefer to pursue a little further the question of what kinds of 'determining ground' reason provides for moral conduct.

Apart from examining, and rejecting, four ways in which Kant may have seen pure reason on the one hand and morality and, more generally, the sphere of practice on the other to be connected, Professor Walsh alludes to three aspects of what he actually takes the rationality involved in moral conduct to be:

(1) Reason is active in the *determination of means and ways* to possible ends (pp. 191, 193, 200, 210). Walsh points out that this is acknowledged by Kant as the rationality of 'prudence' and by Hume as the only role that reason plays in action (apart from establishing the real existence of the objects of the 'passions': Hume, *Treatise*, ed. Selby-Bigge (Oxford, 1965), p. 416).

(2) Kant casually recognizes the relevance of *practical intelligence* to the exercise of theoretical reason (p. 190) but not to the rationality of conduct. Walsh emphasizes this element of practical reason, which consists in *knowing how* to apply one's practical principles in a particular situation (pp. 193, 209, 211).

(3) Reason provides one, thirdly, with *possible objects of wanting* which cannot be drawn from perception and sensory imagination alone.

(This classification is not Walsh's; nor does he claim to have touched on all of reason's functions in the realm of conduct.)

Under the heading of 'providing possible objects of wanting' can be brought at least three distinguishable kinds of contribution which reason makes:

(3*a*) A thinking being has the power to relate particular situations to 1. *more general* and 2. *less immediate* aims. Thus, even the intemperate man goes after not only, say, what is sweet here and now, but, more basically, after sensuous pleasure; this general and enduring objective cannot be attributed to an animal. Kant recognizes this difference;[1] Walsh speaks of 'acting to promote one's long-term interests' (p. 191), and of actions 'finding their grounds in thoughts' (p. 198).

(3*b*) There are things, however particular, which only a rational being can desire because their *attainment* involves the possession of reason. A clear enough example is doing geometry. But the object of desire does not itself need to involve an *exercise* of reason: a man, but not an animal, can want to be honoured. Kant is obviously aware of this.[2]

(3*c*) One can want things whose description cannot take the form 'doing, or being, such-and-such', a form which any characterization of a sensuous desire can be given. I shall soon say more about this.

Kant attributes to reason the power of directing the will in a way other than by the presentation of objects, viz. by *maxims*, which he defines as 'subjective principles of wanting'.[3] In the

---

[1] Cf. pp. 191–2 f. of Professor Walsh's paper. For the convenience of some readers I have added the relevant references to the (German) Academy edition (which Walsh also uses). Its full title is: *Kant's gesammelte Schriften herausgegeben von der Königl. Preussischen Akademie der Wissenschaften* (Berlin, 1910 ff.). I quote from two of Kant's works: *Grundlegung zur Metaphysik der Sitten* = Vol. IV (1911); *Kritik der praktischen Vernunft* = Vol. V (1913).

[2] Cf. Walsh's reference to 'refined desires' (p. 192). In the *Groundwork* ('Kant's Critique of Practical Reason and Other Works on the Theory of Ethics', trans. by Thomas K. Abbott, London 1883, p. 12 = Acad. ed., IV, 396: *Bedürfnisse (die sie zum Theil selbst vervielfältigt)*, Kant says of reason that 'it to some extent even multiplies' a man's wants; and, later (p. 35 = Acad. ed., IV, 418: *seinen Begierden, die ihm schon genug zu schaffen machen, noch mehr Bedürfnisse aufzubinden*), of knowledge that it might 'impose more wants on his desires, which already give him concern enough'.

[3] Abbott, p. 17 n. 1 = Acad. ed. IV, 400 Fn.: *'Maxime' ist das subjective Princip des Wollens*; cf. also the account of practical principles given on pp. 29–31.

case of a moral man they must be maxims which he could want to become universal laws of nature. Kant's own examples of maxims include the following: not to suffer any insult without revenge; to curtail one's life if it threatens to bring more evil than pleasure;[4] to promise insincerely when in a situation of stress;[5] to preserve one's life;[6] to be benevolent where possible;[7] to promote one's own happiness;[8] and honesty.[9]

It is doubtful whether such a maxim is anything fundamentally different from an object of wanting. We must here remember that, when an apple, or a game, or honour, are 'objects of wanting', i.e.: what one wants, it will be, say, eating an apple, playing or watching a game, being honoured, in short: *qualities or activities of oneself*, that count as fulfilments of those wants, and, in that sense, as what one wants. Now to promise insincerely when in a situation of stress, or to be benevolent whenever possible, can, it would seem, be objects of wanting by this reckoning.

One might object to this—and, in fact, to Kant's talk about maxims—that someone whose *policy* it is to promise insincerely in a situation of stress, does not necessarily *aim* at promising insincerely in a situation of stress. This is an instance of a more general problem that I cannot follow up here. In the present context it must be enough to point out that such a man *will* always have the aim—a subsidiary aim, no doubt—of not letting his conduct be influenced by the aim of honesty. Also *when* in

---

[4] 'To shorten one's life when its longer duration is likely to bring more evil than satisfaction' (ibid., p. 39 = Acad. ed. IV, 422: *ich mache es mir aus Selbstliebe zum Princip, wenn das Leben bei seiner längern Frist mehr Übel droht, als es Annehmlichkeit verspricht, es mir abzukürzen*).

[5] 'When I think myself in want of money, I will borrow money and promise to repay it, although I know that I never can do so' (ibid., p. 40 = Acad. ed. IV, 422: *wenn ich in Geldnoth zu sein glaube, so will ich Geld borgen und versprechen es zu bezahlen, ob ich gleich weiß, es werde niemals geschehen*).

[6] Ibid., pp. 13f = Acad. ed. IV, 397: *sein Leben zu erhalten.*

[7] P. 14 = Acad. ed. IV, 398: *Wohltätig sein, wo man kann.*

[8] P. 15 = Acad. ed. IV, 399: *seine Glückseligkeit zu befördern.*

[9] P. 13 = Acad. ed. IV, 397: *Grundsätze der Ehrlichkeit.*

the right kind of situation, he will have the aim of making an insincere promise.

According to Kant the moral law or its 'legislative form' is a 'determining ground' (*Bestimmungsgrund*) of wanting quite different from any object.[10] But this distinction collapses if the moral law is operative only through people's maxims which I have shown to be nothing but a somewhat general kind of objects of wanting. For to act, not only in accordance with the moral law, but *out of duty*, is to act on 'the maxim to follow such a law even against all my inclinations',[11] or again on a maxim (e.g.: never to promise insincerely) corresponding to a rule, or precept, which can be shown to be a categorical imperative.[12] In either case, moral people are distinguished by something only they consistently want to do or to be, not by something that determines their conduct apart from anything they might want to do or to be.

That the moral law comes in the form of an imperative is no argument against this. Kant says that, in an imperative, the word 'ought' only indicates that what it proposes does not determine the will inevitably.[13] And, as we have seen, the moral man's objective is simply 'to follow the moral law . . .', i.e. to do what he ought to do, to do what he could want to be a universal practice.

Nor is it relevant to my point if the moral law is, in whatever sense, *a priori*. Firstly, Kant fails in his attempt to establish that the moral law differs in this respect, from the objective of

[10] E.g.: *Critique of Practical Reason*, Abbott, p. 117 = Acad. ed. V, 29: §6. Aufgabe II.
[11] 'The maxim that I should follow this law even to the thwarting of all my inclinations' (*Groundwork*, Abbott, p. 17 = Acad. ed. IV, 401: *einem solchen Gesetze selbst mit Abbruch aller meiner Neigungen Folge zu leisten*).
[12] *Critique*, Abbott, p. 107 = Acad. ed. V, 21: *weil sie ein kategorischer Imperativ ist*.
[13] *Groundwork*, p. 30 = Acad. ed. IV, 413: *Alle Imperativen werden durch ein 'Sollen' ausgedrückt und zeigen dadurch das Verhältniß eines objectiven Gesetzes der Vernunft zu einem Willen an, der seiner subjectiven Beschaffenheit nach dadurch nicht nothwendig bestimmt wird (eine Nöthigung)*.

being happy, which is not supposed to provide a unique 'determining ground' of wanting. The idea of, and the desire for, happiness could be *a priori*, even if it were not clear *a priori* what happiness consisted in for any individual man. Secondly, supposing the moral law alone provides an *a priori* 'ground' of wanting, why should this mean that here reason can determine the will in a way other than by presenting it with a possible object?

But does not Kant say that any *object* attracts one's desire only in virtue of a *pleasure* that it promises to bring, whereas no prospect of pleasure moves one to adopt a maxim of morality?—Well, Kant does make this claim. But if his argument to the effect that any object of wanting is wanted under the aspect of pleasure were valid, it would hold for everything one could want, including conduct in accordance with the categorical imperative.[14]

The hedonistic thesis that the object of any wanting is, basically, pleasure could not even look plausible if it were admitted that not every fulfilment of a want is something concerning oneself, or better: that there is a kind of wanting which is not, in the last resort, wanting to do, or be, such-and-such. For where this latter kind of wanting is not in question, there will be no presumption that the person whose want is fulfilled must be affected by, or aware of, this fulfilment; and one does not take pleasure in what one is not affected by or aware of.

We could look at Kant's practical philosophy in this way: In distinguishing, within determining grounds of the will, between pleasure on the one hand and a formal law on the other, he was guided, *inter alia*, by the vague idea that in the objective of a

---

[14] 'For then (in the case of an empirical principle) what determines the will is the idea of an object, and that relation of this idea to the subject by which its Faculty of desire is determined to its realization' (*Critique*, p. 108 = Acad. ed. V, 21: *Denn der Bestimmungsgrund der Willkür ist alsdann die Vorstellung eines Objects und dasjenige Verhältniß desselben zum Subject, wodurch das Begehrungsvermögen zur Wirklichmachung desselben bestimmt wird.*) Cf. also Walsh's remarks (pp. 207–9) on the concept of moral feeling.

moral action, as opposed to a 'prudent' one, the agent himself should not occupy a privileged position among his fellow men.[15] This characteristic of moral conduct was to be guaranteed by reason. But how?

With this question I take up the reflections Professor Walsh develops in his paper under (3) and (4). He there submits that Kant's way of connecting morality with reason was partly a result of his speculations about a community of spirits governed by 'purely spiritual' universal (and thus impartial) laws that are geared to a general good and impose themselves on us merely by virtue of their rationality. In this scheme, reason is the warrant of morality by bringing in (*a*) the idea of independence of the world of sensation and, connected with this, (*b*) abstraction from the individual and particular in favour of universality.

Thus, the categorical imperative is to provide the will with a 'determining ground' that treats the good of *all* rational beings, as opposed to a man's individual objectives, as the overall aim of his behaviour. It fails in this because, as long as one's basic maxim, however universalizable[16] and moral, is *to act in such-and-such a manner*, it is like a maxim of 'prudence' or an object of non-rational inclination in one respect, viz. that one plays a logically privileged role in it.

At this point I must say more about that practical function of reason which I described as 'providing one with objects of wanting whose description cannot be reduced to the form "doing, or being, such-and-such"' (3*c* on p. 213). I shall call them *propositional* as opposed to *attributional objectives*; and I want to use the distinction to present a new approach to the Kantian theme of impartial maxims.

A propositional objective occurs in, for instance, someone's wanting John and Jane to be happily married. Or consider this example: a just man wants equal treatment for everybody

---

[15] Cf., e.g., §3 (Theorem II) in ch. 1 of the *Analytic of Pure Practical Reason* (Abbott, pp. 108 f.)

[16] I leave aside here the problem whether there always is such a thing as *the* maxim according to which one acts in a given case.

regardless of their race; i.e. he wants it to be the case that every-body be treated without regard to their race.

In the context of our discussion I am chiefly interested in those cases of wanting that ... where the objective is not in-tended, in the last resort, for the sake of a further objective that is attributional. If I only want John to be happily married to Jane in order to have peace and quiet, my final objective is not *that something be the case.*

I want to suggest that, in order for someone to be a good man, *some* of his *basic* objectives must be propositional.

But cannot every instance of wanting that ... be turned into an instance of wanting to do, or be, something or other? Can-not a man be said to want that no one be discriminated against on account of their race, if and only if he wants to do what is in his power to prevent racial discrimination?

Let me remark first that someone who is against racial dis-crimination, i.e. wants no one to be discriminated against on account of their race, need not want to do everything in his power to prevent racial discrimination. On the other hand it won't be enough if he only wants not to discriminate against anyone on account of his race.[17] 'Being against racial discrimina-tion' may be a vague expression. But then my question is: Must there be some description of an attributional objective—apart from 'wanting to do what befits a man who is against racial discrimination'—which will match that vagueness?

My main complaint, however, against the proposed equiva-lence is this: Wanting that p, is not generally the same as want-ing to do something or other conducive to its being the case that p. Let me try to prove this. For either kind of wanting to be attributable to a person, the most basic test is, in general, whether he does, or tries to do, the kind of thing that is likely to bring about that p or to contribute to its coming about. But other factors are vital in the case of propositional objectives. Someone who, through imprudence, fails in his attempt to do

[17] More than this maxim would not be required by Kant's test: if it were everyone's maxim, there would be no racial discrimination.

something about interracial relations, might feel pity for himself if his objective was just to do that kind of thing; he will feel
pity for those suffering in the existing racial situation only if his
objective was, in the last resort, better interracial relations.
Again, only someone with that latter objective will have a reason
to be glad when someone else achieves what he aspired to
achieve; and he must regret it when others don't care.

This observation might suggest that he who wants that *p* is
simply someone who *wishes* that *p* and *wants* to bring about that
p. Well, if this were the case, this would not necessarily affect
my claim that there is a kind of wanting which cannot be
equated to any wanting to be, or do, such-and-such. But is it
the case?

To the extent that there is a difference between wishing and
wanting, a situation like the following is possible: A doctor
wishes the severe suffering of one of his patients to come to an
end but knows of no cure, and so his wish is that the patient
would die. One day the patient's relatives, who are after his
fortune, turn up and bribe the doctor into giving him an over-
dose of morphine. Now what moves him to the murder is the
objective of getting a lot of money, not that his patient will be
dead. So, in a sense, he can be said to wish that his patient
be dead, and to want to kill him, but not to want his patient to be
dead.

If it is true that criteria for someone's wanting something to
be the case include elements not occurring in criteria for someone's wanting to be, or do, this or that, then morality might
depend on a function of reason that 'prudence' (in Kant's
sense) does not depend on, viz. the presentation of a logically
distinct kind of basic objective. For I would argue that non-
rational wanting cannot have that kind of objective since this
would show up in attitudes over and above behaviour apt to
contribute to the realization of the objective (p. 218; see also
p. 216).

Even if there is this special connection between rationality
and morality, it is, obviously, not one that makes immoral

conduct somehow irrational, as Kant would have liked to make it out.

A further point must be noted: I have suggested that morality involves propositional objectives. This seems to agree, e.g., with our vision of the social reformer, whose primary consideration is not what he ought to do but what ought to be the case. It also agrees with our concepts of justice and charity: a man is not really just or charitable unless he is, in the last resort, interested in people's well-being, rather than in being a virtuous character—though it may be true that the virtues as such are indispensable conditions of his happiness. However, not all morality comes in objectives of this kind.

This seems clear from the virtues which are primarily geared to one's own well-being: in an act of courage or temperance one will often aim at things like one's health, one's reputation, one's wealth. But not even all the demands of justice can be presented in the form of propositional objectives. Consider, e.g., Socrates' Principle, that it is better to suffer wrong than to do it. It makes no sense to suggest that, concerning any man x, it is better *that* x suffer wrong than that x do wrong.[18] And if I make it my objective that I suffer wrong rather than do it, this does seem to be reducible to the (attributional) objective of suffering wrong rather than doing it.

I hope these few examples show that, even if it will often be doubtful whether someone's objective in doing something should be called propositional or attributional, the distinction is not idle, or irrelevant to moral philosophy.

[18] Hence Socrates' Principle (cf. Gorgias 473a5 and 509c7) refutes utilitarianism, or at any rate act-utilitarianism, which is based on a comparison between the intrinsic values of states of affairs only.

Comment: 'Kant, Conduct and Consistency'[1]

BY M. J. SCOTT-TAGGART

Professor Walsh argues to two general conclusions: (1) that 'Kant has nothing of real interest to say about practical reason generally', and (2) that without the nonsense of noumenal causality, Kant's 'all important connection between morality and rationality cannot be made intelligible'. His subsidiary conclusions are variants of these themes, with the exception of his entirely correct conclusions developed in the middle of the paper that two possible lines we might have wished to exploit, in order to find in Kant some reason for connecting morality and rationality, are dead-ends.

In an earlier encounter Professor Walsh has disapproved of a paper I read on the grounds that its approach to Kant was solely historical and barely if at all philosophical. The criticism was perhaps sound: but I here wish to reproach Professor Walsh for the same reason that he previously reproached me. I would defend taking the history of philosophy as sometimes emphasizing history: it is valuable if it prepares the way for the more important task of the history of philosophy. This task I take to be the attempt to fit contemporary theory on to historical fact. We shall never get an exact fit, but the inexactitude often leads us to look again at our theories. History is fruitful not so much for generating insights as for correcting them: to fully validate Kant's contemporary relevance presupposes, therefore, the adumbration of a theory prior to historical investigation. I clearly do not have time to perform both tasks here, but my theoretical commitments should be evident from my fairly clearly defined preference for certain contemporary writers or positions.

My quarrels with Professor Walsh will only emerge after a

[1] I would like to gratefully acknowledge the aid of the Alexander von Humboldt *Stiftung*, who purchased me the time during which was formulated the material upon which much of this reply has drawn.

great deal of stage-setting. My terminal quarrel will be with his first general conclusion, namely the negative relevance of Kant to the proceedings of this conference. I shall argue that there is a difference between intelligent and rational behaviour, and that the know-how envisaged by Professor Walsh has much to do with the former but nothing to do with the latter, and thus the fact that Kant allegedly ignored or overlooked know-how does nothing to establish that he had nothing of interest to say about rational behaviour. I shall approach this conclusion, however, by arguing that Kant *did* have something of interest to say about rational behaviour, and in the course of this approach I shall have something to say about Kant's alleged failure to connect morality with rationality.

First, Kant does indeed make a distinction between speculative reason and practical reason. In both capacities reason has the task of establishing propositions which are 'genuinely universal', and by this he means establishing propositions which would be accepted by any rational being.[2] The difference between speculative and practical reason lies in the fact that speculative reason is concerned to establish factual propositions, while practical reason is concerned to establish what I am going to call advisability propositions. This term is not particularly apt, but I am going to use it for propositions about what should or should not be done. I shall leave largely unexplored the differences between factual propositions and advisability propositions beyond endorsing Kant's view that it is not the case that the former are objective in some sense in which the latter are not. The differences lie partly in their different connections

[2] Kant thought that a proposition was genuinely universal if and only if it was necessary. Because of the biconditional he used the words 'genuinely universal' and 'necessary' in an extremely loose and muddled way: the nearest he came to clarity was in the *Prolegomena*, §22 Ak. IV, 304–5, in connection with his talk about *Bewusstsein überhaupt*. An adequate reconstruction of Kant's views, by which I mean an interpretation concerned to eliminate inconsistencies in the most defensible way, should view him as primarily concerned to establish certain propositions as having *eine wahre Allgemeinheit*, which he thought he could do only if he showed those propositions to be in some sense *nothwendig*.

with the concept of intention, and partly in the different grounds on which they are based. Kant does define his position in regard to the first issue, but it is the investigation of the latter kind of difference that most concerned him, and on which he has most to contribute.

Beyond the distinction between speculative and practical reason, it is fair to say that Kant sub-divides the latter into empirical practical reason and pure practical reason.

My first contention is that Kant did not say anything interesting about empirical practical reason, but that there are things of a Kantian kind which may be said about it.

Let us first take Kant's views on problematic-technical imperatives rather than those which are assertoric-pragmatic. That is to say, we are dealing with reasoning as it is involved in such arguments as the following:

> I want to be fit
> Swimming would make me fit
> So: it is *prima facie* advisable that I should take up swimming.

Such arguments raise serious problems: and I do not wish to deny that these problems and their solution belong to the problematic of practical reason. But I wish to distinguish these problems from others that belong to that same problematic. For the problems raised by the above kind of argument are concerned peculiarly with the formal study of what we might call simple advisability operators, or the relations of and differences between, for example, simple and conclusive advisability operators. Although I have conceded that such a study belongs within a theory of practical reason, it does not fall within the scope of this paper,[3] and I shall speak of such a study as the investigation of practical *inference* in order to distinguish it from other problems concerned with practical reason.

Of all the other problems that cluster around practical reason,

[3] Cf. footnote 7 below. I also fail to consider the sort of practical reasoning involved in the following sequence: My appointment is at ten; the eight-thirty is usually late; so I will catch the seven-thirty. I think an account of such reasoning can be given within the general framework to be outlined.

the one that will concern me will be the content of just *one* of the different kinds of premiss that occur in arguments whose conclusion incorporates, or may incorporate, a conclusive advisability operator. For I take it that a distinctively Kantian contribution to the problematic of practical reason would be the provision and defence of *principles* that may distinctively occur in practical arguments. And here I am using the word 'principles' in such a way that no empirical statement may count as a principle: this satisfies one of Kant's strictures on what is to count as a *Vernunftregel*, although I relax a second requirement that he might have wished to impose, namely that principles should not involve a *ceteris paribus* clause.[4]

Let me now illustrate that there are things of a Kantian kind which can be said about empirical practical reason. To do this we have to turn to Kant's assertoric-pragmatic imperatives, i.e. advisability propositions connected with the putative analytic truth that we each desire our own happiness. I will instance just one principle that is operative in this area. This is Professor Rawls' principle of inclusiveness, which states that if of two or more alternatives open to someone there is one alternative which procures all the benefits of the other and, in addition, further benefits beside, then, other things being equal, it is rational to prefer that alternative.[5] Using this principle an argument might on some occasions be constructed whose premisses fell into the following groupings:

(1) The principle of inclusiveness.
(2) A batch of premisses which I shall speak of as being about a person's desires: this blurs important differences, but I am,

[4] Note that I am saying that a *ceteris paribus* clause may attach to some, although it need not necessarily to all, principles. I am not saying, what would be nonsense, that it may attach to a conclusive advisability proposition.

[5] Cf. John Rawls: *A Theory of Justice* (Clarendon Press: Oxford, 1972) p. 412. §§63 ff. gives the first plausible attempt that I know of to provide a systematic account of the principles of prudential reasoning. Arguably, his Aristotelian principle, namely that of two capacities that a man might have, he will enjoy more the exercise of the more realized capacity, might be construed as an empirical statement.

as I said, investigating only one of the different kinds of premiss that distinctively occur in practical arguments.

(3) A list of all the relevant alternative actions open to the person.

(4) A series of hypotheticals, stating for each of the alternatives in (3) which of the desires of (2) would thereby be satisfied.

(5) A premiss that the *ceteris paribus* clause of (1) is, in fact, fulfilled, i.e. that none of the alternatives is, for example, to be preferred according to the principle of effective means, and that none of the alternatives is to be disbarred on the ground of moral principles (strictly speaking, even if moral principles do have the status of reasons for acting they should still not be introduced at this stage of the argument, but this very important technicality I shall ignore for the moment).

Quite apart from any possible interference from morality, it is clear that operating any such argument requires a great deal of insight. In only the simplest, and extremely rare, cases will we be dealing with a closed system of desires, i.e. operating within a determinate and proximate temporal horizon. In most cases the system of desires will be an open one, which is to say, it is a system in which at the time the argument is deployed the person in question does not dispositionally, let alone episodically, desire certain things which he nevertheless has a disposition to desire (a disposition that would, perhaps, become manifest if he went through an appropriate training schedule), and we must be very careful therefore not to exclude premisses which are relevant under (2) or (3). But an argument of this kind can be a good one, in the sense of including all relevant premisses and (for the sake of elegance) excluding all those which are irrelevant, and it will follow under the postulated circumstances that one of the hypothetical statements of (4) clearly exhibits the advisability of one of the alternatives in the light of the principle of inclusiveness. Thus the conjunction of all these premisses will constitute a reason for adopting some one of the alternatives. Or, to put it in what I think is simply another form, a person cannot assent to the truth of all these premisses and yet deny that there is a conclusive advisability proposition which follows from them expressing the fact that they do constitute good reason for one course of action rather than any other.

A theory which is to be an adequate theory of practical reason must find a place for principles like the principle of inclusiveness: to this extent, therefore, I would deem Kant's contribution to the theory of practical reason to be incomplete. His theory positively requires supplementation by something like the Rawlsian theory of prudence.

Such supplementation would make it easier to see that a prevalent misinterpretation of Kant is not only a misinterpretation, but is also false. It is often said that hypothetical imperatives are analytic in that they rest upon or incorporate the analytic statement that he who fully wills the end also wills the means. Far from being an analytic statement—unless, for no good reason, we make it so—this is quite patently false. It is false if only because of the frequent occurrence of prudential *akrasia*.[6] And Kant does not overlook this fact. Although he is in fact talking about problematic-technical imperatives the following passage will be true of all hypothetical imperatives if we make the necessary Rawlsian supplementation, and the passage will answer the question of how hypothetical imperatives in general are possible: 'he who wills the end, wills (*so far as reason has decisive influence on his actions*) also the indispensably necessary means thereto, provided that they are in his power'.[7] What this amounts to is that the conclusion of a bit of practical reason is not an action,[8] but rather a proposition preceded by

[6] Cf. D. Davidson: 'How is Weakness of the Will Possible?' in J. Feinberg, ed., *Moral Concepts* (Oxford, 1969), pp. 101–2.

[7] *Grundlegung*, Ak. IV, 417. My italics. Reflection on this totally typical quotation makes clear that Kant is envisaging inferences of the form 'Would that *q*, unless *p* then not-*q*, so: it is *prima facie* advisable to bring it about that *p*.' Since this is only one amongst a number of valid forms of practical inference, it is clear that we may expect little help from Kant on what I earlier characterized as the study of practical inferences, which is why I have filtered off that area of the problematic of practical reason.

[8] A view apparently attributed to him by Professor Edgley, although the charge is later implicitly abandoned: cf. *Reason in Theory and Practice* (Hutchinson, 1969) p. 28 and pp. 137–47. I only lately remarked that Professor Edgley had noticed the significance of the

some kind of advisability operator (this should, in any case, be clear from the fact that Kant speaks of them as imperatives).[9] The more important of Kant's concerns is with how we establish advisability propositions. And it is, of course, of crucial importance that we clearly distinguish this concern from a second concern, which is with the step from establishing and accepting such a proposition to our acting upon it. Other philosophers than Kant have confused the two (perhaps they, unlike myself, do not daily perform acts of omission which they recognize to need defence and yet to be indefensible): Kant was particularly tempted to it through his use of the terms *Bestimmungsgrund*, *Bewegungsgrund*, and *Bewegursache*. But while Kant had much to say that was valuable about the first matter, the second is something about which, at least throughout the period of the three *Critiques*, he had little of interest to say because of the hedonistic psychology to which he was rather unfortunately bound.[10]

Let me now begin to sort out the differences between, and the relations of, hypothetical and categorical imperatives. The parenthetical clause, although I differ from him about what precisely the significance is: cf. footnote 37 below and the paragraph to which it pertains. I remain, however, greatly indebted to this book and to the author's 'Practical Reason' in *Mind* (N.S. Vol. LXXIV, 1965).

[9] Professor Beck appreciates the point but expresses it with slightly less than his usual felicity: cf. L. W. Beck: *A Commentary on Kant's Critique of Practical Reason* (Chicago, 1960), pp. 84–7.

[10] This is a point that Professor Walsh has, of course, stressed, but he has made things rather more easy for himself than he might through ignoring the later writings and the development of a systematic distinction between *Wille* and *Willkür*. I cannot here explicate or defend this distinction, and so concede Professor Walsh his point, although that there is *something* to be gleaned from it cannot, surely, be doubted by one who has read Professor Silber's honest and forceful account of Kant's use of it, cf. J. R. Silber's Introduction to Kant: *Religion Within the Limits of Reason Alone* (Harper & Row, 1960). If we called upon this distinction, then the quotation of footnote 6 would amount to: he who accepts as true and complete the premisses of a valid practical argument ought to form the intention to do that action for which the argument gives conclusive reason. And will as practical reason amounts to: reason is practical to the extent that it validly infers an advisability proposition and *ipso facto* recognizes that an intention ought to be formed to do that action for which the argument gives conclusive reason.

first stage will be the introduction of a prudential advisability operator, although at this stage I leave it open whether or not this is distinguishable from a conclusive advisability operator. I shall suppose that we have developed an adequate theory of prudence along Rawlsian lines, i.e. that we have a set of principles which a man may consult and use when asking the question 'What shall I do to be happy?' A conclusion that is reached by means of an argument proceeding from these principles alone I shall speak of as a prudential advisability proposition.

Permit me now to make two points which will facilitate discussion of the relation of such propositions to morality. First, given our set of prudential principles, it is clearly false to say as Kant did—cf. Professor Walsh's exegesis of this point (supra p. 196)—that assertoric-pragmatic imperatives are not universally valid. Given the complete set of premisses, the prudential advisability proposition will logically follow, and thus will hold for any rational being. This will remain true even if, as Kant believed, they had a *ceteris paribus* rider (although Kant might have bamboozled even himself by expressing this in terms of 'conditionality'). What perhaps confused Kant here is that because the premisses include statements about particular desires, desires which may not be universally shared, the conclusion may not be universally *relevant*: but relevance is clearly distinct from validity. This point will become clear when we see that it is at the basis of Kant's distinguishing the prudential advisability operator from the conclusive advisability operator.

Secondly, let me eliminate the problem that many have felt derives for the 'application' of the categorical imperative from the possibility of alternative descriptions of an action. Thus many suppose that, for any action, it is always possible to find at least one description under which it may be thought as a universal law 'without inconsistency', and thus it is always possible to make, in Kantian theory, any action morally permissible. The way in which I would deal with this trouble is to point out that

Kant is quite definite about the categorical imperative 'applying' to the action advised by a bit of prudential reasoning, and *this action is made highly specific*[11] if we break up the prudential reasoning in the way I exampled earlier and check back to see the desires which the action is designed to satisfy. The question that he asks—as we can see if we transpose the way in which he handles his examples into the Rawlsian context—is therefore quite determinate: Can I 'will and/or think without inconsistency' that everybody in the situation defined by the desires and options occurring in the premisses should act on the advisability proposition that they imply? Thus I deal with one problem: the second major problem, which is that of what Kant means by talking of inconsistency in this connection, I leave to one side for the moment.

With these explanations it is fairly easy to see how Kant views the relation of prudential principles to the principles of morality. The Rawlsian theory of prudence is straightforwardly utilitarian: this is to some extent hinted at by the fact that the principle of inclusiveness that I chose as an example of a prudential principle is simply the principle of Pareto optimality applied to one man's desires rather than to the desires of a collection of men. The Kantian claim is that having derived a prudential advisability proposition, a second argument must be run through before we arrive at a conclusive advisability proposition, where this second argument will involve the use of moral principles. Of course, what is advised at the end of the second argument may be the same as that which is advised at the end of the first argument. The point is that it is only at the

[11] I do not mean to imply that only one description is possible, but rather that alternative descriptions will hang together in ways which are, or ought to be, structurally defined by a theory of practical inference. It is important to remark that Kant's concept of action as a topic for moral appraisal differs totally from that of, for example, Mill, in that for Kant the motive is built into the description of the action so that the appraisal of an action as good is internally related to the appraisal of the agent. Had Professor Anscombe appreciated this difference between Kant and Mill she would not, perhaps, have been quite so hard on the former in her 'Modern Moral Philosophy' (*Philosophy*, Vol. XXXIII, 1958).

end of the second argument that it rests upon secure foundations: a point that should be clear when we recall that if we are trying to prove a theorem by natural deduction, then the conclusion may be derived several times in the course of its proof, depending each time upon different assumptions, and we do not have the required proof until it is derived on the basis of no assumptions. I intend the analogy to suggest some part of what Kant might have meant—whether legitimately or no—when he spoke of the moral law as 'unconditional'.

Let us call the two arguments, or two phases of one argument, the prudential and the moral argument. As I pointed out above in connection with a felt problem about the 'application' of the categorical imperative, the moral argument is always sequent to the prudential argument. Only in this way do we have a determinate 'maxim' to 'test'.

At this stage I must make the rather uncomfortable transition from exegesis to argument in that, reluctantly because with little hope of success, I had liked to pick up the gauntlet which Professor Walsh has thrown down in his second general conclusion, namely that Kant had no good reason for connecting morality and rationality. Or perhaps it would be more proper to speak of gauntlets, in that there seem to be several distinct issues involved, on one of which I do not really wish to quarrel here. Thus when Professor Walsh begins the argument that leads to this particular conclusion, he asks three questions: (1) given that most people do care about moral issues, 'does this show that pure reason can be practical?' (2) 'Why was it that Kant supposed that moral behaviour must be rational behaviour?' and (3) 'Why did he say that moral concepts "have their seat and origin in reason completely *a priori*"?' I think that this is a very deft way of dividing up the problem, because I think that we have three distinct questions here, but unfortunately the treatment by Professor Walsh suggests what I am by no means sure that he would affirm, namely that returning a negative answer to (1) will involve returning a negative answer to (2) and (3). I shall, however, sketch reasons for thinking that some part of the Kantian doctrine on (2) and (3) can be saved, i.e. shall sketch reasons for supposing that moral behaviour involves practical reason and, moreover, pure practical reason at that. But because it is difficult to see how this can be maintained if we return a negative answer to (1), saying that pure reason cannot be practical, I shall first look at the reasons that we have for declaring this negative.

The separation of the first question from the others is a matter of some urgency in view of Mrs. Foot's contention, that parallels in many ways that of Professor Walsh, that morality does not involve such animals as categorical imperatives.[12] The point is certainly important, in that it would seem that if Mrs. Foot is correct then establishing a conclusive advisability proposition will not be the two-phase affair that Kantian theory essentially demands. All that we shall need will be a theory of prudence combined with a very liberal idea of the range of items that people may declare themselves to want. As a result, the virtuous man will qualify as such even if he acts out of other motives than respect for the moral law, which latter, with its connotations of noumenal causality, is dismissed. Theory will still, of course, admit a place for virtue, in that a person acting out of certain desires, namely those which involve in an essential way the consideration of other people's desires and interests, will exhibit actions that can quite properly be qualified as virtuous. Thus no reason, it is suggested, can be adduced for saying that actions done from tact, sympathy, or consideration should not qualify as virtuous.

What would be Kant's reply? I think he has two suggestions which have been thought to possess cogency. The first is that actions which are so qualified as virtuous are not actions which always work out to the benefit of their designed recipient—and this in other cases than those where there is some executive

[12] 'Morality as A System of Hypothetical Imperatives' in *Philosophical Review* (Vol. LXXXI, 1972) and 'Reasons for Actions and Desires' in *Aristotelian Society Supplementary Volume* (Vol. XLVI, 1972). Cf. also a lucidly argued special case by P. Mercer: *Sympathy and Ethics* (Clarendon Press: Oxford, 1972), ch. VII.

fumbling.[13] In relation to some of the putative virtues that Kant mentions, the case does seem valid, but in relation to such virtues as those cited above, although the fact lodged in objection does seem to be a fact, it could be counter-claimed that the fact that actions done from these motives are sometimes bound, if successfully carried through, to work out to the disadvantage of the designed recipient is due to lack of intelligence or human insight on the part of the agent, and is not due to the fact that the actions are not related to a 'good will' as their 'condition'. This counter-claim is, I think, sound in principle. To counter the counter would involve us in giving so cerebral an interpretation of the good will that it would no longer be the Kantian concept. Let us remark Kant's second reply, which is a little more tricky. It starts from the assumption that a man cannot qualify as virtuous through, say, his tactfulness, unless it is the case that he is not tactful only when he *happens or chances* to feel like being so.[14] His tactfulness, if it is to qualify him as virtuous, must have a subjunctive character: it must be a settled disposition to act tactfully, even when the man feels inclined to be cutting and hurtful. Of course the virtues can support one another: tact may be made more easy through the fact that the tactful man is also considerate, and thus generally feels inclined not to hurt others, and this desire may override any momentary inclination to be hurtful through being tactless. But to depend upon feelings here would be to depend upon something fairly weak: a person who feels inclined to be tactless will generally also be inclined to view the world in a jaundiced fashion and to see others as 'not really worth the trouble'. Thus the tactfulness which is to be a virtue must have a subjunctive character which enables it to exist through a very various array of affective states. At the same time this subjunctive aspect must not be based in habit.[15] It seems to me that Kant is right that the virtue is found in what we might call an intellectual set: the recognition

[13] *Gundlegung*, Ak. IV, 392.
[14] *Grundlegung*, Ak. IV, 397–9.
[15] MdS Ak. VI, 407; *Anthropologie* Ak. VII, 147.

that the situation calls for tact is able to negotiate tactful conduct even if, on at least some occasions, the person doesn't actually *feel* tactful. Where Kant is perhaps wrong (and here I am acceding to a point that Mrs. Foot made in the discussion of the paper as read) is in supposing that this intellectual set requires any noumenal mechanism, or special talk of respect, to make it intelligible: we can acquire this intellectual set as a result of a course of discipline that might have as empirical a basis as one could wish.[16] What remains to Kant is that virtue rests upon what he sometimes calls *Denkungsart*, or way of thinking, as opposed to *Sinnesart*, although we do not preclude the possibility that the way of thinking might have an empirical foundation in the way of feeling, even if it later escapes from this basis and can operate in relative independence of it. This, I think, does something to save the Kantian doctrine that virtue relies upon a person's having a good will in *some* sense of this phrase: even if, as is necessary, we have to cut the Kantian concept of a good will down to a more manageable size.

At this point we can see how Mrs. Foot and Professor Walsh are at one in liberalizing the range of possible items of desire and eschewing Kant's psychological theory, although the theory with which they replace it will still, of course, permit a place for the phenomenological facts of 'the war of morality with self interest'. This war will be analogous to the war that I win when I pick up Henry James rather than Raymond Chandler. Or, Mrs. Foot's example, the war that I win when I force myself to get up in the morning which, incidentally, Augustine compares to his situation when he was still a slave to the pleasures of lust even though he was convinced that the words of God were true, and against the charge that he was doing as

[16] I have said that I am abandoning Kant's notion of respect: but this is purely within the limits of this paper. Of course we cannot salvage all of Kant's uses of this notion, but following the strategy suggested later in this paper—that, namely, of operating centripetally rather than centrifugally, i.e. working from the 'peripheral' uses of a concept to its more 'central' uses—I think something can be saved if we commence with the Kantian distinction between self-love and self-respect.

he believed he ought not 'the only answers I could give were the drowsy words of an idler—"Soon", "Presently", "Let me wait a little longer". But "soon" was not soon, and "a little longer" grew much longer.'[17]

I can see no reason for not concurring with this programme of liberalization: and in particular I would welcome the resultant extension of the possible range of moral judgements through the revised basis for a theory of virtue, although I do have my small Kantian caveat that such a theory of virtue needs to give an account of the subjunctive character of virtuous qualities of a man. I have suggested that there is a connection here with a thinned down concept of the good will: and it would be surprising indeed if nothing could be salvaged from a concept that so many have felt to possess significance.

In allowing so much I think I have allowed almost as much as I wish to the position of Mrs. Foot and Professor Walsh. I have allowed to the former that moral qualities may be exhibited by actions negotiated by hypothetical imperatives. I have allowed to the latter much of his position[18] that moral qualities may be ascribed to the 'whole man' rather than merely to the rational part of man in so far as it 'wins out' over the sensual part. I have at the same time conceded the substance of the claim that Kant is wrong to say that pure reason can be practical, for this thesis is construed by Kant in terms of a peculiar mental mechanism, and I have effectively allowed, through abandoning the concept of respect so far as this paper is concerned, that Kant is wrong to say that only action determined by reason without any pathological *Triebfeder* qualifies for moral epithets.

I should now like to proceed—even though what I have so far said stands in need of far more discussion—to challenge the claim that we have thereby shown the disconnection between morality and rationality to be complete: I shall explore a little the connections between morality, consistency, and reasons for

---

[17] *Confessions*, Book VIII §5, trans. R. S. Pine-Coffin (Penguin Books, Harmondsworth, 1961).
[18] Cf. his *Hegelian Ethics* (Macmillan, 1969), especially ch. V and VI.

acting. The thesis that I had liked to defend is that it is irrational to be immoral, but in this notoriously difficult area my argument will have to be sketchy in the extreme, and I apologize in advance for the fact that at a crucial stage I shall have to rely upon arguments advanced by others. If these arguments appear weak then I am not altogether dissatisfied, for the problem that they concern is, to my mind, the most pressing in moral philosophy today, and the fact that nobody has done better may encourage others to try harder.

I shall begin this new phase by considering an unease which may be felt about the liberalized theory of prudence whose examination I broke off in order to clarify what I think it *had* quite properly established. This unease arises because the principles involved in the Rawlsian theory of prudence would, by themselves, and even with the required derestriction on the idea of what people may want, negotiate for different people in the same physical circumstances quite different advisability propositions. This is simply the point that I noted earlier about the conclusion of a good prudential argument being universally valid, although not necessarily universally relevant. It is a point with which I think Mrs. Foot would agree, in that she has by no means abandoned her position, which she established through her classic example of rudeness,[19] of what we might call the self-possession of evaluative language, although she is now arguing that the self-possession of evaluative language does not imply that it should possess us. Put in rather summary fashion, she combines the view that moral judgements are objective with the view that moral judgements *as reasons for acting* are subjective.

A good Kantian would wish to show that no conclusion of any (even liberalized) prudential argument ever presents a course of action as being more than *prima facie* advisable. He would wish to show that to all conclusions of prudential arguments there is the rider: if this is not inconsistent with the

[19] 'Moral Arguments' in *Mind* (N.S. Vol. LXVII, 1958).

requirements of morality, and thus he would maintain a distinction between prudential and conclusive advisability operators. I am afraid that a good Kantian will find little support in the central Kantian texts upon which to base such an argument, but it is worth looking in passing at how such an argument would run, for we can find a place for his argument within a larger framework that we shall then turn to.

Kant's texts suggest the following argument:[20] if people acted on the different advisability propositions that were prudentially negotiated for them in the same physical circumstances, then they would frequently be brought into conflict of one kind or another. It is not the case that all varieties of conflict are undesirable (one interesting variety is the sort of conflict which, given men as they are and have been, is desirable but which it cannot be a man's duty to promote: I am thinking of Kant's acceptance of the prevalent belief that the 'cunning of reason' uses war as a means for cultural and moral progress at certain periods of the world's history). Nor is it the case that the conflict is ever likely to become total war: there is no reason that I can perceive why the reaction of other people, whether exercised judicially or through public and private opinion, should not be considered amongst the consequences of an action and go quite straightforwardly into the prudential reasoning.[21] But it would be unrealistic to suppose that the resultant social divisiveness would not involve gross injustices. There would be

---

[20] Cf. L. W. Beck, op. cit., chs. 6, §§5 and 7, §6.

[21] This is to confess an inability to understand those philosophers who still threaten us with a Hobbesian state of nature: as, I believe, Professor Watkins does in his contribution to this volume. The games-theoretic approach to moral questions to which these arguments are allied is helpful in many ways and does give us one method which, judicially applied, will rank some reasons as better reasons for acting than others. But I fail to see how this approach can establish that what morality requires provides good reason for acting to someone who doesn't care about morality and—the two test cases by which a well grounded moral theory must assess itself—who can either tie a knot in the social fabric and get away with it or else slip a fast one through. I personally learnt a great deal about the possibilities and limitations of such an approach from D. K. Lewis, *Convention: A Philosophical Study* (Harvard, 1969).

frequent occasions—indeed, are there not already—where a conflict of interests arose, and what was prudentially advisable for the stronger party was not what was prudentially advisable for the less powerful party—the more powerful party not, as a matter of fact, being imbued with an altruistic disposition and high ideals about wishing to live a just life or the like—and the outcome would be recognizably unjust. Thus equating prudential with conclusive advisability would often imply the rationality of some unjust actions.

As an argument this would look like an attempted *reductio*: and perhaps to men of the Enlightenment it was deemed successful. But as an attempted *reductio* against Mrs. Foot's position it is a palpable misfire, since the conclusion is apparently not an unwelcome one. If I might state the case in terms with which I do not think that Mrs. Foot would agree, what we are being challenged to produce is a *strict reductio* such that we can convict someone who denies the truth of ' "*x* is unjust" is a better reason for not doing *x* than "*x* is prudentially advisable" is for doing *x*' of the straightforward inconsistency of both believing some proposition while also believing its contradictory.[22] And I am quite sure that this cannot be done. Of course a person who denies this statement is *wrong*: but a person can be wrong without being inconsistent.[23] And of course a person who really

[22] I use the example of injustice as a paradigm of conclusive moral and overriding reason. I do not claim that it will always be such a paradigm, and, if someone does not care for the example they are at liberty to substitute one of their own.

[23] I am here presupposing the solution of the fundamental methodological question as to how we might rank reasons for acting as better or worse: the basic idea is Hegelian, and it in no way implies that reasons for acting should not change their relative positions in the hierarchy. I remain unconvinced by the traditional methods as found, for example, in Professor Baier's *The Moral Point of View* (Cornell, 1958), pp. 308–15, or to the view developed with great subtelty and deceptive lucidity by Professor G. R. Grice in *The Grounds of Moral Judgement* (Cambridge, 1967). Contemporary positions with which I feel more sympathy are Professor Rawls' view in his 'Outline of a Decision Procedure for Ethics' in *Philosophical Review* (Vol. LXVI, 1957) and ch. 1, §9 of his *A Theory of Justice*. The same kind of analogy between knowledge in morality and science—where both are liable to conceptual revolutions and the replacement of a less adequate by a more adequate

believes this is *corrupt*:[24] but lacking a strict *reductio* it seems that this is quite compatible with consistency. Thus a person can hold thoroughly villainous views without necessarily being inconsistent.

I think that the position just sketched differs from that defended by Mrs. Foot in that, I believe, she would wish to say —and certainly suggests—that a person who was 'indifferent to' or 'didn't care about' injustice because 'he couldn't see the point' was a person who was *not* wrong to deny the statement ' "*x* is unjust" is a better reason for not doing *x* than "*x* is prudentially advisable" is for doing *x*'. I have allowed that such a person would not necessarily be inconsistent but, for reasons

---

scheme—is exploited by Professor Schneewind in 'Moral Knowledge and Moral Principles' in *Royal Institute of Philosophy Lectures, Volume 3: Knowledge and Necessity* (Macmillan, 1970), although I naturally dissent from his view that the categorical imperative is not a supreme moral principle: its lack of content makes it precisely possible for there to be development of lower order moral principles. This methodology, incidentally, corresponds in spirit to Kant's regressive argument to the categorical imperative (cf. KdpV Ak. V. 8) and, in the light of it, Professor Matson's article on 'Kant as Casuist' in *Journal of Philosophy* (Vol. LI, 1954) must be written off. I do not see that Kant's synthetic argument, or transcendental deduction, of the categorical imperative, can get very far from its premiss that human agents are often in situations where they ask practical questions: a brave attempt is, however, made by L. W. Beck in his 'The Fact of Reason: An Essay on Justification in Ethics' reprinted in *Studies in the Philosophy of Kant* (Bobbs-Merrill, 1965). I would emphasize, however, that the problem to which I am here suggesting, without fully arguing, a solution, namely that of how we establish the truth of statements of the kind 'R^1 is a better reason for doing *x* than R^1 is for doing not-*x*', seems to me to be the most urgent problem in moral philosophy today.

[24] Sometimes I have managed to believe this. More often I am persuaded by Professor Holland's somewhat Platonic position in 'Moral Scepticism' in *Aristotelian Society Supplementary Volume* (Vol. XLI, 1967), where such a denial would be taken to show that the person does not understand what he is saying, i.e. does not know what justice *is*. We need to distinguish the morally blind from the morally corrupt: the former would be one who *really* didn't understand what he was saying while the latter would be one who *pretends to himself* to believe what he is saying. It is only the latter who really is corrupt. I do not, however, wish to build acceptance of the better-reason proposition into an implicit requirement of understanding what injustice is: I explain below why I think that a normal person who denies the proposition only pretends to himself to believe what he is saying.

which I have roughly sketched in footnotes 23 and 24, I do not allow that such a person would not be wrong: after all, a person can be wrong on other grounds than that what he believes is self-contradictory! That a person might not see the point (or might pretend to himself not to see the point) of morality does not imply that morality has no point. A person who is indifferent to injustice (or pretends to himself that he is so) lacks a moral disposition,[25] and a person who suffers such a lack will not be a person for whom the recognized injustice of some action will be behaviourally effective. Such a person may *have* no reason for refraining from doing *x* where doing *x* is something he recognizes to be both unjust and prudentially advisable, but this is not to say that *there is no* reason for refraining.

It is perhaps instructive to remark that the above argument applies—or apparently applies: I am here posing a challenge to those who do not accept that argument—to the theory of prudence as well as to moral theory. A person who fails to accept the principles of the Rawlsian theory need not necessarily be convicted of inconsistency. A person lacking a prudential disposition will not be able to recognize what is a better reason for acting than something else as being such, and such a person will consequently be imprudent. But he is not necessarily inconsistent. If we had not been blinded by centuries of stipulation I feel sure that we could all recognize amongst our acquaintances people of whom it was not natural to say that they desire their own happiness, and psychiatrists could provide case after case of people who are indifferent to it. Such people I find much more easily intelligible than their moral analogues: perhaps we should bear in mind Nietzsche's declaration that 'man does *not* strive for happiness; only the Englishman does that'.[26] To take a different example—Kierkegaard's thoroughly

[25] I use the phrase 'moral disposition' to carry only a part of the weight carried by Kant's *'moralische Gesinnung'*: I drop from the latter concept, in the light of what I have said earlier about temporarily abandoning the notion of respect, everything except the virtues and their subjunctive character.

[26] *Werke*, ed., K. Schlechta (Darmstadt, 1966), II, 944.

consistent aesthetic personality—is a man who quite consciously devotes his life to the pursuit of his whims behaving in some way inconsistently? Yet such a man would be wildly imprudent: and we should say of such a man that although he may have no good reason not to follow his whims, since he lacks a prudential disposition, there nevertheless is good reason not to do so. Or rather: we *either* say that such a life is based on error, in the sense of a mistake of principle, *or* we must abandon the whole enterprise of attempting to show certain reasons for acting as being better reasons (in themselves) than others. Since I take the second disjunct to be unacceptable, the substance of my challenge is: Are there criteria for ranking some reasons for acting as better reasons than others which will 'pass' paying our endowment policy premiums as good reason for not maximizing present satisfactions which will not *also* 'pass' being unjust as a good reason for not doing so? Or have we all been conditioned by our upbringing to accept without question that putting pence into a piggy bank is 'a good thing' and hence unproblematic?

To conclude this phase of the argument: a person who doesn't accept the principles of prudential reasoning is silly, and a person who doesn't accept the principles constitutive of the disposition of at least a central core of our moral concepts is corrupt. Neither person is necessarily inconsistent. Sheer consistency cannot require anything from us in this area: we need first a point of leverage. But it would be a mistake of the first order to suppose that because a person can be consistent without being either moral or prudent he can therefore be *rational* without being either. People lacking a moral or a prudential disposition may not have reasons for being moral or being prudent: but this is not to say that there are not reasons which favour being moral and being prudent. I shall later suggest such a reason in the moral case which I do not see that any person can deny to be a reason, and this will give us a point of leverage for charges of inconsistency. If this is correct then those who wish to disconnect morality and rationality are guilty of the error of tying the concept of rationality too closely to the concept of consistency.

There is, therefore, a sense in which 'if rational, then moral' is true: even though we have rejected the mechanistic way in which Kant thought he had to establish the conditional. I turn now to the question of whether being, or intending to be, moral requires the use of reason. And I think that Kant is quite right to say that it does, for being moral involves more than acting in conformity with a set of principles that one has learnt by rote. The principles themselves have their rationale, and Kant would say that the formula which is constitutive of such reasons is the categorical imperative: and thus the categorical imperative is the principle of moral reasoning which is analogous to the principles of the Rawlsian theory of prudence, and I have already suggested that what we might hope for from Kant in relation to the topic of practical reasoning is the provision and defence of the principles which occur in such practical reasoning rather than illumination of other premisses that may occur in such reasoning. Whether Kant had anything interesting to say in this area depends upon whether we can accept the categorical imperative as a satisfactory principle of moral reasoning.

To avoid one possible misapprehension from the start: Kant is not committed to saying that somebody who rejects the categorical imperative is inconsistent. What he claims is that somebody who rejects the categorical imperative—'I don't accept that as a reason . . .'—is irrational or morally blind and not entitled to the treatment we accord the majority of persons (who, I suppose, being in the majority, are to be classified as 'normal'). And that this will follow from what I have said *if* the categorical imperative is a satisfactory principle that accounts for the disposition of a nuclear group of more down-to-earth moral concepts.

For myself, I believe that it comes very close to being so, although an adequate defence of this claim would have to be lengthy and involve going into matters that are not strictly germane to the proceedings of this conference. But some clarification is needed. The formulation of the categorical imperative that I shall be concerned with is the famous formula: 'So act that the maxim of your will could always hold at the same time as the principle of a universal legislation.'[27] To put this in other words—justified in the light of what I have already said—this amounts to: Perform those actions, and only those actions, which are advised by a bit of prudential reasoning if you can at the same time will that actions of those kinds should always be performed by persons of whom the premises of the bit of prudential reasoning are true. The other formulations of the categorical imperative, in the *Grundlegung* as elsewhere, I view not as deductions from this formula, but, for the most part, explanatory notes to it.

I should not, of course, find this at all a defensible formula if it were the case that many of Kant's examples which he believed to follow from this principle did in fact follow from it: and that altogether apart from the notorious mistake about the absolute obligation not to lie under any circumstances.[28] Whether Professor Schilpp is or is not right when he says that 'Kant seems, practically from the first, to have thought of reason as a tool to be used and shaped according to the requirements and exigencies of changing situations in a never static world',[29] it

[27] KdpV Ak. V, 30. I use this formula rather than that more widely known from the *Grundlegung* Ak. IV, 421 because the latter is apt to mislead. Through beginning 'Act only on those maxims which you can . . .' this formula suggests that the categorical imperative operates merely as a veto to proposed actions, while the former formula makes clear not only that actions are prohibited but also that certain action can be required.

[28] That this is a misapplication is now estabished. And Mrs. Foot has drawn attention to the fact that in the early lectures Kant did not claim so much, where I think the undocumented passage she is thinking of is that where Kant says that if, under duress, a thief asks me where I keep my money, I am under no obligation to tell the truth because 'he knows I will not tell the truth if I can help it' (*Eine Vorlesung Kants über Ethik*, ed., P. Menzer (1924), pp. 286–7). As a matter of slight interest, it might be noted that the same view is to be found in the (late) *Anthropologie* Ak. VII, 151, which makes the view of *Über ein vermeintes Recht* very curious indeed.

[29] *Kant's Pre-Critical Ethics* (Northwestern, 1960), p. 2 *et passim* where he argues that Kant never regarded the categorical imperative as an inflexible 'mould'.

is certainly true that Kant *ought* to have thought of reason, and the categorical imperative, in this way. Kant's historical situation, where the prevailing moral attitudes were still dominated by dogmatic Christian attitudes, would naturally have led him to very different conclusions, based on the categorical imperative, from those which the most of us would today draw from the same basis.

To counter the tendency to think that Kant constantly mishandled the categorical imperative let me give an example from his political writings which will help bring out its plausibility (as well as serve a purpose a little later in this paper). Here he utilizes the categorical imperative to argue for principles which will secure for each person a sphere of liberty in so far as that liberty is consistent with the like liberty for others. This is clearly analogous to Professor Rawls' first theorem of justice. In the contemporary climate (hopefully on the decline) of welfare economics guided by utilitarian principles we may think this undesirable in that we might think it requires backing by the mistaken idea that if we preserve liberty it would be promoting happiness through the fact that each would be able to pursue his own good, within the constraints of the equal liberty principle, in his own way. This is indeed a mistaken idea in that there are people living at or beneath the utility floor of whom the suggestion that they are able to pursue their own good in their own way is totally vacuous because such people do not have the means to achieve a good for themselves that is worth a nickel. Kant does not ignore this possibility. A first consideration might suggest that he does, in that he deemed it desirable to extend franchise only to those who are—in an inadequately defined but intuitively clear sense—economically self-sufficient: but we must remember his historical situation as well as the connection between such self-sufficiency and the concept of freedom that he valued so highly. But at the same time he is quite clear that those with franchise would be acting unjustly if they instituted legislation which prevented those who were not economically self-sufficient from becoming so: indeed, he believes it to be a requirement of justice that legislation should actually promote their chances of becoming so, although he did not go far enough in this direction, and did not see (what is by and large accepted in the Western world today) that welfare and education programmes should be introduced to promote these chances for those living at or below the utility floor from moving to some other position within the social fabric. This is part of his thesis that power would be unjustly used if it was not employed to promote the chances of any individual, *whatever his position by birth*, from moving to some other position than that to which he was born (and that such movement did take place may be seen, for example, in Wolff and Wincklemann, who were the sons of a tanner and a cobbler respectively). It is clearly not too far from such a position to Marx's claim that 'the criticism of religion ends with the doctrine that man is the highest being for man, and thus with the categorical imperative to overthrow all conditions in which man is degraded, enslaved, and a neglected being'.[30] Although Kant was not Marx's target, it was indeed Kant's religious views that would have prevented him—on the grounds that the end does not justify the means—from accepting the militant action that Marx's position implies. Reason may, however, favour the use of force on occasions: it was Kant's faith in reason that made his argument for the separability of prudential and conclusive advisability operators weaker than it might have been. It was Marx's economic analyses that transformed the Kantian view that man should be treated as an end in himself, which amounts to saying that no man should be taken for a ride, into the doctrine that no man should be exploited. But Kant may readily be forgiven, in view of the inadequate theories of economics at his time as well as the religious climate, from developing his political theories further than he did.

What, now, might be said for the categorical imperative as *the* principle of moral reasoning if we separate it from so many of Kant's examples illustrating its application?

[30] *Fruhe Schriften* (Stuttgart, 1962), I, p. 497.

Perhaps the most important point is that it implies that I should perform no action that affects other people if I should not be prepared for others, in the same situation, to perform a like action where it is I that is affected by it. But what is being meant by the phrase 'being prepared' in this formulation? I have elsewhere suggested that there may well be people so insulated by fortune that they would well be prepared to permit others in the same situation (objectively considered) to perform a like action because, things being as they are, they are never likely to be affected by their actions.[31] But I think Kant's formulation of the categorical imperative escapes such a charge that there may be people who are beyond or above morality. If a man's 'maxim' is to be thought as a universal law, then all we need is the premiss that those people who are so insulated are so as a result of nature's lottery, and that if their proposed action were viewed as a law of nature, and nature has provided him with his privileged position only as a matter of chance, then he must view his action—in relation to his being prepared to have it as a law of nature—from the point of view of the least privileged of men. I think that this condition may legitimately be extracted from the categorical imperative: and certainly with other interpretations of 'being prepared to' that have been proposed we reach morally undesirable results. If Kant was less inclined to stress it than he should have been, it may well be that he lived in an age when reversal of fortunes was far more frequent than it is today: something we can establish as historical fact, or legitimately infer from Rousseau's constant insistence in *Emile* that a man should be educated for all stations— educated to be 'economically self-sufficient'—because one can never rely upon fortune continuing to smile upon a man.[32] But

[31] 'Recent Work on the Philosophy of Kant' in L. W. Beck, ed., *Kant Studies Today* (Open Court, 1969), pp. 44–6.

[32] My exposition can be seen to correspond to some degree with Professor Rawls' veil of ignorance: a device that he introduces to dramatize our basic moral intuition that no man should be handicapped by the contingent circumstances of his birth. And if one is justified in ascribing this view to Kant then the arguments of Professor Walsh (*Hegeliean Ethics*, ch. IV) that Kant's ethics is contentless will miss

I think we can also find support for this interpretation of the notion of 'being prepared to' if we recall Kant's political theory that I have just briefly sketched, where we saw him advocating a form of society in which each man was to be able to reach the social position that he merited, which would imply a great deal of persons both rising and falling in the social hierarchy.

The second particularly important point about the categorical imperative is that it requires actions to possess 'transparency': no man should perform an action where he was not prepared to disclose the nature of that action as defined by the cluster of premisses which give it its determinate character. This follows from the fact that if our 'maxim' were to be a law of nature then, since laws of nature are essentially discoverable, their transparency would be a natural result. Kant does at one point make this explicit in relation to the doctrine of right, if not the doctrine of virtue, when he gives as a transcendental formula: 'All actions affecting the rights of other human beings are wrong if their maxim is not compatible with its being made public.'[33] Perhaps he was right to restrict transparency to the doctrine of right, for one can easily envisage situations where it could be argued that concealment of our motives is desirable, even although the categorical imperative appears to entail that this is always impermissible: this is a point which, so far as I know, has not been recognized as a corollary of the Kantian position, and I proffer the topic to some aspiring doctoral candidate short of a problem. For the moment I am going to take it that the categorical imperative entails the transparency of an action.

The two points I have just made about the interpretation of the categorical imperative have important consequences: the first makes it morally impermissible for those who can tie a

their mark, for they share the interpretation of Kant that I have criticized. This is not, however, to say that it is easy to get from the position of one who takes seriously 'There but for the grace of God . . .' to any concrete social policy. But there is no reason to think that there is *any* easy way of getting to a concrete social policy.

[33] *Zum ewigen Frieden* Ak. VIII, 381. The converse, of course, does not hold true.

knot in the social fabric and get away with it to do so, while the second makes it morally impermissible for those who can slip a fast one through to do so. And these two cases represent the main cases where we feel that morality stands in need of defence, in that they are the main cases where people lacking a moral disposition, and thus having no reason to be moral, are apt to go against what morality requires.[34] To the extent that the categorical imperative generates the conclusion that such actions are immoral I would take it that there is a strong case for saying that it is indeed *the* principle of moral reasoning. Of course the case needs further argument but, unfortunately because I had liked to develop the line, this is not the place for it.

Having prepared the ground, let me now return to the main theme of connecting morality with consistency and rationality. We have so far established that it is rational to be moral, although an immoral man is not necessarily (although he may be) inconsistent. Let me now try to make clear, and defend, Kant's claim that a man would be guilty of some sort of inconsistency if he could not will his maxim as universal law, i.e. who would not be prepared to have others in the same situation performing the action that is prudentially advised. I have already said that in order to bring a charge of inconsistency we need some point of leverage: no charge of inconsistency can be brought against a person lacking a moral disposition (or, rather, no charge of a kind that is of interest to us here). But if we are dealing with a person with a moral disposition, i.e. who recognizes that there are good reasons for acting morally, we are dealing with a person who may not always do what morality requires, but his having a moral disposition will be exhibited in such a case by his reactions, as, for example, being ashamed and remorseful, or engaging in rationalization and offering specious excuses.[35] But could there be a person who lacked a moral disposition? As I have unpacked this disposition, as involved in the categorical

---

[34] Cf. footnote 21.
[35] Cf. the recent return to this topic by Irving Thalberg: *Enigmas of Agency* (Allen & Unwin, 1972), ch. 11.

imperative, we have the two main requirements of (*a*) a preparedness to abstract from one's personal circumstances, and
(*b*) the transparency of one's conduct. The first condition is the
most important, for it seems likely that a certain amount of
deviousness *may* be legitimate so long as it is exercised within
the limitations imposed by (*a*). Now I wish to state dogmatically
that a person who is not prepared to abstract from his personal
circumstances when he is in a situation of some sort of conflict
is not—whatever ultimate account of 'being a reason' may be—
accepting as a reason in that situation what *is* a reason, and
although there may well be people who deny this in principle (as
opposed to conceding it but applying it partially or with poor
insight) they are either mentally sick or else are being extremely
dishonest with themselves and others. A person who denies that,
for example, different inherited status is relevant to his conduct, and that he of the less privileged status has rights against
he who is more privileged, is a psychological possibility, but he
is someone who does not measure up to the requirements for
being a person in any proper sense of this word. Any person who
is not mentally sick must (overtly or in his heart) concede us (*a*)
and, therewith, a point of leverage for charges of inconsistency.

What now can we make of Kant's claim that an inability to
will universally one's maxim is guilty of inconsistency? First:
what is it for actions to be inconsistent?[36] It is clear that actions
cannot satisfy logically incompatible descriptions, so that
actions can be inconsistent only if they are done on different
occasions: thus differing from beliefs, which can be inconsistent
and held simultaneously. But it might seem that any two
actions can qualify as inconsistent since it will always be possible to find a description of the one which is logically incompatible with some description of the other. The difference,
however, between actions which are merely different, and those
which are inconsistent, lies in the fact that there are certain
descriptions of actions which are *privileged*: and amongst these

[36] This paragraph is derived from Professor Edgley, op. cit. ch. 4,
although it involves considerable simplification of his views.

(although not totally exhaustive of these) are descriptions which relate to the intention with which the action was performed and the reasons for which that intention was formed.

Now we have already seen—in our examination of the theory of prudence which provides us with advisability propositions (albeit of a *prima facie* nature)—we do have available to us quite determinate and privileged action descriptions. And it is clearly seen that if a person cannot acknowledge that an action prudentially advised to him is one which he would be prepared for others to perform in like circumstances, then if he acts as he is prudentially advised to do, he is thereby performing an action which may not be inconsistent with any other action that he *actually* performs, but which is inconsistent with other actions which are 'virtually' his own, in that they may be subjunctively ascribed to him. He is thus involved in inconsistency since, conceding preparedness to abstract from his personal circumstances, he is performing an action which he recognizes not to be favoured by reason. It is therefore quite natural to speak of him as performing an action that he cannot will as universal law, and thus as being inconsistent.

A result similar to this may be reached by a shorter route, although again we require acceptance of the salient feature of the categorical imperative. To recognize a conclusive advisability proposition involves, because such is involved in understanding what a conclusive advisability proposition *is*, the recognition that it would be inconsistent (although not, of course, impossible: *akrasia* is a frequent condition) to fail to do the action that is advised or, at least, to form the intention not to do what is advised.[37]

[37] I am here partly explicating the notion of an advisability proposition which, as I remarked earlier, would have to be done by seeing its distinctive relation to the concept of intention as well as its relation to distinctive types of grounds (and *not* by the presence of certain semantic features, which is why I have chosen to speak in a language of art, that may have been off-putting to many, about advisability propositions rather than 'ought judgements' or 'evaluative judgements'). The conclusion here, incidentally, helps to clarify my quarrel with Professor Edgley on the interpretation of 'he who wills the end

It seems, therefore, that Kant's position is defensible when he says that there are certain actions which cannot be willed as universal laws without inconsistency, and that a person who performs an action that he cannot so will is himself being inconsistent. His further claim, that there are certain actions which cannot be *thought* as universal laws without inconsistency, is a lot more tricky to handle, and I do not have space to go into it here. But suffice it to say that almost all of the actions which fail this stronger criterion will also be actions which are ruled out by the weaker one.

I have so far defended several of Kant's claims about the connections between moral and prudential arguments, rationality, and consistency. Let me tidy this part of my account by defending what was previously left to one side: the claim that the prudential argument needs to be followed by the moral argument, of which the categorical imperative is the principle, if we are to arrive at a conclusive advisability proposition. We have seen that the prudential argument may well, for those with altruistic feelings, negotiate conclusions advising actions which, although conditional upon the agent's desires, may be classified as virtuous. It might seem a pointless procedure to follow such a prudential argument with the moral argument, but there are two reasons for supposing that it is not. (1) We may, in the first place, be unclear or mistaken in supposing that a certain type of action is or is not virtuous and thus good without qualification, or, more pertinently here, we may be unclear or mistaken as to

wills the indispensably necessary means thereto'. He takes this (op. cit., p. 147) to mean that if a person intends to do *x*, and if doing *y* is a necessary means or is analytically related to doing *x*, then the person must in consistency intend to do *y*. But if a person *really* intends to do *x*, then he *logically* cannot, under these circumstances (where foreseen but not intended consequences gain no grip) intend not to do *y* (even though, of course, he may not *wish* to do *y*). I would place the gap that is required if logic is to have normative bearing not, as does Professor Edgley, between two intentions, but, rather, between the recognition of an advisability proposition and the intention that is thereby required if consistency is to be maintained. Such cases are frequent: I myself often recognize the truth of an advisability proposition but come nowhere near forming an intention to do what is advised.

whether a given action of that type is what the situation requires. Let us suppose that someone believes that benevolent action is virtuous: and such action may well be advised by a bit of prudential reasoning. But benevolent actions as such cannot under all circumstances be considered without qualification as being good, since there are certain situations where it is not in place. If, for example, the benevolent action happens to be the action of a judge in a court of law, we cannot consistently will that actions of this kind under these circumstances should become universal law or else the law would be brought into contempt.[38] Thus following the prudential argument with the moral argument acts as a check or control on whether the situation calls for the particular sort of virtue that—if we are fortunate—the prudential argument advises. (2) The second reason is more important, in that with the aid of the categorical imperative that small grain of a moral disposition that is to be found in all psychologically sound persons can be made to go a long way. For the categorical imperative makes clear, in concrete cases, why it is that certain actions are good without qualification, and, understanding this, a person who is prepared to abstract from his own personal circumstances may be led from small to larger moral concessions in his behaviour. Thus making the moral argument sequent to the prudential argument acts as a check or control on whether a virtuous action is really what the situation requires and, if it is so, it explains why actions of that sort are to be encouraged.

There is a third question with which I said I would deal, namely the question of why Kant said that moral concepts have their origin in reason completely *a priori*. To answer this question fully would take considerable time, and to answer it at all breaks the flow of the argument: let me therefore deal with it in summary fashion in one paragraph. Roughly speaking, Kant's central reason for this assertion is the same reason that led him

---

[38] *Eine Vorlesung Kants*, p. 134. This does not, of course, imply that a judge should under no circumstances be lenient or merciful, although Kant is notorious as being more of a legal rigorist than most.

to say that we should define what is right before we define what is good,[39] and in view of the contemporary reaction against utilitarianism in favour of defining terms in this order it would seem that Kant has a lot going for him.[40] Kant's own reason for adopting this strategy lay in his recognition that freedom is the *ratio essendi* of the possibility of the justified use of any moral concepts. Rather than showing (if such be possible) that freedom in the required sense demands this ordering of our concepts, which would be a long task, let me mention two small considerations (apart from the obvious consideration that what is done is not legislative for what ought to be done) which led him to this result, even though, taken by themselves, they fall short of a demonstrable proof of what we need. The points relate to the two empirical considerations that occur in prudential reasoning as I have sketched it above, these being (A) the desires of particular people, and (B) the strategies, involving knowledge of causal laws, that are considered in relation to the satisfaction of the desires mentioned in (A). The two points are, of course, related, and the points I wish to make about them both stem from the influence of Rousseau upon Kant, which is, of course, well acknowledged: 'After Newton and Rousseau God is justified and Pope's dictum is seen to be true.'[41] On (A): it is a common thought that man is possessed by his possessions, and Rousseau brought forcefully to Kant's attention that such possession can corrupt morality. Man craves—here Rousseau learnt from Mandeville, but went into a puritanical reaction— luxury and the admiration of others: this, for Rousseau, was progress, from which he tended to retreat into his dreams of a simple agrarian community. Kant (like most figures of the Enlightenment in Germany) was more realistic, and departed from Rousseau in approving of luxury because it was civilizing, although he says that a man *must be able to* live without luxury:

[39] KdpV Ak. V, 62–5.
[40] Such a mode of procedure is the avowed policy both of G. R. Grice's *The Grounds of Moral Judgement* and of John Rawls' *A Theory of Justice*.
[41] Ak. XX, 59.

the more dependent that he is upon it 'that much less free he is, and that much more near vice'.[42] That is point number one for Kant's being chary of policies conditional upon agents having desires which are not under the watchful guidance of our thought. On (B): Kant valued scholars, but in arguing against Rousseau's extreme thesis that man was not made for scholarship he writes: 'Why should a citizen who is industrious in his profession, cares for his family, and behaves in a decent way, be held as of less worth than the scholar?... All men are equal, and only he who is morally good has intrinsically greater worth than others.'[43] What follows from this? First, decision as to what is right and wrong 'must not be so difficult that even the commonest and most unpractical understanding without any knowledge of [the causal] ways of the world should go wrong in making it'.[44] Second, it must be within everybody's power to do what morality requires of them.[45] On both counts it follows that a man may not be free to do what he ought to do if we define what he ought to do in terms of actions leading to a previously defined good: he may lack the causal knowledge and he may, even if he has the causal knowledge, lack the causal power. Development of these points would, I think, show that our moral knowledge is arrived at independently of anything other than minimal knowledge of the causal ways of the world, for in morality what interests us is the action and not the object of the action,[46] and it is this that Kant means when he asserts that moral concepts have their origin *a priori*.

[42] *Eine Vorlesung Kants*, p. 217.

[43] *Eine Vorlesung Kants*, p. 307. Cf. Ak. XX, 59.

[44] KdpV Ak. V, 36. I have departed from Beck's translation who reads my 'knowledge of [the causal] ways of the world' as 'worldly prudence'. Kant's term is *'Weltklugheit'*, and an account of his use can be found at *Grundlegung* Ak. IV, 416 footnote 45.

[45] A passage bearing on this thesis that is important but, so far as I know, lies unnoticed is *Anthropologie* Ak, VII. 418.

[46] *Grundlegung* Ak. IV, 413 footnote. I am not going to pretend that this is not a dark saying, but I take it to mean that the object of the action advised by a bit of prudential reasoning is, so to speak, bracketed out when we go into the sequent moral argument.

If I am right to any degree in what I have said rather lengthily, although even so not lengthily enough, then Kant did have a great deal to say which is valuable about the subject of practical reason. I am therefore faced, in conclusion, with the problem of what to do about Professor Walsh's first general conclusion, namely that Kant had nothing of real interest to say about practical reason. His charge is that Kant's importance in this area is negligible because he gave no place to know-how: a concept that must be taken into account even when dealing with speculative reason.

While I willingly concede that an understanding of know-how is of great philosophical importance, I would challenge that Kant was unaware of it and, more seriously, charge that the concept of know-how is *irrelevant* to the concept of rational action, so that, even if Kant did neglect it (as he did), then this would in no way prejudice his contribution towards our understanding of the concept of rational action.

The examples of know-how that Professor Walsh gives are (*a*) knowing how to physically manipulate the environment, (*b*) knowing how to recognize an instance of a concept when one is encountered, and (*c*) knowing how to recognize morally relevant features of a situation: a know-how that singles out some men as more morally perceptive than others.

It is certainly true that Kant nowhere (to my knowledge) deals with (*a*), but he did have a clear grasp, which he may nevertheless may be accused of failing to exploit, of the lessons of (*b*). In relation to Professor Walsh's own exampled profession, Kant points out quite correctly that we should have an infinite regress of rules if our conceptual thinking were not supplemented by native wit in applying our concepts (which equals, in the Kantian idiolect, rules). He points out that there may well be 'doctors or lawyers who have performed well during their schooling, but who, when they have to give advice, do not know how to set about it'.[47] And what goes for (*b*) also goes for

[47] *Über den Gemeinspruch* Ak. VIII, 275. Clear insight into the point at issue is also evident in *Anthropologie* Ak. VII, 199.

(*c*): there may well be men versed in moral theory who are absolutely lost when it comes to moral practice because they lack the perceptiveness to recognize in practice what they well know, or would know, to be morally relevant in theory: such men lack what Kant calls the rare talent of *judicium discretivum*. Kant quite deliberately neglected this area—even that part of this area where we can give rules governing in part the application of our concepts—because he was above all interested in developing a theory of reason that was *normative* for such practice.[48]

'But', it will be charged, 'this is beside the point. The point is that Kant failed to appreciate that practice precedes theory— that knowing how to speak a language, for example, precedes the development of linguistic theory, or that knowing how to reason properly precedes the development of logical theory.' Again the charge that Kant overlooked this is unfounded: it seems to have been an annual example in his logic lectures that we all know how to speak a language before we come to formulate its grammar. But let us admit the charge that Kant neglected the importance of this: we then come to my question of whether *if* he had failed to see any of this it would follow that he had nothing interesting to say about rational action.

According to Rylean orthodoxy, know-how is introduced to undercut the idea that all intelligent action is preceded by a bit of theorizing. Action not preceded by a bit of theorizing can be intelligent: and it is intelligent if it shows that at some time past a person has learnt to adapt his behaviour to novel circumstances or if it shows that the man is currently modifying his behaviour patterns to circumstances that are in some way nonstandard. Of the second variety would be, for example, the apt metaphorical extension of some concept to cover new cases, which is matched by the behaviour of the person of novel and innovative moral insight: and it is certainly a pity that Kant, being more (even though not exclusively) concerned with 'the logic of justification' rather than the 'logic of discovery' should

[48] See, for example, MdS Ak. VI, 205.

have neglected intelligent behaviour of this sort. The question that presses, however, is, conceding the relation of know-how to intelligent behaviour, what is the relation of intelligent behaviour to rational behaviour?

Considerations could be multiplied of the following sort as to the differences between appraising an action as intelligent and appraising an action as rational. In the latter case, to say that someone did something irrational is to commit us to a charge that his action was inconsistent with beliefs that he held, or that he should have held, and perhaps with actions that he has performed or judgements that he has made about the actions of others. To appraise an action as unintelligent, however, commits us as a matter of necessity to *none* of these things. If we are tempted to think of them as the same it is perhaps because we use 'stupid' quite frequently as the negative correlative of both 'rational' and 'intelligent'. In the light of considerations such as these it seems to me that the crucial and self-evident point is that *rational* action is *action which is or should have been preceded by a bit of theorizing*. Since theorizing involves know-how it will follow that rational action requires intelligence, but the converse does not hold: intelligent action does not require (although it may in some varieties need) reason. To speak of an action as rational or irrational is to speak of it as conforming or failing to conform to an advisability proposition which expresses the reasons which bear normatively upon the action in question. And thus to speak of an action as rational or irrational is to speak of it in relation to the various propositional attitudes involved in theorizing (including such disparate attitudes as believing, inferring, and deducing).

If this sketch of the difference between intelligent action and rational action is on the right lines, it follows that know-how has nothing to do with a theory of practical reason, since a theory of practical reason will be a theory about the normative relations between one proposition and another, or between propositions and actions, and while know-how will be involved in the exercise of practical reason, it will not be involved in the theory of practical reason as such.[49]

[49] I am indebted to the translations of the *Critique of Practical Reason* by L. W. Beck (Liberal Arts, 1956) and the *Groundwork of the Metaphysic of Morals* by H. J. Paton (Barnes & Noble, 1967). For the rest I have neither used, nor intend to use, translations which do not have the courtesy to include canonical pagination, which will usually be that of the *Akademie Ausgabe* of Kant's works published by Walter de Gruyter & Co.

Index